THE PETRO-DEVELOPMENTAL STATE IN AFRICA

JESSE SALAH OVADIA

The Petro-Developmental State in Africa

Making Oil Work in Angola, Nigeria and the Gulf of Guinea

HURST & COMPANY, LONDON

First published in the United Kingdom in 2016 by
C. Hurst & Co. (Publishers) Ltd.,
41 Great Russell Street, London, WC1B 3PL
© Jesse Salah Ovadia, 2016
All rights reserved.
Printed in India

Distributed in the United States, Canada and Latin America by
Oxford University Press, 198 Madison Avenue, New York, NY 10016,
United States of America.

The right of Jesse Salah Ovadia to be identified as the author
of this publication is asserted by him in accordance with the
Copyright, Designs and Patents Act, 1988.

A Cataloguing-in-Publication data record for this book is
available from the British Library.

978-1-84904-476-9 *hardback*

This book is printed using paper from registered sustainable
and managed sources.

www.hurstpublishers.com

CONTENTS

ACKNOWLEDGEMENTS

There are more people to thank than I could possibly mention for the support and encouragement that allowed me to pursue this project. Richard Saunders guided me from the earliest stages of thinking about my project to the final stages, with the help of Greg Albo and Anna Zalik. My mentors John Saul and Bruce Berman were important influences. My publisher Hurst, and particularly Michael Dwyer and Jonathan de Peyer, also showed great enthusiasm for bringing this book forward. The field research for this project was carried out with the aid of a grant from the International Development Research Centre, Ottawa, Canada. Information on the centre is available on the web at www. idrc.ca. I was also generously supported by York University and the York Centre for International and Security Studies. In Angola, Acção para o Desenvolvimento Rural e Ambiente (ADRA) and Sérgio Calundungo, ADRA's Director Geral, were very welcoming. In Nigeria, I was supported by Chris Newsom, Jo Croft, Inemo Semiama and Stakeholder Democracy Network (SDN), as well as by Issac (Asume) Osuoka and Celestine Akpobari at Social Action. I received a great deal of support for my research from Daniel dos Santos, Ricardo Soares de Oliveira, Tako Koning, Sylvia Croese, Peter-Jan van As, Lucy Corkin, Ricardo Cardoso, José de Oliveira, Belisario dos Santos, Ike Okonta and Gboyega Bello. I am also forever indebted to the numerous friends and informants who participated in my research. I would like to thank my parents, Anne Gewurtz and David Ovadia, as well as my partner Diana Radulescu. I am particularly grateful to Cara Goldberg for many years of love and friendship and to other friends and supporters in Toronto including Leah Breslow, Emily Blackmoon and Lilian Yap. Last but certainly not least, I would like to thank the people of the host communities in both Angola and Nigeria. It is my sincere hope that one day soon you can claim the benefits from petroleum resources that are rightfully yours.

PREFACE

In recent years, I have witnessed an explosion of interest in local content policies and the larger connected theme of natural resource-based development. A few years ago the topic was barely on anyone's radar. The global commodities boom, the oil and gas boom in the Gulf of Guinea and across sub-Saharan Africa and the concerted efforts of Angola and Nigeria, as well as Norway, Brazil and others, have helped put local content on the global policy agenda.

Traditionally, experts have understood the economic benefit of resource extraction for host countries and communities to be limited to the revenues paid to the state for royalties and taxes. It is now well-known from the history of oil in Angola, Nigeria and elsewhere in the Global South that such petroleum rents are often less of a blessing and more of a curse.

Local content policies (LCPs) promote indigenous participation in economies otherwise geared for the export of raw materials. They also encourage the development of local manufacturing and service provision through backward, forward and sideways linkages along the petroleum value chain. In Angola and Nigeria, billions of dollars are invested annually in the highly capital-intensive activity of crude oil exploration and production. Retaining even a small portion of this investment to benefit local economies is a powerful tool for economic diversification and job creation, which are two of the most important objectives for resource-dependent African states.

The new emphasis on local content coincides with a series of changes since the early 2000s in domestic and international contexts. In this book, I argue that new political and economic conditions have been created as a result of these changes, opening up new policy space for resource-rich states to pursue petro-development. In addition to using the revenues from oil and gas in developmental ways (i.e. productive investments in health, education, training, infrastructure, social assistance and other important activities), a defining feature of the petro-developmental state is that it puts in place LCPs to nurture capitalist development.

More work is needed to identify and test the characteristics of the petro-developmental state. Similarly, more time is needed to see if the potential for petro-development is transformed into reality. However, I believe that through a combination of sound investment of revenues and local content policies the petro-developmental state can emerge. At the same time, good governance, redistribution of the benefit from resource-based development, and the active participation of citizens and civil society organizations are needed to ensure a sustainable and just impact from these gains. This is the message I would like to drive home with this book.

Despite the changes I've noted, local content policies have until recently been largely ignored by academics. This is surprising given that these policies appear to me to be related to numerous important academic and policy debates. In putting local content policies at the centre, my approach allows for connections to be made between seemingly separate questions related to the political economy of development and for the integration of a number of extremely significant yet seemingly disparate ideas and modes of analysis.

Interest in local content coincides with the popularity of global value chain analysis, popularized by Gary Gereffi and others.[1] While investment rises and falls with the price of petroleum resources, the amount spent every year on extractive industries in Angola and Nigeria is enormous. Capturing a larger percentage of this money in the local economy could mean billions of dollars that were previously going abroad can now be used to promote economic development. Particularly in the context of the recent oil price shock, the significance of LCPs for late industrialization and development compares favourably to development through natural resource revenues alone. This is because local content policies produce developmental outcomes regardless of commodity prices as long as resources continue to be extracted. In effect, the same costs and services are required whatever the price. Therefore, the potential for LCPs remains, although the bargaining power that states hold to insist on their implementation may shift.

The dilemma of how to accomplish structural transformation in economies dependent on exporting primary commodities is not new and is faced by a number of Latin American and African countries whose economies were structured by the logic of colonialism. The notion of petro-development is similar to what in Latin America is called 'new developmentalism'[2] or 'neoextractivism'.[3] As a set of policies that foster industrialization and diverse economic growth, LCPs should be considered essential components of any approach to the emerging movement for global resource justice.[4] However, the literature on global resource justice has largely failed to make the connection between underdevelopment, resource-dependent economies and LCPs as mechanisms of structural transformation.

Through the Africa Mining Vision, the African Union is advocating strongly for local content policies as part of its vision of 'transparent, equitable and optimal exploitation of mineral resources to underpin broad-based sustainable growth and socio-economic development'.[5] International oil companies as well as institutions such as the World Bank, Organization for Economic Cooperation and Development (OECD), United Nations Development Programme (UNDP), African Development Bank and many others are now also waking to the significance of LCPs and are exploring their potential.

Local content policies are only the most recent manifestation of state-led economic development. The lineage of these policies can be found in earlier manifestations of national content and control. Local content is also part of a longer history of late industrializing states nurturing capitalist development, as described by Amsden (1989), Wade (1990) and Chang (2002). The role of the state in promoting economic development has been identified and discussed by countless scholars going back at least to the German economist Friedrich List in the nineteenth century. Yet, in recent decades the World Bank and International Monetary Fund (IMF) put forward a vision of development through the free market in which the state plays only a minor role. These policies of market liberalism—or neoliberalism—proved disastrous across Africa.

While local content policies are enacted by government, oil and oil service companies are crucial partners in their implementation. In discourses related to the extractive industries, the notion of corporate social responsibility (CSR) has become so ingrained that it is taken for granted that CSR activities are required to make a claim on a 'social license to operate' (Hilson, 2012). Similarly, I believe that local content, which goes well beyond CSR in that it applies to all of a company's activities across the value chain, should be seen as a second and perhaps more important element of the requirements for such a social licence.

The reason I focus on local content policies is because in a petro-developmental state, LCPs incorporate and organize many of the mechanisms of state-led development typical of the East Asian developmental states. It is List whom Ha-Joon Chang credits with originally coming up with the metaphor of 'kicking away the ladder'. Chang builds this metaphor into a set of 'catch-up' interventionist strategies that states use to promote economic development. Most of these strategies involve what Chang calls 'activist industrial, trade and technology' (ITT) policies. These policies promote infant industries through tariff protection, state-directed research and development, strategic use of state-owned enterprises, and other measures. Various ITT policies such as the ones mentioned above, but also joint venture provisions, royalty and taxation policy, technology transfer policy and investment promotion are subsumed under local content policy in Angola, Nigeria and other resource-rich countries. Given the prominent role of oil and gas in the Angolan and Nigerian economies, it is natural that local content in oil and gas would be the organizing principle for state promotion of economic development.

As I argue within these pages, local content policies have a dual nature: they are both mechanisms for promoting development and at the same time mechanisms that can allow a local elite to prosper with only minor benefits reaching the majority of citizens. Where local content is simply about promoting ownership by the elite, it risks repeating the mistakes of Nigeria's experience of indigenization in the 1970s. However, where it promotes in-country value-added economic activity and upgrading along the value chain, it offers enormous potential, as in the cases of Norway and, more recently, Brazil. It is my sincere hope that this analysis helps advance at a theoretical level the understanding of capitalist development for resource-rich countries in the Global South, while at the same time advocating in practice for redistribution of the benefits of petro-development.

For over fifty years, states like Angola and Nigeria have collected rents and royalties from oil extraction, yet have little to show for them. In fact, revenues are only the first and least effective way that states can benefit from petroleum resources. In this book, I will show how local content policies offer a second and more powerful tool for fostering industrialization, economic growth and possibly even social development—capturing and utilizing investment in extractive industries to benefit local economies and create developmental outcomes.

Jesse Salah Ovadia
December 2014

ABBREVIATIONS AND ACRONYMS

ADRA	Acção para o Desenvolvimento Rural e Ambiente
ANIP	Angolan Agency for Private Investment
AOPIG	African Oil Policy Initiative Group
AOS	Africa Oilfield Services Ltd
BD	Bloco Democrático
BNA	National Bank of Angola
BP	British Petroleum plc
CABGOC	Cabinda Gulf Oil Company Ltd
CAE	Centro de Apoio Empresarial
CBA	Collective Bargaining Agreement
CCIA	Angolan Chamber of Commerce and Industry
CDC	Community Development Committee
CEIC	Centre for Scientific Studies and Investigations
CEO	Chief Executive Officer
CISLAC	Civil Society Legislative Advocacy Centre
CSO	Civil Society Organization
CSR	Corporate Social Responsibility
D.NEG	Negotiations Directorate
D.PRO	Directorate of Production
DAP	Discretionary Allocation Policy
DEC	Directorate of Economy and Concessions
DFE	Department of Enterprise Development and Promotion
DPR	Department of Petroleum Resources
DW	Development Workshop
E&P	Exploration and Production
EFCC	Economic and Financial Crimes Commission

EITI	Extractive Industries Transparency Initiative
EOI	Export-Oriented Industrialization
EPF	Egi People's Forum
ERA	Environmental Rights Action
EYF	Egi Youth Federation
FCPA	Foreign Corrupt Practices Act
FEED	Front-End Engineering and Design
FESA	José Eduardo dos Santos Foundation
FHN	First Hydrocarbon Nigeria Ltd
FNLA	Frente Nacional de Libertação de Angola
FpD	Frente para a Democracia em Angola
FPSO	Floating Production, Storage, and Offloading Vessels
GADA	Gender and Development Action
GDP	Gross Domestic Product
GONGO	Government-Organized Non-Governmental Organization
GRN	Gabinete de Reconstrução Nacional
GURN	Government of Unity and National Reconciliation
HRW	Human Rights Watch
ICPC	Independent Corrupt Practices and Other Related Offenses Commission
IMF	International Monetary Fund
IOC	International Oil Company
ISI	Import Substitution Industrialization
JOA	Joint Operating Agreement
JV	Joint Venture
LCV	Local Content Vehicle
LNG	Liquid Natural Gas
MAT	Ministério da Administração do Território (Angola)
MD	Managing Director
MDAs	Ministries, Departments, and Agencies
MEND	Movement for the Emancipation of the Niger Delta
MINPET	Ministry of Petroleum (Angola)
MITI	Ministry of International Trade and Industry (Japan)
MOSOP	Movement for the Survival of the Ogoni People
MOU	Memorandum of Understanding
MPLA	Movimento Popular de Libertação de Angola
NAOC	Nigerian AGIP Oil Company
NAPE	Nigerian Association of Petroleum Explorationists

NAPIMS	National Petroleum Investment Management Services
NBS	Nigerian Bureau of Statistics
NCA	Nigerian Content Act
NCD	Nigerian Content Division
NCDMB	Nigerian Content Development and Monitoring Board
NCLCD	National Committee on Local Content Development
NEITI	Nigerian Extractive Industries Transparency Initiative
NEPAD	New Partnership for Africa's Development
NGO	Non-Governmental Organization
NIC	Newly Industrialized Country
NipeX	Nigerian Petroleum Exchange
NNPC	Nigerian National Petroleum Corporation
NUPENG	Nigeria Union of Petroleum and Natural Gas Workers
OIWA	Orlean Invest West Africa Ltd
OML	Oil Mining Lease
OPEC	Organization of the Petroleum Exporting Countries
OPL	Oil Prospecting Licence
OPSA	Observatório Político e Social de Angola
OSC	Oil Service Company
PDP	People's Democratic Party
PDPN	Projecto de Desenvolvimento da Participação Nacional
PETAN	Petroleum Technology Association of Nigeria
PENGASSAN	Petroleum and Natural Gas Senior Staff Association of Nigeria
PIB	Petroleum Industry Bill
PMA	Plataforma Mulheres em Acção
PSA	Production Sharing Agreement (Angola)
PSC	Production Sharing Contract (Nigeria)
SAECGOC	Sindicato Autónomo dos Empregados da Cabinda Gulf Oil Company
SAP	Structural Adjustment Programme
SDN	Stakeholder Democracy Network
SEFL	Sahara Energy Field Ltd
SIIND	Sonangol Industrial Investments
SNG	Save Nigeria Group
Sonangol	Sociedade Nacional de Combustíveis
SPDC	Shell Petroleum Development Company
SSA	Sub-Saharan Africa

ABBREVIATIONS AND ACRONYMS

TEPNG	Total E&P Nigeria Ltd
TNC	Transnational Corporation
UNCTAD	United Nations Conference on Trade and Development
UNEP	United Nations Environment Programme
UNITA	União Nacional para a Indêpendencia Total de Angola
US	United States

1

INTRODUCTION

THE EMERGENCE OF THE
PETRO-DEVELOPMENTAL STATE

Stretching from Liberia and Sierra Leone at the western tip of Africa, along the coast past Nigeria and south to Angola, the Gulf of Guinea has been a site of profound change over the past decade. The impact of that change has reverberated from the countries that surround the Gulf throughout Africa and around the world. The nature of the change affecting the region is both internally driven and brought about by changed international forces. It is at the same time political, economic, social and technological and is rooted in one particular commodity which, although it is of immense value and strategic importance, has for many years been seen as a terrible curse. That commodity is oil.

Until recently, the development prospects of the region and of sub-Saharan Africa (SSA) as a whole seemed bleak. Following on the heels of slavery and colonialism, decades of structural adjustment imposed by international financial institutions such as the International Monetary Fund (IMF) and the World Bank reinforced the continent's underdevelopment. Africa was part of the global capitalist system, but it was not benefitting from capitalist development. The continent's seven oil-exporting countries—Angola, Cameroon, Chad, Equatorial Guinea, Gabon, Nigeria and Republic of Congo[1]—seemed particularly imperilled. In these countries, the state functioned not on the basis of domestic taxation and the consent of the governed, but on the basis of external sources of income from petroleum rent. Despite the amount of

1

wealth being extracted and the revenues flowing into state treasuries (if they made it that far), quality of life was in sharp decline and there seemed to be little reason for optimism.

Today, the situation has changed. In the last decade, as a result of a complex set of new domestic and international realities, the possibilities for economic growth and social development in the Gulf of Guinea have been dramatically transformed. This new moment opens new opportunities for state-led development and capitalist transformation, at a time when new producers of oil and gas are sprouting up across Africa. At the centre of this shift are local content policies, which open a path to economic development through natural resources.

By questioning academic knowledge on concepts such as the 'resource curse', 'rentier state', state-led economic and social development and indigenous capitalism in Africa, I intend to demonstrate the emergence of a moment pregnant with new possibilities and new geopolitical realities in terms of development,[2] class relations and strategies for national and international capital. Integrating and updating disparate literatures with in-depth on-the-ground research, this book traces my search for an answer to the question of how countries in sub-Saharan Africa can throw off the subordinate place they have had in the global capitalist system due to centuries of imperialism and underdevelopment[3] to make oil work for development. For the oil-exporting countries of the Gulf of Guinea my answer is a new form of developmental state—the 'petro-developmental state'.

Dynamics of Change in the Gulf of Guinea

The traditional oil-exporting countries, all of which are linked by the Gulf of Guinea,[4] were among the most resistant to the wave of democratization across sub-Saharan Africa in the 1990s characterized by the adoption of the formal veneer of liberal democracy. Instead, many continued to experience stubbornly resistant and intractable civil strife. As shown in Table 1.1, two countries in the region—Angola and Nigeria—account for roughly 75 per cent of total crude oil production. These two countries are often associated with the notion of a resource curse due to their histories of conflict, civil war and corruption. Poverty and underdevelopment, according to the resource curse hypothesis, existed not despite petroleum and mineral wealth, but because of it. The situation seemed hopeless. And yet, a decade later, Angola and Nigeria are the leading examples of Africa on the rise.

Table 1.1: Production of Crude Oil Including Lease Condensate
(Thousand Barrels Per Day)

	2008	2009	2010	2011	2012	2013
Angola	1,946	1,867	1,899	1,746	1,777	1,831
Cameroon	81	77	65	62	63	63
Chad	127	120	123	115	105	98
Equatorial Guinea	337	322	298	278	289	270
Gabon	248	242	246	245	242	243
Ghana	6	6	7.2	77	78	98
Nigeria	2,165	2,208	2,455	2,550	2,520	2,367
Republic of Congo	233	268	305	290	280	265

Source: US Energy Information Administration (http://www.eia.gov/).

Frequently the subject of profiles in the *Financial Times, Forbes, The Wall Street Journal, The Economist* and other business periodicals,[5] Angola and Nigeria are now seen as up-and-coming emerging markets for new investment, even as questions of corruption and low-level conflict (or not so low-level conflict in the case of Boko Haram in northern Nigeria) remain unresolved. The change in discourse has gone from one extreme of abject poverty and hopelessness to another of exuberance and unbounded opportunity. Undoubtedly, the new discourse is rooted in real change. Economic growth, stagnant for decades, has begun to increase throughout SSA. Real Gross Domestic Product (GDP) growth over 2001–10 is estimated to be 5.7 per cent, compared to 2.4 per cent in the 1980s and 2.3 per cent in the 1990s. The oil-exporters of the Gulf of Guinea generally outperformed the rest of SSA, averaging 8 per cent growth in the same period.[6] Nowhere has the shift been more apparent than in Angola and Nigeria. In fact, in January 2011, *The Economist* published data showing that over the last decade Angola had the world's highest GDP growth rate, while Nigeria had the fourth highest.[7]

Perhaps taking a cue from this impressive reversal, there has been a noticeable shift in the language used not only by business periodicals, but also by international policy-makers. In the foreword of a report from the Africa Progress Panel of distinguished African leaders and international partners, Kofi Annan writes that many resource-rich countries have sustained high growth and improved their citizens' daily lives, in defiance of the notion of a 'resource curse'. Arguing that a 'commodity supercycle' offers new opportunities to the continent, he argues for national strategies to 'set out how the extractive sector fits with plans for poverty reduction, inclusive growth and social transformation' and better manage the continent's vast natural resource wealth (Africa Progress Panel, 2013: 6–7).

Even international financial institutions such as the International Monetary Fund (IMF) have changed the tone with which they discuss sub-Saharan Africa. The IMF's Regional Economic Outlook for SSA, published in May 2013, is decidedly upbeat:

> Sub-Saharan Africa has performed strongly and should continue to do so. Output grew, on average, at a rate of 5.1 per cent in 2012, and is projected to accelerate to 5.4 per cent in 2013 and 5.7 per cent in 2014. Drivers of growth include investment and exports on the expenditure side, with the production side led by construction, agriculture, and new extractive industry capacity coming onstream. (2013: 1)

The IMF's tone is a marked change from the tone of the first regional economic outlook, released in June 2003. After noting some 'bright spots', including the New Partnership for Africa's Development (NEPAD) and 'progress' on 'good governance', that report went on to say:

> The sombre side of the economic outlook reflects the fact that many sub-Saharan African countries continue to experience weak policies, bad luck, or both. Among the various impediments to higher economic growth in many countries is a weak institutional framework—a catchall for poor governance, corruption, and public sector inefficiencies. (IMF, 2003: 3)

Even in more sophisticated analyses of Africa's changing potential, development is generally portrayed as a linear progression similar to early modernization theory of the 1950s and 1960s. While the change is undoubtedly real, it needs to be concretely analyzed in a rigorous theoretical and historical context. The histories of imperialism and underdevelopment in Africa do not need to be rehashed in this work—especially when there is already so much excellent scholarship on the topic—though much of that knowledge has informed my approach to the question of how to promote development in sub-Saharan Africa.[8] Therefore, I begin at my own point of entry into this topic: the Gulf of Guinea's 'oil boom' and the twenty-first-century scramble for Africa's resources.

A New Moment for Development in the Gulf of Guinea

The history and political economy of development and underdevelopment in Africa teaches that Africa is only a peripheral[9] part of the world system—connected to the centres of global capitalism but disconnected from any of the benefits associated with capitalist development in North America, Europe and elsewhere. Capitalist development was built upon the underdevelopment of the periphery while economic growth at the centre relies on a continual process of what David Harvey (2003) calls 'accumulation by dispossession'.

As a postgraduate student, my interest in the Gulf of Guinea was sparked by a concern over the George W. Bush administration's approach to oil and how Africa fitted into this approach. Petroleum is a commodity of unparalleled importance in the new global economy. By the early 2000s, the search for new sources of oil to reduce the US dependency on the Middle East had created what was soon labelled an 'oil boom' in the Gulf of Guinea.[10] The extent of the offshore reserves in the Gulf of Guinea is unknown. Only a few years ago, the technology to perform deep-water drilling was prohibitively expensive. New technologies of exploration and production, updated geological knowledge of deep-water hydrocarbon basins and higher global oil prices have been central to making exploration and extraction of Africa's offshore oil feasible. Since the mid-2000s, new technology originally intended for the Gulf of Mexico has made it possible to drill for oil in 'ultra-deep water' beyond 1,500 m in depth.

Meanwhile, Africa's proven reserves have grown immensely. Before the boom, oil extraction was already well-established onshore and in shallow waters in Nigeria and Angola. By the end of the first decade of the twenty-first century, virtually every country in the Gulf of Guinea was inaugurating or significantly expanding its oil production; Ghana's massive Jubilee oilfield began production in late 2010, while oil was also found or was being sought in Sierra Leone, Liberia, Côte d'Ivoire, Togo, Benin and São Tomé and Príncipe. This new oil boom has led to what many observers have called the 'new scramble' for Africa's resources.[11]

When I began looking into the oil boom, I saw that it was being fuelled by competition amongst the major Western international oil companies and state oil companies from China, India and elsewhere in Asia. During the Bush administration, the Cheney National Energy Strategy Report highlighted the importance of West African oil, leading to the formation of the African Oil Policy Initiative Group (AOPIG). Shortly afterwards, access to Africa's oil supplies was declared a 'strategic national interest' for the United States. Meanwhile, China began a much-studied new engagement with Africa in the same period. This engagement produced a series of massive oil-backed loans in Angola[12] and various loans and infrastructure projects in Nigeria[13] as well. In my own analysis of this competition (Ovadia, 2013a), I have argued that the US and China are best understood as competitors that seek favourable conditions for their own capitalist classes to engage in capitalist accumulation and accumulation by dispossession, as opposed to states competing in classical inter-imperialist rivalry. China in particular is best understood as both imperialist and at the same time a new hope for economic and social development.

The pursuit of untapped oil resources is part of what Michael Klare calls 'the race for what's left'. This race involves 'a concerted drive by governments and resource firms to gain control over whatever remains of the world's raw materials base' (Klare, 2012: 12).[14] Due to large-scale depletion and unrelenting demand, Klare notes that the race involves an 'invasion' of the last frontiers, including deep-offshore oil and gas. Emblematic of the hype surrounding the oil boom, the Gulf of Guinea was called a 'new strategic Gulf' by J. Peter Pham.[15] This 'new Gulf' has many advantages over the Persian Gulf. Deepwater drilling, which predominates in the Gulf of Guinea, is less prone to sabotage and the threat of civil strife. This threat causes a great deal of risk and loss in Nigeria and other countries with significant onshore resources. With offshore oil extraction, new floating production, storage and offloading vessels (FPSOs) act as massive factories that process and store petroleum and then offload it to supertankers without it ever having to go onshore. Unfortunately, as happened in the Middle East, the oil boom in the Gulf of Guinea has also been accompanied by increased militarization, notably with the creation of the United States (US) Africa Command and increased violence in the form of physical displacement.[16]

Unfortunately, in this new moment, some dynamics are a reminder of past injustices. The first scramble for Africa was launched with King Leopold of Belgium's famous remark 'I do not want to miss a good chance of getting us a slice of this magnificent African cake.' In the opening of his book *Untapped: The Scramble for Africa's Oil*, journalist John Ghazvinian describes his experience attending the opening dinner of the 18th World Petroleum Congress, held in Johannesburg, South Africa:

> And it has to be said that the evening would not have been the same without the desserts. The organizers had decided to give us each a little chocolate mousse and sponge cake carefully moulded into the shape of Africa. It was hard not to admire the culinary artistry involved, but as I looked round the Dome, I wondered: was I the only one to pick up on the symbolism of 3,500 drunken oil executives devouring the Dark Continent, bite after dribbling, chocolaty bite? (Ghazvinian, 2007: 5).

I began to realize that the 'oil boom' in the Gulf of Guinea, combined with a geopolitical environment increasingly shaped by the US and China's thirst for petroleum (particularly petroleum from outside the Middle East), created a new moment and new possibilities for the development of the Gulf of Guinea. At the same time, the political economy perspective I was familiar with made me realize that it also created new possibilities for underdevelopment and what Paul Baran (1957) called the 'appropriation of economic surplus'. The economic surplus can be appropriated by both domestic elites who are now more plugged into international circuits of capital and by international capital itself. With this in mind, I turned to focus on the question of how the oil boom could be made to work for development instead of underdevelopment. To begin to answer this question, I began looking at scholarly knowledge about the role of oil in development and underdevelopment.

The Rentier State and the so-called 'Resource Curse' in the Context of African Development

I was soon immersed in literature about the 'rentier state' and the 'resource curse'. Coming out of the 1970s, the 'rentier state' literature was the first that was specific to development and underdevelopment in resource-rich countries. It narrowed down to focus on the economic effects of petroleum rent. As shown by Hossein Mahdavy, oil rents prevent significant social and economic advancement. Mahdavy used the term 'rentier state' to describe 'any country that receives on a regular basis substantial amounts of external economic rent' (1970: 428). To date, this has been an accurate description of the situation in Angola and Nigeria. However, there are examples of economies that have managed or appear to be managing a larger transformation—the most obvious examples being Norway and Brazil—suggesting that such transformations are indeed possible.

Since the rentier state revenue predominantly accrues directly from abroad, it then ends up allocating these revenues. This leads to Luciani's (1987) distinction between 'productive' versus 'allocative' states. If a state is able to domicile sufficient economic activity linked to the oil industry internally, the state ceases to be rentier, moving from a state primarily focused on allocation to one with significant productive activity. However, Mahmoud Abdel-Fadil writes: 'Linkages between the oil sector and the rest of the economy are very limited in oil-rentier states, as its main contribution to economic activity has been mainly through the availability of financial resources and government spending' (1987: 84). This is the challenge that rentier states face.

The concept of 'resource curse' is a particular outgrowth of rentier state theory. The term gained popularity after being used by Richard Auty (1993),

Jeffrey Sachs and Andrew Warner (1995; 2001) and others. The basic premise of the resource curse, also called the 'paradox of plenty' (Karl, 1997), is that the rapid accumulation of surplus through resource exports erodes social cohesion, encouraging spending on conspicuous consumption and imported goods rather than industrialization.

In short, the resource curse holds that, due to petroleum resources, other kinds of capitalists will fail or be less unsuccessful. Michael Ross (2001) specifies three different aspects of the curse, arguing that it can produce a 'rentier effect', a 'repression effect' and a 'modernization effect'. Of the three, the rentier effect is most often at the core of explanations for the curse, while conflict, violence and other outcomes may also be seen as secondary or associated tendencies produced by the operation of the curse in a given political economic context.[17]

While the literature on the resource curse has been highly influential, it can at times be overly deterministic. In his latest book on the curse, Ross (2012) links the resource curse directly to the properties of petroleum revenues in terms of scale, source, stability and secrecy because oil revenues are unusually large, do not come from taxation, are extremely volatile and can easily be concealed from the public. This kind of thinking leads to the fallacious idea that how a state extracts, collects and utilizes or distributes revenues defines its nature—a common misreading of rentier state theory, which was meant to be separately applied to individual states. This fallacy in turn leads to a sameness in how some scholars understand institutions and elite behaviour in resource-dependent countries—basing their entire analysis on a highly deterministic notion of a resource curse.

The resource curse thesis informs much of the literature on oil and development. However, the evidence on the resource curse has been challenged by numerous scholars in recent years. Brunnschweiler and Bulte (2008), for example, argue that the literature tends to ignore reverse causality. They show that, with a different measure of resource endowment, resource dependence is not correlated with conflict or low levels of economic growth. Haber and Menaldo (2011) have also challenged the notion that resource dependency promotes dictatorial forms of governance. Even Michael Ross, a leading advocate of the oil curse hypothesis, admitted in his 2012 book that new comprehensive research on the topic suggests that there is actually not much evidence supporting claims that oil extraction is linked to slow economic growth or weak, corrupt or less effective governments.

Saad Filho and Weeks write: 'The essential flaw in these hypotheses is that the 'disease' and the 'curse' are outcomes rather than causes... It follows that what writers call diseases and curses are the result of failures to implement effective macro-management policies' (2013: 1–2). Along with what many others are now saying, they are arguing that policy matters. I reached this conclusion myself after reviewing this literature, and later on I heard it over and over again from civil society activists on the ground in Angola and Nigeria. If the negative developmental outcomes associated with the resource curse can be avoided by some resource-rich states in particular contexts and using the 'right' policies, there is a need to theorize alternative state responses in light of the particular context of African development and underdevelopment. This was my next task on the road to understanding how to make oil work.

* * *

After independence in the 1960s, African states faced a choice between capitalist and socialist development. Shortly thereafter, the extent to which capitalism existed in sub-Saharan Africa became the subject of intense scholarly debate. The question most commonly debated was whether capitalism would be positive or negative. Among Marxists, an important question was whether or not African capitalism needed to be promoted as a first step toward the conditions under which socialism could emerge. Additionally, and of particular importance for this work, the study of regimes that actively promote or 'nurture' capitalist development produced rich theoretical contributions to the overall study of African capitalism and African development.

By the 1970s it was clear that there were many varieties of experiments in African capitalism (just as there were many varieties of experiments in African socialism). In *The Emergence of African Capitalism*, historian John Iliffe presents three types of regimes that emerged in post-colonial SSA: 'anticapitalist', 'parasitic capitalist' and 'nurture capitalist'. The final category, nurture capitalism, refers to 'a deliberate attempt by the state to create an economy in which at least substantial areas of enterprise would be in the hands of private capitalists' (Iliffe, 1983: 82).

Following Iliffe, Paul Lubeck undertook a study of nurture capitalism focusing on the cases of Nigeria, Kenya and Côte d'Ivoire to determine 'the degree of autonomy possible for indigenous accumulation under the external structural constraints imposed by the capitalist world economy and state system' (1987: 3). Anticipating later efforts to bridge internal and external factors, Lubeck's approach allows for the study of 'internal microlevel factors, such as capitalist class formation, conflict within and between classes, efficient resource allocation, following market signals instead of unrealistic state planning, and allowing indigenous accumulations to produce without intervention from rent-seeking state elites' (1987: 3–4), while acknowledging the importance of external constraints in delineating the limits of possible development. Lubeck's list of internal microlevel factors is a starting point for identifying the internal variables that today structure development and change in the Gulf of Guinea.

With regard to Senegal, Catherine Boone (1998) asked: 'will Africa's political classes use their power to expand the scope of local capital accumulation, especially by supporting and facilitating local private investment in industry?' Boone writes that in most of Africa, 'no significant stratum or fraction of the wealth-accumulating political class invests in productive activities... in these situations, political classes are predominantly "rentier" in nature.' She explains that while indigenizing capital accumulation is in the interest of *some* political classes, the political project of consolidating internal political dominance and retaining control over the state apparatus is central in all cases (Boone, 1998: 186). In the case of the Gulf of Guinea, however, a shift by the elite to embrace capitalist accumulation may be possible due to the changed internal and external variables structuring the current historical. This possibility suggested to me the need to explore what kind of state configuration would in fact nurture capitalist development. In order to explain how I proceeded, I must first review some key aspects of the theoretical approach I used to analyze internal and external dynamics of change in the Gulf of Guinea.

New Imperialism and a Framework for Understanding Oil and Development

As I became interested in the oil boom in the Gulf of Guinea, I realized that recent scholarship had not yet absorbed the changed context for oil production in that region or the impact this new moment has for our understanding of what oil means for a developing economy. What has previously been understood about oil and development and about sub-Saharan Africa's place in the global economic system is outmoded and in need of re-evaluation. To evaluate the factors influencing the emergence of indigenous petro-capitalism in Angola and Nigeria, I needed a framework that would facilitate analysis of the internal dynamics such as class formation, state structures and the agency of civil society actors along with external factors such as inter-state economic rivalry, competition for resources, changing international norms and the interplay between the interests of various fractions of finance capital. I found such a framework in literature on the new imperialism, and in particular in David Harvey's concept of accumulation by dispossession.

As Saad Filho (2007) writes with reference to the notion of the resource curse, without bringing in power and class, a deficiency in the social organization of society can only be understood superficially as a curse focused on the qualities of the point of production, divorced from the wider structure of class and power relations. I see the concept of accumulation by dispossession as linking internal and external explanations for sub-Saharan Africa's underdevelopment by linking the accumulation strategies of international capital with those of national elites and focusing on the way these groups work together to dispossess communities of their resource wealth.

Kolstad and Wiig argue that in order to avoid the resource curse, 'it is crucial to avoid policies that are particularistic, i.e. interventions which make power and representation even more uneven than they already are' (2009: 5322). However, in Nigeria, the political elites have engaged in massive appropriation of the country's oil revenues and amassed untold wealth. The 'achievements' of Nigerian oil development include 85 per cent of oil revenues accruing to 1 per cent of the population. In fact, Michael Watts has estimated that of US$400 billion in revenues, as much as US$100 billion have 'simply gone "missing" since 1970' (2006: 11–12). In Angola, according to Philippe Le Billon, 'abundant and secure oil rent allowed the [governing] party to wage a long and violent civil war against the National Union for the Total Independence of Angola (UNITA) since the 1970s' (2007: 39). Frynas and Wood argue that oil revenues not only financed Angola's civil war, allowing it to continue well beyond the Cold War, but also shaped the contours of the war: 'Access to oil resources can also, to some extent, explain the timing of the government's military campaigns against UNITA in the 1990s, which was particularly visible in the case of the 1999 military setbacks and advances' (2001: 594).

Given how oil has resulted in underdevelopment across SSA's oil exporters, it is not surprising that several oil-rich developing countries—notably Ecuador and also Nigeria—have witnessed large-scale social movements to leave the oil in the ground.[18] However, given that these campaigns are unlikely in the short time to halt the centrality of oil to the functioning of the world system or to the economies of underdeveloped countries that possess significant petroleum resources, an alternative must be sought. I sought such an alternative in policies that would lead to real capitalist economic development instead of the further underdevelopment brought about by peripheral capitalism. The theoretical approach of the new imperialism was the key to my realization that the enactment of such policies could be part of a larger transformation in the social relations of production; and that this transformation is possible due to the changed dynamics of oil extraction in the Gulf of Guinea.

Unfortunately, while the 'new imperialism' articulates a critical approach to studying capitalist accumulation and neo-colonial or imperial relations between North (or West) and South, like other literature on the new imperialism, David Harvey's work is primarily concerned with the US, Europe and global capitalism. At the same time, it also raises questions about China and a new era of inter-imperialist rivalry. Other authors have further expanded the field. For example, Biel (2000) has written broadly on north–south relations, Petras and Veltmeyer (2001) on Latin America and Bond (2006) on post-apartheid South Africa as a sub-imperial power. Nonetheless, a major gap remains in the literature when it comes to analyzing new imperialism in SSA. Harvey himself is not particularly concerned with microlevel factors, but the literature in general simply does not speak to the Gulf of Guinea and the value of the concept of accumulation by dispossession for understanding elite behaviour, international capital and the state.

Peripherally capitalist countries continue to experience accumulation by dispossession as fractions of foreign capital seek to expand in the Global South. However, they do so without any of the benefits of capitalist economic development. In the case of Angola, and more obviously in the case of Nigeria, this concept explains continued underdevelopment and ecological destruction. In the case of rentier states, a much larger share of the extracted surplus is transferred to the political elite due to the specific fixed nature of petroleum resources. Surplus is therefore extracted directly by foreign capital but also by the domestic elite through capital flight. These are some of the internal and external dynamics of new imperialism that must be understood before beginning to understand how the current moment offers the possibility of a different outcome.

Saul and Leys (1999) write: 'After 80 years of colonial rule and almost four decades of independence, in most of [SSA] there is some capital but not a lot of capitalism. The predominant social relations are still not capitalist, nor is the prevailing logic of production.' Today, while social relations are still not capitalist, what must be established is whether the 'internal microlevel factors', to use Lubeck's term, may be aligning to offer certain countries—those with petroleum resources that in a previous historical moment acted as more of a curse than a blessing—the possibility of significant economic growth, the emergence of a 'real' capitalist bourgeoisie and the beginnings of capitalist development. While Amin considered a few cases of countries that transitioned successfully to central capitalism (South Africa, Israel and Japan), he did not at the time he was writing about peripheral capitalism really consider the possibility of future cases outside the Soviet mode of production. This oversight suggested to me the need to look to East Asia for a model of a (relatively) successful transition to capitalism (with reservations about its long-term sustainability where economic growth is not accompanied by democratization and social development).

The Return to State-Led Development

The new moment of change and new prospects for the Gulf of Guinea raises important questions about how development (understood as meaningful and positive economic, political and social change in people's everyday lives) occurs and how it can be promoted. Taking a step back, developmentalism, or a concern with how to bring about development, has been the subject of intense research and scholarly debate since at least the mid-twentieth century. At the centre of many of these debates is the role of the state in development—particularly in relation to the market. To understand how state policy can promote more developmental outcomes from resource extraction, I first had to understand the history of state-led development.

Breaking from both modernization theory and Keynesianism, which saw the state as complementing and promoting the market, the neoliberal ideology of the Washington Consensus held that the state should perform only the most basic and necessary of functions. To devastating consequence, these ideas became hegemonic in the 1980s with the rise of Margaret Thatcher in the United Kingdom and Ronald Reagan in the United States. Almost exactly at the height of the popularity of the neoliberal approach in the Global North, Chalmers Johnson put forward an alternative view of the state based on his analysis of Japan. He noted that Japan was successful in achieving economic growth because of the interventionist policies of the Ministry of International Trade and Industry (MITI). Johnson (1982) argued that MITI perfected what he called 'market-conforming' methods of state intervention in the economy in order to achieve its developmental goals. Johnson's analysis led to a debate about the extent to which Japan, where state intervention was obvious, as well as many of the other countries in the region from South Korea and Taiwan to Singapore, Hong Kong and others, developed as a consequence of state policy or through the invisible forces of the free market. For those who argued the latter, the idea of a 'developmental state' emerged as an explanation for the East Asian 'economic miracle'.

Johnson (1999) shows that the Japanese developmental state had four elements: a small and professional bureaucracy within the state to select and promote industries and to supervise competition; a political system that enabled the efficient functioning of this bureaucracy; a method of state intervention that complimented the market system; and an organization, such as MITI, to effect implementation. The role of the state was, through professional government agencies, to coordinate and lead industrial development.

Describing the case of South Korea, but also of the NICs, Ha-Joon Chang (2003) shows that the state played a large role in regulating finance, setting priorities for industrial growth and using taxes, subsidies and other policies to grow priority sectors. Chang (2006) contends that in terms of human resource endowments, natural resource endowments, physical and social infrastructure, previous industrial experiences and foreign aid, 'the advantages enjoyed by the East Asian countries [over sub-Saharan Africa] in terms of initial conditions are nowhere as great as they are commonly assumed to be'. Finally, in a book about the prospects of a democratic developmental state in South Africa, Chang (2010) writes that the experiences of East Asia, as well as of states that were similarly developmental or were developmental through different strategies and alliances, can all provide important broader lessons about state intervention (developmentalism). So how do you create a developmental state in sub-Saharan Africa?

The lineage of the developmental state stretches back at least as far as nineteenth-century Prussia. In Latin America and sub-Saharan Africa, one of the most well-known attempts to kick-start industrialization was import substitution industrialization (ISI). The later failure of ISI was followed by the emergence of the East Asian developmental state and later by theories of a democratic developmental state and an African developmental state that mobilizes support and participation from various civil society actors. Just as the rentier state was a specific intervention into wider conversations about development and capitalism, the idea I eventually constructed of the 'petro-developmental state' is intended to capture the possibilities and historical specificity of the current moment for oil extraction in the Gulf of Guinea.

At the core of the idea of the developmental state is a belief in state intervention in the market. Despite claims to the contrary by modern neoliberal theorists, state intervention was prescribed by many classical political economists, including Adam Smith. In one of the most famous passages in *The Wealth of Nations* discussing the idea of the 'invisible hand', Smith writes:

> By preferring the support of domestic to that of foreign industry, he intends only his own security; and by directing that industry in such a manner as its produce may be of the greatest value, he intends only his own gain, and he is in this, as in

many other cases, led by an invisible hand to promote an end which was no part of his intention (2008: 339).

Although he is today upheld as the most famous advocate of free trade, Smith only supported free trade when it did not interfere with domestic industrialization. In order to support local industry, most countries turn to some form of protectionism.

John Waterbury writes that 'Protection is probably as old as trade' (1999: 324). As Ha-Joon Chang argues in his influential book *Kicking Away the Ladder* (2002), every major developed country has used interventionist economic policies to promote industrialization. Once these countries had reached a certain level of industrial development, Chang explains they then adopted free market discourses in order to ensure open markets for their own goods and services, and to prevent others from using the same protectionist strategies that led to their own industrial development.

Reviewing the commonly understood limitations for economic development in 'late industrializing' countries, Amsden writes: 'Late industrializers must grow exclusively by borrowing technology. Denied a competitive advantage from new products and processes, they initially have only their low wages to rely on in wresting market share from countries with higher productivity' (1992: 53). The countries of the Gulf of Guinea, however, do have another advantage—one that may in the current historical moment offer not the certainty, but the possibility of producing successful developmental states. Effectively managed, the oil and gas resources of the Gulf of Guinea can kick-start industrialization—first in the oil service sector and then beyond. To accomplish this goal, they will have to take full advantage of the idea of promoting 'local content' to turn themselves into petro-developmental states.

How Local Content Can Foster State-Led Development

When I began researching the question of oil and development, I had only a vague notion that the new millennium had ushered in a new moment in which the Gulf of Guinea states would have to use their changed domestic and international circumstances to seek development through petroleum resources. This notion was not enough to answer the question posed above: 'So how do you create a developmental state in sub-Saharan Africa?' What I was lacking was a specific mechanism for how this new development would take place. Little did I realize that just prior to the oil boom, the first steps had been taken to implement a set of policies in Angola and Nigeria that would provide just that mechanism for making oil work: local content.

Local content is a strategy in the model of ISI strategies attempted throughout the Global South in the 1960s and 1970s. In essence, ISI is a strategy of using tariffs and quota restrictions on imports, controlled access to foreign exchange and other forms of state protection to encourage domestic industry to supply products previously only available via imports. The domestic industries may be locally owned (either privately or by the state) or foreign owned. In practice, the countries that adopted ISI encountered many problems, both internal and external. Lewellen notes three main problems: 1) in general, the quality of indigenously produced goods was lower than that of imports and the prices were higher; 2) the discrepancy in quality and price leads inevitably, where a country with high tariff protection borders one without, to smuggling; and 3) countries with small populations have little demand for manufactured goods (1995: 85–6). These problems must be overcome for local content to succeed where ISI failed.

ISI was abandoned by most states in the 1980s in the context of a worldwide debt crisis and the rise of global neoliberalism, which advocated free markets and export-oriented industrialization (EOI). Those that tried to stick with ISI policies were forced by the World Bank and IMF to adopt EOI as conditions of the new loans under structural adjustment programmes (SAPs), which were needed to correct balance of payments deficits. Unlike traditional ISI, local content has proven successful in several cases. To begin with, local content focuses support and protection in a key sector of the economy. This approach was an important aspect of how the East Asian NICs developed. Problems with quality and price can be countered by the involvement of international companies in manufacturing that occurs in-country. Additionally, as I will show below, oil-exporting countries have a unique ability due to the significance of petroleum to force international capital to play by their rules. Finally, demand for oil services is assured where petroleum reserves are significant due to global dependence on petroleum and petroleum products.

In order to understand the potential of local content as a new form of ISI, I found it necessary to go deeper into the East Asian developmental state. The work of Johnson on Japan in the early 1980s was followed by a whole host of researchers investigating the emergence of the developmental state. The first task was to define concept. To date, one of the best definitions comes from Castells:

A state is developmental when it establishes as its principle of legitimacy, its ability to promote and sustain development, understanding by development the combination of steady high rates of growth and structural change in the productive system, both domestically and in its relationship to the international economy... Thus, ultimately for the developmental state, economic development is not a goal but a means. (cited in Fine, 2006: 103)

Evans (1995) enriched the concept of the developmental state by suggesting that it needed to be 'embedded' in the structure of the political system and in society in a functional fashion to create an alliance between the agents of the state and an important interest group (i.e. industry) in order to lead to economic growth. This alliance between the state and a particular group creates a powerful force for economic development, but also suggests the need to analyze power relations, the state and class interests in order to understand the effects of rentierism and possible openings for development in petro-economies.

Chang (2006) suggests that three important aspects of the East Asian model were investment policy, trade policy and industrial policy. To begin with, investment and re-investment were promoted through maintaining stability, controlling capital outflows and inflows, luxury consumption control (through heavy tariffs, domestic taxes and banning of certain imports) and disciplining producers receiving state-created rents to ensure they raised productivity. Trade policy concentrated on promoting 'infant industries' and exports, while industrial policy involved organizing mergers and negotiating market segmentation, subsidizing capital equipment upgrading, subsidizing research and development or training in specific industries and spreading information on best-practice technologies. These are precisely the policies being attempted through the promotion of local content in Angola and Nigeria.

* * *

As the debate around the developmental state continued, attention turned to the fact that successful developmental states are largely authoritarian in their political orientation. Robinson and White (1998) observe that the debate on developmental significance of democratic states is premised on the assumption that democracy and socio-economic development are complementary. However, they suggest that many developmental states are actually 'illiberal' states where capital accumulation is by means of corrupt and illegal practices. Robinson and White conclude that while developmental democracy is not an assured outcome of economic and political liberalization, 'nor is it an illusory ideal' (1998: 4–5). They therefore turned their attention to the concept of a 'democratic developmental state'.

Arguing that 'hidden' or 'surrogate' social policies were of major importance in the East Asian developmental experience, Chang (2004) contends that the 'economic' cannot be separated from the 'social' in understanding what makes a developmental state successful. In East Asia, he argues, social policy broadly defined was 'crucial in generating social cohesion' (Chang, 2004: 255). Similarly for Mkandawire (2010), a big concern is that the question of social policy and social development is neglected in the dominant literature on the developmental state. He argues that attention to these questions is needed for political stability, which is, in turn, necessary for longer-term economic growth. Mkandawire argues that if natural resources can be used to earn the foreign exchange required for industrialization, instead of ending up harming the manufacturing sector, this would give African countries an advantage compared to the East Asian developmental states, who had to earn all of their foreign exchange for industrialization from exports from the industrial sector itself (Mkandawire, 2010: 74–6).

These debates around the developmental state and its possible application in the African context brought me back to the specific historical situation of the Gulf of Guinea's oil-producing states. In analyzing the possibilities for the twenty-first-century developmental state, Evans (2008) writes that the developmental state in the twenty-first century will differ due to changing sector dimensions (i.e. the declining centrality of manufacturing). Historically, manufacturing involved moving people out of a sector (such as agriculture) with declining marginal returns and into one where unions could promote higher wages and productivity gains and where technological progress from machine-production could allow increased productivity (and thus increased income).

However, Evans argues that 'By the late 20th century, manufacturing was going the way of agriculture in the rich countries of the North', while 'In the Global South, even impressive increases in manufacturing output proved incapable of generating a blue-collar class of a size and prosperity sufficient to anchor general increases in well-being' (2008: 9, citing Amsden 2001). The challenges of developing through manufacturing in the south are significant. However, I knew that the petro-developmental state could conceivably enjoy an advantage given the fact that industrialization could be anchored in a large and significant industry that is tied to its extraction location. This scenario becomes more realistic for the Gulf of Guinea states given that local content is a policy of industrial protectionism that has strong and almost universal legitimacy in the current moment. With a basic grounding in theory and in recent history, I was ready to begin gathering empirical evidence in support of my ideas.

INTRODUCTION

The Gulf of Guinea as a Region and Other Methodological Questions

My study began with the question of how new or newly accessible offshore oil resources would impact the development potential of the countries of the Gulf of Guinea. From this research question emerged a hypothesis about the possible emergence of what came to be called a 'petro-developmental state'. As I set out to gather evidence in support of this hypothesis, I developed an approach to collecting and interpreting data which must be appreciated in order to understand the explanatory power and limitations of my findings. In the section below, I will explain my selection of case studies, my approach to studying the Gulf of Guinea as a region and other aspects of my methodology.

Through my study of local content policy in Angola and Nigeria, I explore the internal and external dynamics of change that have emerged in the last decade and that stand to shape the region for years to come. To this end, I focused on understanding changing geopolitical dynamics, changing class dynamics, the role of civil society and social movements in these processes of change and the potential of the new local content policies being implemented in Angola and Nigeria.

The emergence of a qualitatively new moment for oil production in the Gulf of Guinea is a phenomenon best investigated by locating the study in what is currently happening on the ground in the region and in a thorough appraisal of the evidence supporting various potential outcomes for the economic and social development. To evaluate how observable trends may play out in SSA's emerging oil and gas exporters, I chose to focus on those countries where oil is currently being produced in large quantities and where the impact of a new geopolitical reality has been felt first.

Angola and Nigeria are useful as case studies for several other reasons. Due to the sheer volume of oil they produce, the two countries are the most strategically significant countries in the region, and indeed in sub-Saharan Africa, for the rest of the world. Nigeria in particular is at the centre of many of the most important debates in African social science, due to the sheer size of its population and economy; while Angola is a useful case, given the dramatic rise in oil production as offshore capacity comes online and the extent of Chinese investment. Both countries see themselves as regional players and have ambitions to set themselves up as regional hubs for the continent's oil and gas industry. To that end, there are nascent indigenous exploration and production companies in both Angola and Nigeria, while Nigerians also own several large multinational oil companies that operate in other nearby countries. The growth of indigenous oil service companies is also a feature in both countries, encouraged by the local content policies that are at the centre of this book's argument about making oil work.

Despite the focus on Angola and Nigeria, the key geographical concern for me when it comes to this changed dynamic for oil and development is the Gulf of Guinea region. Ricardo Soares de Oliveira writes: 'For the first time, the Gulf of Guinea is being approached as a vast oil province that is ignorant of borders and conventions.' Yet, as Soares de Oliveira himself notes, only decades ago, 'no group of countries perceived itself as "Gulf of Guinea", no international organization addressed it as a unit and, more importantly, no one spoke if it' (2007b: 2–3). The relatively recent creation of the concept of 'Gulf of Guinea' suggests that some attention should be paid to its 'regionness' and to whether it makes sense to analyze a group of countries together as constituting the Gulf of Guinea region.

Discussing the 'regionness' of southern Africa, Sandra MacLean writes: 'regions are almost always more than geopolitical divisions; they are also "social constructions", i.e. processes based on shared interests and intersubjective understanding. So, how to establish the Gulf of Guinea as a region?'[19] MacLean suggests that 'a particular area or group of states must, over time, develop a sense of "regionness"'. Citing Bjorn Hettne, MacLean argues that an empirical demonstration of an area's 'regionness' requires it to possess 'a higher degree of economic interdependence, communication, cultural homogeneity, coherence, capacity to act and, in particular, capacity to resolve conflicts in the region concerned' (MacLean, 1999: 947). Whether or not the Gulf of Guinea meets this standard (MacLean doubts whether even southern Africa does), it is clear that the countries of the Gulf of Guinea are engaged in a project to construct and promote such characteristics. This project is seen most clearly in the creation of the Gulf of Guinea Commission as a regional organizing body.

Established in 2006, the Gulf of Guinea Commission currently has eight member countries: Angola, Cameroon, Democratic Republic of Congo, Equatorial Guinea, Gabon, Nigeria, Republic of Congo and São Tomé and Principe. The preamble of the Treaty Establishing the Gulf of Guinea Commission speaks of the need to 'reinforce and consolidate the fraternal relations existing among our people'.[20] The treaty also mentions several objectives, displaying a full agenda of region-building. These objectives include promoting consultation and policy harmonization in the exploitation of hydrocarbon resources to promote development and the preservation of the natural environment. It also calls for member countries to work together to formulate common immigration policy and strengthen communications and transportation networks and commits members to promote 'integration of the Gulf region'.

In explaining the origins of the Commission, Ambassador Florentina Adeneke Ukonga, one of two Deputy Executive Secretaries, notes:

> All our countries, except São Tomé and Principe which hasn't started exploiting, we are so rich in hydrocarbon resources, fisheries, quarries... principally the objective is that since we are so rich in natural resources which everybody wants given the geostrategic importance of the region in the supply of oil to other countries of the world such as the US, Europe and China... our heads of state felt that it would be better if our countries get together so that when the exploration and exploitation is done, it will not be to the detriment to our countries and their people.[21]

Creating a common identity and background for sub-Saharan Africa's oil-producers is a large part of the Commission's project. José Mba Abeso, the other Deputy Executive Secretary, explains:

> Oil and gas reservoirs are geological phenomenon. Countries' borders are a political phenomenon. In many cases, oil reservoirs cross borders... We need to resolve our common problems in a way that will not create difficulties in our economic and social environment... Our boundaries were created by our colonizers. We are the same people... We need cooperation because of the environmental impacts. One part can affect the other parts. We have the same ecosystem and the same environment.[22]

The contents of the treaty establishing the Gulf of Guinea Commission and the comments of its two Deputy Executive Secretaries demonstrate a project to establish the Gulf of Guinea as a region with a shared interest in promoting and facilitating resource extraction, particularly of oil resources, for the purpose of national and regional development. However, the states of the Gulf of Guinea are vastly different in terms of structure and the amount of oil production and reserves they possess, not to mention their vastly different histories and cultural and linguistic backgrounds. What they do possess in common is that their economies, to different extents, are based on the extraction of oil.

It is not necessary to view the Gulf of Guinea states as existing in a functional community in order to analyze many of the structural forces affecting the region. For the purposes of this study, what is important is that it is possible to speak of an overall transformation producing a historically new conjuncture for understanding oil and development in these countries. The specific cases of Angola and Nigeria differ in important ways from the region as a whole due to pre-existing oil extraction, not to mention size and significance. However, these two emerging petro-developmental states may still provide a model for the region as whole to follow, just as Japan became a model for the East Asian developmental state.

* * *

When I set out to conduct field research for this study,[23] I employed the qualitative methods of key informant interviews, case study analysis and participant observation. While I select and present quantitative data in some places, I do not dwell on explaining or analyzing such data in great detail. Instead, statistical data collected during field research and from international organizations are used primarily to illustrate trends that were identified in the interviews or to provide additional depth to an argument. The core activity of my research was to live in the case study countries, get to know their respective oil and gas industries and conduct interviews. It was in this way that I developed and refined my arguments. The mix of data from different sources and approaches helped to deepen the study and verify the evidence gathered.

Another important aspect of the research was the selection of case studies of individual companies in the oil and gas industry. Although I attempted to familiarize myself with the industry in advance of the fieldwork and identified several foreign and indigenous companies, selection was done in-country, largely on the basis of contacts I could access. I approached several companies directly and formally to request interviews, but also conducted interviews with subjects I met informally while I was in the field. I actively sought out expatriate communities in Angola and Nigeria to identify expatriates working in the oil sector, and also made connections with nationals where possible. In the end, I chose to focus on building case studies of three indigenous oil exploration and production companies and seven oil service companies in each country. For Angola, two of the oil service companies have majority foreign ownership, while in Nigeria all seven oil service companies are majority Nigerian-owned. In both countries I interviewed employees of other companies—both foreign and national. I also interviewed staff from seven foreign oil exploration and production companies in Angola and from four such companies in Nigeria.

The argument made and the evidence gathered is intended to support the tendencies I saw emerging. Given the qualitative nature of my research and the importance of the research experience I had and relationships I formed, I believe it necessary to reflect on my own positionality and the privilege I had as a researcher. My position as a white, male, foreigner and non-native speaker of Portuguese and other local languages was both positive and negative for the research. No doubt it has a significant impact on who I was able to speak to and what they said. The results, therefore, reflect a particular standpoint and are framed by the theoretical lens through which I understand them. My standpoint is articulated not to invalidate the evidence, since all qualitative and quantitative data is collected by some person or group with a particular subjective position. Rather, it is to help the reader interpret the evidence and evaluate its explanatory power.

Angola and Nigeria are difficult places to collect data. Additionally, the oil industry is notorious for its opaqueness. As a white foreigner, I found it much easier to gain access to the industry and industry officials. While it may be difficult to do research about these industries from abroad, researchers of the right race and gender who present themselves in the field in the right manner are likely to be treated with all the privileges enjoyed by expatriates. Although my race and gender may have influenced what locals said to me as well as how I understood it, I believe my outsider status encouraged leading Angolans and Nigerians to grant my interview requests. The long list of high-ranking officials and industry insiders I spoke to is an indication that I enjoyed a status that local researchers would not enjoy. I am indebted to my two partner organizations for their guidance and to numerous people I met who helped me in my research, some of whom I have named in the acknowledgements, but many of whom I cannot name.

Conclusion

The journey that I have traced in the sections above moved from my early introduction to the changed dynamics of oil and development in the Gulf of Guinea through my grounding in several important debates about imperialism, capitalist development and the so-called resource curse. From there, I arrived at new contributions to the new imperialism and the possible emergence of a petro-developmental state that nurtures local capitalism and has unique power in a moment of global neoliberalism to adopt protectionist policies that work to bolster domestic industry in the oil and oil services sectors.

What many popular analyses of new opportunities and of 'Africa rising' fail to integrate in a sophisticated way is that this new moment presents new possibilities for accumulation by the ruling elite of local states and by international capital and for the agency of various actors to influence the above-mentioned structural changes in complex and disparate ways. This complexity is something I hope will come out in the chapters below.

The Angolan and Nigerian cases presented below are intended to produce a broader comparative picture of the current moment and future possibilities of oil extraction in the Gulf of Guinea. It will add depth to key dynamics of change in an under-studied and under-theorized part of the world and link issues that have attracted significant attention, such as Chinese engagement in Africa and the new 'oil boom' into a broader analysis incorporating theoretical work that has already been done on new imperialism, patron-client relations in Africa, the resource curse and African capitalism.

In this opening chapter, I have set the stage for evaluating my hypothesis that transformation in the Gulf of Guinea may allow for the emergence of petro-developmental states and may even open the possibility of wider transformations in social relations and the dominant mode of production. Although oil is being discovered throughout the region, the internal and external dynamics of oil extraction in the current conjuncture may not yet be apparent in the majority of these countries due to the lack of significant current oil production. It may be several years before it is possible to analyze the new political economy of oil extraction in the Gulf of Guinea in a proper and in-depth way.

This new moment involves the transformation of the African state and class relations in oil-producing countries. I present the new moment by discussing the structural transformation of oil sectors (with a focus on upstream operations),[24] changing strategies of elite accumulation, legal and institutional reforms, new strategies of ruling class legitimation and, potentially, new opportunities for improvements in the quality of life of the majority of the population in oil-producing and exporting states.

In this new moment, one of the biggest changes is the decision by the Angolan and Nigerian governments to pursue local content in their respective oil and gas industries. The adoption of these policies and the historical, political, economic and class contexts in which they are emerging will be the focus of much of the remainder of this book.

What makes local content important in the current moment of global neo-liberalism is that it is a development strategy premised upon protectionism, state-led development, import substitution and other strategies consistently dismissed by the Washington and post-Washington Consensus. Due to the strategic nature of many natural resources and the fact that they cannot simply be moved out of a particular jurisdiction to a more favourable fiscal or regulatory regime, countries with petroleum wealth can insist on these policies and have significant leverage to ensure their implementation. The benefit in terms of capital retained in the local economy from local content policies has the potential to be larger than the royalties and taxes from petroleum extraction. For this reason, local content may be the single most significant innovation in energy policy in the Global South in recent decades.

Chapter 2 will cover a brief history of oil extraction in Angola and Nigeria before presenting the genesis of local content policies in the oil and gas industries of the two countries. In my research, I began to see local content as a concept at the centre of virtually every important issue facing Angola and Nigeria today. For this reason, a specific focus on local content policy in Angola and Nigeria guided the collection of data and provides much of the empirical substance for the discussions and analysis herein.

Chapter 3 brings the topic of local content in Angola and Nigeria into the current moment to discuss ongoing dynamics and issues. Whether examining questions of development and underdevelopment, surplus appropriation, elite accumulation, or conflict and corruption, local content is a useful entry point into modern debates. The chapter discusses the roles of various stakeholders, including the international oil companies (IOCs), presenting both the promise of local content to achieve significant economic development and the concerns or pitfalls in its implementation.

Moving to discuss the internal dynamics of the potential impacts of local content policy, Chapter 4 presents questions of elite accumulation and class transformation and argues that the Angolan and Nigerian petroleum elite have made an organized and concerted effort to design and implement local content in such a way as to maximize their benefit in terms of power and wealth. Given the behaviour of international capital and national elites, a case is made in Chapter 5 for understanding the transformation currently underway in Angola and Nigeria as a movement to a more capitalist mode of production and accumulation based on structurally different social relations. Evidence bolstering the claim that elite accumulation is undergoing profound change and for understanding this shift in terms of a new, more capitalist logic is presented in the chapter in the form of case studies of various oil exploration and production companies, as well as oil service companies operating in Angola and Nigeria.

Finally, Chapter 6 brings the local back into the overall argument by looking at the ways in which local content is connected to ongoing struggles on the part of various non-governmental organizations, activists, media outlets, labour unions and communities in oil-producing areas. The consideration of these struggles allows the limits of the possible for this new historical moment to be better understood and suggests how the different possible outcomes for both Angola and Nigeria, but also the wider Gulf of Guinea, will be mediated by the way various types of agency play out within the confines of future structural realities.

There are three main avenues of change explored below. Firstly, there are new possibilities to pursue the kinds of state-led approaches to development that have been closed to most developing countries since the rise of neoliberal growth theory. The findings of this study suggest that avenues for state-led development which were previously dismissed may now be open and exploitable. Secondly, the elites may have greater incentive, or it may now be more in their own self-interest in the current moment to pursue capitalist accumulation strategies instead of strategies of rent seeking. In this way economic development, and in turn a transformation of social relations of production, may be successfully pursued through top-down leadership instead of pressures from the bottom-up. Finally, there may be new room for civil society to push for social change from below. The forces of change may structure the current conjuncture to allow for economic and even social development simply through various actors pursuing their own self-interest. Ultimately, my analysis rests largely on the first two, yet civil society may still be the key factor in shaping the outcomes of the current moment of transformation and determining whether the new possibilities are possibilities for development or for underdevelopment.

While the petro-developmental state may be initiated by state actors and local elites following their own self-interest in a structurally new and different historical conjuncture, I contend that ultimately whether development or underdevelopment results from the transformation will depend not only on historical conditions, but also on power relations and struggles on the terrain of civil society. In a context where political struggle alone is unlikely to improve development prospects, local content represents a set of policies that can find widespread backing by the state, national elites, international capital and local communities. Given the right combination of agency and decision-making by government officials, the national elite and civil society actors, these conditions could allow for sustainable economic and social development. At the same time, new possibilities of underdevelopment are also created by the same new conditions, suggesting a need for informed policy-making and struggle to achieve the best possible outcomes.

2

WHAT IS LOCAL CONTENT, WHERE DID IT COME FROM AND HOW CAN IT SUCCEED?

Chapter 1 introduced the key concept in this project—local content. Local content policies provide the mechanism by which resource-rich countries can emerge from centuries of underdevelopment and transform themselves into sustainable and democratic petro-developmental states. But what is local content precisely, where did the idea come from, why was it implemented when it was and what will it take for local content to succeed? These key questions, among others, will be taken up in this chapter with reference first to Angola and then to Nigeria.

As explained in Chapter 1, local content policies require local participation in a particular productive economic activity; for example, of particular importance for this study, the extraction of crude oil. This is precisely why I argue that local content policies offer new possibilities for making oil work. In the case of both Angola and Nigeria, local content emerged out of dramatic moments of change. These moments, occurring around the turn of the millennium, happened within three years of each other. In 1999, there was a transition back to civilian rule brought about by the death of Sani Abacha. In 2002, the death of Jonas Savimbi brought an end to Angola's civil war and marked the beginning of a new era of peace and reconstruction. In different forms, policies to promote national participation were tried in both countries decades prior. Therefore, the individual histories of both countries must be explored to determine what, if anything, makes local content in the twenty-first century different.

In this chapter, I will set the historical context of oil production and early attempts to promote national content and control in both Angola and Nigeria, before moving on to describe the legal frameworks in which national content was promoted and in which local content now operates. National content and control is my term for policies that were first implemented in the 1970s and that attempted, for reasons discussed below, to regulate increased employment of national citizens in the foreign multinational companies involved in oil production. These policies may be referred to as 'Nigerianization' or 'Angolanization', depending on which country is being described.[1]

To a lesser extent, especially in Nigeria, policies of national content and control also attempted to promote indigenization, or the participation of firms owned wholly or partly by citizens. These policies set the context for the current push for local content in twenty-first-century Angola and Nigeria. Through their failure, it is possible to describe what makes local content unique and in what ways it attempts to succeed where the policies of the twentieth century failed.

Oil Extraction in Angola and Nigeria[2]

Polices promoting national content and control have a long history in Nigeria's oil and gas industry—dating at least as far back as the passage of the Petroleum Act in 1969. For the following three decades, national content in Nigeria was defined by policies of indigenization. Underlying these policies were three sets of rationales or justifications. The policies would, in theory, provide revenue to the government of Nigeria, empower Nigerians by providing them with new opportunities and give Nigeria control over key industries of strategic significance. In practice, in each of these respects, national content was a complete failure. By exploring these failures, we can begin to understand the ways in which local content seeks to propose something qualitatively different.

The first attempts at indigenization in the Nigerian oil and gas industry focused both on ownership and on the training and participation of Nigerians. In the Petroleum Act of 1969, there are some very basic protections for Nigerian companies, as well as a number of regulations regarding training and human capacity development. The basic protections for Nigerian oil companies are found in the First Schedule of Section 23, which allow for the revocation of an oil prospecting licence or oil mining lease where the licensee or lessee is controlled by a country which does not permit citizens of Nigeria or Nigerian companies to acquire, hold and operate petroleum concessions.

More ambitiously, the Petroleum Act called for the large-scale 'Nigerianization' of top-level positions over a defined period of time. As Atsegbua (2004) argues, the day-to-day running of the oil industry has to be in the hands of Nigerians in order for Nigeria to have *de facto* control of the sector. Part IV of the Act requires the holders of all oil prospecting licences (OPLs) and oil mining leases (OMLs) to submit to the government 'a detailed programme for the recruitment and training of Nigerians... in all phases of petroleum operations' and to submit twice-yearly reports on the execution of the programme. This requirement works together with the First Schedule of Section 37, which requires the holder of an OML to employ Nigerians for 75 per cent of managerial and supervisory positions within ten years of the grant. Despite these lofty ambitions, targets were never achieved. Although progress could have been much quicker had policies been properly implemented and enforced, decades of slow Nigerianization are responsible for the significant numbers of Nigerians that work at almost all levels of the Nigerian oil and gas industry.

Unlike Nigerianization, indigenization was an unqualified failure. In 1972, the government of Nigeria instituted the Nigerian Enterprises Promotion Decree, often called the 'Indigenization Decree'. This marked the beginning of the policy of indigenization in Nigeria, pursued most explicitly from roughly 1972 to 1979. The policy was nationalist in nature, but also inspired by neo-Marxist approaches to development. The aim of the decree was to encourage the participation of Nigerians in the economy by requiring the transfer of foreign capital to indigenous hands. It was vigorously opposed by international capital, with several major multinational firms leaving the country, as well as comprador fractions of the Nigerian bourgeoisie.

In two schedules, the decree listed 22 industrial and service activities exclusively reserved for Nigerian citizens or associations (Schedule 1) and 33 commercial and industrial activities also reserved for Nigerians, but which could be carried out by expatriates under certain conditions (Schedule 2). Some notable areas affecting the oil industry included:

- Haulage of goods by road (Schedule 1);
- Manufacture of blocks, bricks and ordinary tiles for building and construction (Schedule 1);
- Boat building (Schedule 2);
- Coastal and inland waterways shipping (Schedule 2);
- Construction industries (Schedule 2);
- Distribution agencies for machines and technical equipment (Schedule 2);
- Manufacture of cement (Schedule 2);

- Manufacture of wire, nails, washers, bolts, nuts, rivets and other similar articles (Schedule 2);
- Manufacture of paints, varnishes or other similar articles (Schedule 2);
- Shipping (Schedule 2).

One of the main methods of skirting indigenization was the practice of 'fronting', in which the former expatriate owner sold the targeted business to Nigerians but retained effective control. This practice severely undermined the policy. Nicholas Balabkins (1982) describes several methods of fronting employed with respect to the Indigenization Decree. One of the major consequences of the Indigenization Decree, described by Balabkins as 'unintended', was 'the concentration of economic power in the hands of a few Nigerians' (1982: 179, citing Chikelu, 1976). Both 'fronting' and the concentration of power are among the most cited reasons for continued underdevelopment in Nigeria. They have also been a concern amongst the planners formulating Nigeria's local content strategy.

Around the same time as the Indigenization Decree, the government of Nigeria began taking equity participation in the IOCs operating in Nigeria. By April 1974, the government had built up a 55 per cent stake in the subsidiaries of all the major IOCs in Nigeria. A new Indigenization Decree was instituted in January 1977. The new decree included all activities carried on in Nigeria and there were no exemptions for any expatriate firms. Three categories of activities were created: one in which activity was reserved exclusively for Nigerians, one in which Nigerians were to have at least 60 per cent equity participation in the enterprise and one in which Nigerians were to have no less than 40 per cent equity participation. All industrial fields not listed were automatically in the third category requiring 40 per cent indigenous equity participation.

By 1979, the government of Nigeria had increased its equity participation in the IOCs to 60 per cent. At the end of that year, with the nationalization of British Petroleum's (BP) 20 per cent stake in Shell BP, the government's equity in Shell Nigeria increased to 80 per cent. The interests of the IOCs led them to increase profit through non-price competition. This was achieved, among other means, by excluding competition, resisting the acquisition of oil expertise by Nigerian nationals and resisting technology transfer (Turner, 1980). Although it had the largest share in all the IOCs, Nigeria did not, Atsegbua contends, have *de facto* control. Additionally, the Nigerian government became responsible for coming up with its share of the capital needed for exploration and production, an obligation that it has over time found quite burdensome. For the oil sector, one of the key lessons of the indigenization experience was the need for Nigerian management in the oil and gas industry.

Their ability to retain managerial control over Nigerian operations was the key reason why most foreign firms were not overly concerned by indigenization. In the summer of 1979, Biersteker interviewed 23 senior executives of the largest transnational corporations operating in Nigeria. None of the executives were concerned about indigenization, precisely because they had been able to maintain control of day-to-day operations. There were a wide variety of strategies to maintain this control. Biersteker writes, 'there are as many different strategies to avoid losing control as there are transnational corporations investing in Nigeria' (1987: 264). These methods included the public sale of shares to ensure that no single Nigerian entity gained a controlling share, technical services agreements with foreign corporations, negotiation of exemptions, strategies of using multiple companies in service areas where different regulations applied, using Nigerian fronts, changing voting rules, dividing the board of directors, adding additional expatriate workers, bribery and unilateral violation of the law (Biersteker, 1987: 264–71).

This impressive list demonstrates the variety of internal factors that can influence the outcomes of political-economic phenomena and policies designed to promote African capitalism. The lack of indigenous managerial capacity was one of the key reasons why the Indigenization Decree was not successful. In Atsegbua's words, 'The inability of Nigeria to exercise *de facto* control over its oil industry is the result of the absence of domestic personnel for management positions in the subsidiaries of the IOCs' (2004: 106–7). Of course, Nigerian personnel do not ensure Nigerian control, as locals appointed to such positions may feel loyalty and affinity to the viewpoints of their overseas headquarters.

A similar process was happening during this period in the oil services sector. Beginning in 1977, the government-owned Nigerian National Petroleum Corporation (NNPC) began holding equity interest in several multinational oil service companies (OSCs). Over the years, while their operations in Nigeria have grown significantly, the asset base of these OSCs has remained stagnant. Despite efforts to exert national control, the industry made few contributions to economic development. Profits reported in Nigeria were very low compared to the turnover, while the multinational OSCs did not have standard fabrication yards in Nigeria. This ensured that fabrication contracts would be handled by their home offices and most materials would be sourced from sister companies. These sister companies could then quote high, noncompetitive prices. They also made little effort to procure widely available chemicals in Nigeria and failed to make any plans to change these practices (Ariweriokuma, 2009: 102–3).

A full study of why indigenization failed, analyzing the political–economic and socio-cultural factors that undermined these policies, is beyond the scope of this work. However, as Claude Ake writes:

> Indigenization was ostensibly intended to localize control of the economy. But what actually happened was that it gave opportunities for some Nigerians who were already very well off to acquire shares in foreign-owned businesses and to enter into partnership with foreign capital. So in the end what was indigenized, was not control of the economy, but rather exploitation. (1982: 188)

The new elite of the indigenization era, as Ike Okonta describes, 'squandered several opportunities to transform into a bourgeoisie proper in the 1960s and 1970s' (2008: 259). They became known not as a class of successful capitalists, but, as Apter relates, 'the Mr 40 percenters'. They were 'a tight circle of comprador cronies around foreign capital' (Apter, 2005: 37), who took their 40 per cent ownership in foreign firms and made little or no contribution to the economy or to their companies.

The lessons of this era's failures have been internalized by the architects of Nigerian content. In summing up the experience of indigenization at an industry conference on local content in August 2010, Austin Avuru, Chief Executive Officer (CEO) of Seplat Petroleum, noted: 'The policy generated handsome profits for Nigerian Dealers without building capacity... The result was economic stagnation and collapse of entire program.'[3] As we shall see, in Nigerian content policy-makers have sought to avoid some of the major pitfalls by building more widespread support for local content policies.

One of the few positives emerging from decades of failed national content policies is fairly strong representation of Nigerian nationals working in the industry, including some in senior management positions—both in exploration and production companies and OSCs. This qualified success has led in recent years to some of the first set of Nigerian engineers employed in such positions to start their own OSC companies. NNPC continued equity participation in multinational OSCs until 2006. Unfortunately, in the near-three decades that NNPC attempted to exert control over the sector, little change was put in place and little was done to increase the sector's benefit to the Nigerian economy (Ariweriokuma, 2009: 103). Even in terms of Nigerian participation, the outcomes have fallen far short of the stated objectives. In terms of indigenization, very little progress was made by the end of the twentieth century.

Table 2.1: Nigerian Oil Production 2004–2013
(barrels per day)

2004	2,329,000
2005	2,627,400
2006	2,439,900
2007	2,349,600
2008	2,165,400
2009	2,208,300
2010	2,455,300
2011	2,550,300
2012	2,520,000
2013	2,367,400

Source: US Energy Information Administration.

Today, Nigerian oil extraction suffers from the inefficiency and incompetency of the NNPC bureaucracy and, more importantly, from the ongoing effects of Niger Delta militancy and oil bunkering, a criminal racket that reaches to the highest levels of the Nigerian state.[4] Despite this seemingly intractable crisis, official Nigerian oil production remains high (see Table 2.1) and Nigerian proven oil reserves, estimated to be 37.2 billion barrels, dwarf Angola's proven reserves of 10.5 billion barrels.[5] The Nigerian experience differs from Angola's in many ways. Despite a long and drawn out civil war, Angola may today be in a better position to benefit from its petroleum resources.

* * *

In Angola, colonial agreements with the Cabinda Gulf Oil Company and other companies pre-dated independence. The 1976 nationalization of ANGOL de Lubrificantes e Combustíveis SARL, a subsidiary of the Portuguese company SACOR, was one of the first actions of the new government. However, lacking the technology or capacity to exploit its petroleum resources, the government quickly announced that it would honour past agreements with US and French oil companies. The nationalization created the national oil company Sociedade Nacional de Combustíveis (Sonangol).

Although policies of national content and control were a priority of the Angolan government, just as in Nigeria, they were largely unsuccessful in promoting the participation of nationals in the industry or the use of goods and services from domestic companies. Angola's General Petroleum Activities Law, written in 1978, made Sonangol the exclusive concessionaire for oil exploration and development and permitted the company to enter into associations with foreign companies. The legislation required Sonangol to maintain a minimum of 51 per cent in all oil-related ventures. However, in terms of ownership and formal control, it was not until 1991 that contractors (IOCs operating under a production sharing agreement (PSA) with Sonangol) could exceed 49 per cent ownership. This change reflected the greater capital investment needed to drill for oil offshore; and the fact that in the midst of a civil war, the Government of Angola needed an arrangement where it was not responsible for fronting any of the capital. The PSA arrangement allowed for the IOCs to recoup costs from oil production instead of from the government.

The earliest law on Angolanization (understood narrowly to mean promoting Angolan employment in the oil and gas industry) is Decree No. 20/82. This 1982 decree set targets in terms of numbers of Angolans employed by the IOCs that operate various oil exploration and production (E&P) activities in Angola and instituted a mandatory framework for the training and promotion of Angolan employees. The law was poorly enforced in a time of great uncertainty and of minimal state capacity to regulate the sector. However, it was a fairly solid instrument and is still the legislation on Angolanization referred to in the current PSAs.

Table 2.2: Oil Production 1980–2000 (barrels per day)

1980	136,000
1985	232,000
1990	474,000
1995	617,000
2000	748,000

Source: Hodges, 2004.

As seen in Table 2.2, oil extraction enjoyed relatively modest growth until the late 1980s, when production began to increase substantially. It remained relatively stable throughout the 1990s, though price fluctuations dramatically affected the stability of the economy overall. By this point, oil revenues had allowed the government to gain the advantage in the ongoing civil war and to defeat the rebel forces militarily.

In Angola, as new offshore fields came online, oil extraction expanded greatly. As Table 2.3 shows, production almost doubled from 2004 to 2008. In 2007, Angola joined the Organization of the Petroleum Exporting Countries (OPEC). Investment and production are expected to continue to increase in the coming years. Angola even briefly became the leading exporter of oil in sub-Saharan Africa when Nigeria suffered from lower production due to the Niger Delta crisis. As Hodges (2008) rightly points out, the growth in production has enormous implications for Angola, given that the country has one-tenth of Nigeria's population. The massive revenue generated for the government from taxes and royalties is a windfall for post-war reconstruction. It also secures the position of the ruling Movimento Popular de Libertação de Angola (MPLA) party and its president, who has been in power since 1979.

Table 2.3: Angolan Oil Production 2004–2013 (barrels per day)

2004	1,051,700
2005	1,239,100
2006	1,398,000
2007	1,723,500
2008	1,945,700
2009	1,866,800
2010	1,898,500
2011	1,745,600
2012	1,777,000
2013	1,830,000

Source: US Energy Information Administration.

Today Sonangol is one of the most successful and powerful national oil companies. The company plays a pre-eminent role in far-reaching areas of the Angolan economy and in maintaining the system of presidential patronage.[6] Under Sonangol's leadership, Angola has become one of the top oil producers in Africa and one of the most strategically significant countries in the region to both the United States and China. Importantly, the high levels of foreign investment in the oil sector, billions of dollars invested every year in both Angola and Nigeria, have not led to industrial growth or economic benefit for the majority. As an expatriate oil worker in Angola explained to me:

> The oil industry is going to invest every year say US$5 billion[7] in Angola. In actual fact, that money isn't all being spent here in Angola. In fact, only maybe about ten per cent is spent in Angola. The rest is spent on drilling rigs made in Korea, tankers made in Japan, pipe which has been rolled in steel mills in Quebec, it will be on electric logging services from whoever. So that has always been a problem with the oil industry. So much of the money is spent out of country. It takes time for the service industry [to develop].[8]

Table 2.4: Crude Oil as a Percentage of Total: Angola
(2007–10 Actual; 2011 Estimated)

	Exports	*Revenues*	*GDP*
2007	95.5%	81.0%	55.8%
2008	96.6%	80.9%	56.9%
2009	96.3%	72.9%	44.4%
2010	96.2%	80.8%	44.8%
2011	96.3%	84.3%	47.5%

Source: IMF, 2010; 2012a.

The government take from petroleum represents an enormous source of revenue for both Angola and Nigeria. In Angola, as shown in Table 2.4, oil represents over 95 per cent of the total value of exports, generally contributes around 80 per cent of government revenues (although 2009 was a slight outlier due to the global financial crisis) and accounts for 40–60 per cent of GDP. Despite the dominant role of petroleum in the Angolan economy and booming production in the oil sector, there has been little benefit to the average Angolan.

Table 2.5: Crude Oil as a Percentage of Total: Nigeria
(2007–10 Actual; 2011 Estimated)

	Exports	*Revenues*	*GDP*[9]
2007	97.6%	77.0%	37.3%
2008	97.5%	81.0%	38.2%
2009	96.7%	63.8%	29.5%
2010	96.5%	69.9%	41.9%
2011	96.6%	78.3%	40.5%

Source: IMF, 2011; 2012b.

The statistics for Nigeria show similar trends to those in Angola. In Nigeria, as shown in Table 2.5, oil and gas represent 96–98 per cent of exports, generally contribute around 80 per cent of government revenues (although 2009 was an outlier due to the global financial crisis and Niger Delta crisis) and account for around 40 per cent of GDP. Despite the incredible financial impact of petroleum, or as some have argued because of it, the non-oil economies of Angola and Nigeria have never been able to transition to capitalist development in the model of Europe, North America and elsewhere.

222

The oil sector, as in many parts of the Middle East, remains an enclave disconnected from the non-oil economy. This fact, which will be discussed further in Chapter 3, drives the current push for local content in both countries. However, before we are able to bring the story of local content into the twenty-first century and begin to discuss what agency would be required for it to come into being and act successfully to promote economic and social development, it is necessary to consider the actually existing legal regimes for local content that have emerged from the earlier efforts to promote national participation in petroleum production.

Legislation and Legal Regimes of Local and National Content

The legal framework of local content in Angola involves several pieces of oil and gas legislation on diverse topics, along with the legal regime of the PSAs. Understanding this legal framework is necessary for understanding the mechanisms though which local content is being implemented. The general lack of information about this framework is one of the key variables allowing the policies to serve as mechanisms for elite accumulation. Given the opaqueness of Angolan oil law, even an overview of the contents of these laws brings new information into the public sphere. This section will review a range of laws related to local content, leaving some of the most recent changes to be discussed in the chapters that follow.

Figure 2.1: Overview of Angolan Legislation Related to Petroleum Extraction

Law	Year	Title
Law No. 13/78 of 26 August	1978	General Petroleum Activities Law
Decree No. 20/82, of 17 April	1982	Mandatory Hiring and Training of Angolans by Foreign Companies Operating in the Angolan Oil Industry
Decree No. 9/95 of 21 April	1995	Internal Regulations of the General Inspectorate of Labour
Decree No. 127/03 of 25 November	2003	General Regulatory Framework for Hiring of Services and Goods from National Companies by Companies in the Oil Industry
Law No. 14/03 of 18 July	2003	Law on the Promotion of the Angolan Private Business Community

Law No. 10/04 of 12 November	2004	Petroleum Activities Law
Law No. 11/04 of 12 November	2004	Petroleum Customs Law
Law No. 13/04 of 24 December	2004	Law on Taxation of Petroleum Activities
Decree No. 48/06 of 1 September	2006	Rules and Procedures of Public Procurement Competitions in the Petroleum Sector
Decree No. 116/08 of 14 October	2008	Training Law
Decree-Law No. 17/09 of 26 June	2009	Training Decree-Law
Executive Decree No. 14/10 of 11 February	2010	Functioning and Management of the Petroleum Training Fund
Law No. 2/12 of 13 January	2012	Foreign Exchange Regime for Petroleum Sector
Decree No. 3/12 of 16 March	2012	Tax Incentives for Private and Public Angolan Oil Companies

In terms of Angolanization, Decree 20/82, mentioned above, was revoked by Decree No. 116/08, which was itself then revoked by Decree-Law 17/09. A further law, Decree 9/95, was passed in the 1990s requiring a 70 per cent national workforce in all companies of more than five employees. However, this was largely ignored in the petroleum sector. In terms of Decree-Law 17/09, a senior manager in one of the IOCs confided that, in his opinion, Decree 20/82 is actually stronger, as 17/09 has no specific targets on Angolanization—only reporting targets for the Ministry of Petroleum.

Decree-Law 17/09, like much of the legislation in Angola, states that the IOCs 'shall be under the obligation to fill their staff positions, at all levels and in all positions, with Angolan citizens', but allows that 'should it be demonstrated that there is not a sufficient number of duly qualified and experienced Angolan citizens available in the national labour market, foreign personnel may only be hired with prior authorization from the Ministry of Petroleum'. This allows IOCs to hire expatriates after having published advertisements for the vacancies in Angola, explaining the daily job advertisements found in the *Jornal de Angola* for impossible-to-fill positions that require of Angolan applicants advanced engineering degrees as well as 15–20 years of relevant experience.

Under Decree-Law 17/09, majority foreign-owned companies are required to enter into a Program Contract with the Ministry of Petroleum (MINPET) related to the development of their human resources. They are also required to submit annual human resources plans and implementation reports. An

OSC is likely to meet with the Director of Human Resources in MINPET for a few hours each year. MINPET is likely to spend an afternoon with a minor operator. Finally, a major IOC is likely to meet with MINPET over two to three days with the minister present to emphasize the importance placed on Angolanization.

One of the more controversial aspects of the law is found in Article 5 and mandates equal monetary and social benefits, as well as equal employment conditions, for Angolan personnel and foreigners employed by the IOCs. Non-observance of this aspect of the law has been a source of deep tension within many international operators and oil service companies. The law calls for a Fund for the Training and Development of Angolan Human Resources in the Petroleum Sector (Petroleum Training Fund). The rules and procedures governing the fund were later defined by Executive Decree 14/10, which came into effect the following year.

In the remaking of the legal framework for resource extraction that occurred in 2004, the General Petroleum Activities Law of 1978 was replaced by Law 10/04, the 'Petroleum Activities Law', which establishes the rules for the exercise of petroleum operations in Angola. At the same time, the government also passed new legislation related to customs and taxation (Laws 11/04 and 13/04). The re-writing of Angolan petroleum law post-civil war reflects new realities and changes in the global oil industry, as well as the new political realities of the government's strengthened position vis-à-vis the IOCs.

Law 14/03 makes reference to preferential treatment for Angolan companies in concessions. Following that, the new Petroleum Activities Law contains several provisions related to local content, requiring the government to promote and encourage investment in the petroleum sector by companies held by Angolan citizens; to promote the use of national products and services in various ways, including by requiring IOCs to use materials, equipment, machinery and consumer goods of national production of the same or approximately the same quality; and to subcontract to local service providers when the price is no more than 10 per cent higher than the imported items or service charges of foreign firms.

Decree 127/03 is the culmination of a push to promote the use of Angolan goods and services in the procurement procedures of the IOCs that was initiated by the Ministry of Petroleum and the Angolan Chamber of Commerce and Industry. The decree created three regimes or systems of categorization of goods and services used in the oil industry (see Figure 2.2). Also under Decree 127/03, national companies enjoy preferential rights in the contracting and subcontracting of goods and provision of support services, provided their proposals are not more than 10 per cent higher than other companies. MINPET and the Angolan Chamber of Commerce and Industry (CCIA) review Angolan capacity annually to determine if activities in the sector can be moved from Regime 3 to 2 or from Regime 2 to 1.

Finally, Decree 48/06 makes some additional changes required to Decree 127/03 regarding public competition. The decree sets regulations regarding pre-qualification for public contracts; requires that three estimates be sought from different entities; and defines the ways in which Sonangol may regulate the bidding for oil service contracts. These regulations allow Sonangol to exercise enormous control over which companies receive oil service contracts in the sector through its Directorate of Production (D.PRO) and Directorate of Economy and Concessions (DEC).

Figure 2.2: Regimes Created by Decree 127/03

Regime 1	Regime of Exclusion for Angolan Businesses	Activities such as transportation, supply, catering, cleaning, gardening, general maintenance, etc. are included in this regime. In law (if not in practice), only Angolan companies (51 per cent owned by Angolan citizens and registered with both MINPET and CCIA) can bid on contracts.
Regime 2	Regime of Semi-Compliance	For areas such as the purchasing and processing of data, surveying, drilling, consultancies, operation and maintenance of pipelines, etc. In this regime, foreign companies must be in an association with an Angolan company. Although some in the industry argue the law is 'confusing' in terms of what this means in practice, Angolan authorities have interpreted this provision to require a formal joint venture.[10]
Regime 3	Regime of Competition	For goods or services that involve 'a high level of capital in the oil industry and in-depth specialist know-how'. Foreign-owned companies are free to participate without entering into a joint venture with an Angolan company. In practice there are very many activities which fall into this category.

Angolan PSAs are a separate legal regime containing their own clauses relevant to local content. Most clauses dealing with local content repeat provisions of the legislation described above, in some cases with stricter terms that enforce a higher standard of local content. Sonangol has preferred to work through the PSAs to promote local content. This preference is logical given 1) that only Sonangol (through the Negotiations Directorate, or D.NEG) is responsible for negotiating the terms of the PSAs, and 2) that IOCs have historically ignored Angolan laws for the most part but have abided more closely to the terms of the PSAs.

Under the PSAs, Sonangol must approve almost all procurement and has effective control over which companies get short-listed and selected. Sonangol's right to exercise control over contracts is established under the PSAs for all contracts over US$100,000. It has developed strong capacity and knowledge about local capacity. Although the PSAs contain the same provision as the legislation regarding a 10 per cent difference allowed for local suppliers, in practice Sonangol exercises a great deal of power over the IOCs with respect to the provision of services. This power has allowed D.PRO and DEC to put pressure on operating companies to take differences of 20–30 per cent in some cases.[11]

Sonangol also has strong powers to enforce local content because it can give preferential treatment to any company it chooses—not just those with 51 per cent Angolan ownership. Sonangol can examine where materials will be made, where goods will be assembled and who the subcontractors will be. Even a 100 per cent foreign company can get preferential treatment and can even get the 10 per cent difference allowed to national companies if it is making products in Angola or incorporating a large amount of local content. Taken together, the legal framework provided by legislation and the PSA regime not only enable the government to promote local content in the Angolan oil industry, but also enable the presidency, through Sonangol, to exercise enormous influence over billions of dollars[12] spent annually by the IOCs on oil service contracts.

* * *

In Nigeria, the Petroleum Act has been in force for several decades and is the most significant legislation currently on the books.[13] However, there are several other legal regimes that are of significance in understanding national content in Nigeria's oil and gas industry. Among these are the petroleum arrangements between the Nigerian National Petroleum Corporation (on behalf of the Nigerian government) and the petroleum operators. The four main types of agreements are joint operating agreements (JOAs), production sharing contracts (PSCs), service contracts and the memoranda of understanding (MOUs) that Nigeria signed with each of the IOCs in 1986. Although they are not public documents, it is well known that there are provisions regarding national content in several of these arrangements.

After entering into partnership with the IOCs in the 1970s, JOAs were signed, setting out the terms of the joint venture. The sections of the JOA related to national content are listed by Etrikerentse (2004: 227–9):

- Article 2.2.8(vi) states 'Operator shall give preference to a contractor that is organized under the laws of Nigeria to the maximum extent possible, provided there is no significant difference in price or quality between such contractor and others';
- In the schedule to the JOA on contract procedure, Section 4.3.2 states that all work done in Nigeria shall use, as far as practicable, indigenous human and material resources;
- Section 4.5 states that the local part of the work done by foreign contractors shall, where practicable, be performed by contractor's local subsidiary;
- Section 5.5 requires the operator to 'maintain policies and practices which create a competitive environment/climate amongst local and/or overseas suppliers';
- Section 5.5.1 states that 'Fabrication whenever practicable shall be done locally provided standards are not jeopardized. To this effect, joint operators recognize and shall accommodate local offers at a premium of 3%.'

Beginning in the 1990s, due to funding problems with the joint venture arrangement, the government of Nigeria began signing PSCs with the IOCs instead of new exploration and production being conducted under the JOAs. Most of the PSCs are for exploration and production in Nigeria's deep water, where the initial investment required is substantially larger. Less is publicly known about the local content clauses in PSCs. Additionally, there may be slight differences depending on when the PSC was signed. However, what is well-known is that in all the PSCs there are clauses requiring the preparation and implementation of plans and programmes for the training and education of Nigerians for all job classifications in accordance with the Petroleum Act 1969, as well as a premium on commercial offers of locally-sourced goods and services (Atsegbua, 2004). Many of these provisions have been completely ignored by both the IOCs and NNPC. As one Nigerian content manager noted during an internal presentation at the Nigerian AGIP Oil Company

(NAOC), in terms of the national content provisions of the JOAs and PSCs, 'the effect was not felt'.[14]

Nevertheless, Nwaokoro insists that 'Nigeria's 1993 model PSC remains an excellent vehicle for enhancing local content'. Explaining, he refers to numerous clauses in the 1993 PSC for offshore deep water that make clear NNPC's authority to assert control by approving work programmes and budgets annually, requiring industrial training and education of Nigerians, employing qualified Nigerians to the maximum extent possible and giving preference to goods available in Nigeria and services rendered by Nigerians provided they are of sufficiently quality, are offered at competitive prices and are timely available (Nwaokoro, 2011: 60–61). Unfortunately, even by the end of the 1990s, forty years after oil extraction began, the government and NNPC were largely unable to exercise control or enforce provisions of the PSCs related to local content.

Two other sets of policies have been used in recent times to promote national content in Nigeria's oil and gas sector. They are the Marginal Fields and Local Content Vehicles (LCV) programmes. Both programmes target Nigerian participation in the exploration and production of oil and gas. While the Marginal Fields Program is ongoing,[15] the LCV programme was used only in the 2005 bid round. These two programmes are the most recent examples of ongoing indigenization efforts which, while they aspire to promote Nigerian participation in the industry, also serve to mask elite accumulation and rent-seeking under the guise of promoting national content and control.

The Marginal Fields Program targets small discoveries within the area of a concession and offers them to Nigerian exploration and production companies. The fields are those that have not been exploited by the operator of the concession, despite the fact that they have proven reserves, because such exploitation would only be of marginal commercial value. The programme was implemented in 1996 through an amendment to the Petroleum Act that allows the head of state to order the farming-out of a marginal field within a larger leased concession if it has been left undeveloped for a period not less than ten years from the date of first discovery.

Of course, only a very small number of Nigerians have the necessary capital or connections to take advantage of the opportunities presented by the Marginal Fields Program. Additionally, the peculiar wording of the amendment (which was passed as a decree under military rule in the final years of the Abacha regime), granting the power to release marginal fields not to the government, Department of Petroleum Resources (DPR) or NNPC, but solely to the head of state, seems to reinforce the idea that this programme was intended more as patronage than as a method of promoting national content.

Although the Marginal Fields Program was conceived in the 1990s, it was stalled by opposition from several quarters until 2002, with much of the opposition coming from the IOCs. In early 2003, awards of 24 fields were finally made to 31 indigenous companies. The awards were granted for a period of five years and were automatically renewable for companies that had begun producing oil in that time-frame. However, by the end of the first five years of the programme, only five fields had entered into production (AOGR, 2010: 4). Additionally, most of the Nigerian companies that won awards were heavily reliant on foreign 'technical partners', which limited the transfer of knowledge, skills and technology.

On the other hand, there are several cases where marginal fields provided profitable opportunities for Nigerian capitalists. As one informant noted, 'Some Nigerian marginal fields would not be thought of as marginal anywhere else in the world.'[16] Additionally, there is some evidence to suggest that in order to make these fields more profitable, small Nigerian companies are more likely to integrate various gas development projects into their E&P activities. Such integration not only allows the country to benefit from another important natural resource, but also potentially provides a source of power to a country that sorely needs energy to kick-start wider industrial development (see Chapter 5).

The Local Content Vehicles Program was a concept developed for the 2005 bid round by then-Minister of State for Energy, Edmund Daukoru. The programme mandated that the government supply a list of Nigerian companies approved to participate in the round as LCVs. Each bid for a licence was required to include a minimum 10 per cent stake for LCVs, which would be involved as full-paying partners. The programme was envisioned as a way to build the capacity of indigenous oil companies, with the IOC taking on particular responsibilities in each bid to train and develop the partnering LCVs' capacity.

Promoting the local content aspect of the bid round during a 'roadshow' speech before the 2005 round, Daukoru argued that one of the major thrusts of the round was: 'To implement a viable and comprehensive local content policy that emphasizes quantifiable and measurable indigene participation, utilization of local goods and services utilization, technology transfer and capacity building, all of which are necessary to transform Nigeria into the hub of oil and gas development in the Gulf of Guinea.'[17]

In the same speech, Daukoru specifically argued that the LCV process 'discourages the hawking of Nigerian acreage abroad'. Unfortunately, the

LCV programme ended up creating several complications in the round. According to a report by Chatham House, the LCV programme: 'produced a rash of shell or paper companies, causing bidders serious difficulty with due diligence'. The authors of the report conclude that the evidence suggests that the LCV scheme was 'a mechanism to reward cronies with a slice of the action', and that bidders were steered to choose particular LCVs. Also of particular significance, the report notes that 'Of the 100-plus LCVs which pre-qualified, only 10% had previous experience in oil exploration and development' (Vines et al., 2010: 13–14). In the end, according to Austin Avuru, most of the companies involved in the 2005 bid round as LCVs were unable to pay their share.[18]

Of course it is important for Nigerian companies to have knowledge, capacity and experience in oil exploration and production. Acknowledging this necessity, the Chatham House Report points to the Marginal Fields Program as a more useful mechanism for promoting national control. Egbert Imomoh, Chairman of Afren plc and a former Deputy Managing Director of Shell Petroleum Development Company (Nigeria), argues that the marginal fields exercise was useful for encouraging indigenous players to get into the upstream sector; however, he does note that although there are many indigenous players in the sector now, there are not many with producing fields. Imomoh says that he never understood the idea of local content vehicles, commenting that they were likely 'good for a few individuals who made a quick buck and then went to bed'.[19]

However, Daukoru argues that the LCV programme is still superior to the Marginal Fields: 'I was always against marginal fields... It does not provide much revenue to the government and involves a lot of inefficiencies.' Daukoru believes that LCVs are a much better way to promote and develop indigenous upstream capacity, since the companies involved will be part of the decision-making:

> Because they are partners, they are entitled to all the documentation, paperwork and can attend meetings and be involved in staffing. That is the surest way in my mind to grow the future E&P integrated companies. Nigerians can be providing welding services for a million years, can be providing diving services for a thousand years, they can do fabricating of wellhead platforms for as long as you like. The combination of a welder and these other professions will never come together to form an integrated E&P company... that is why we came up with the concept of local content partners.[20]

Daukoru does admit that a major problem was that many of the LCVs sold their stake shortly after the round. His view is that if these transactions were disallowed in future rounds, the programme would be much more successful. 'If they continue, they could be fixed as time went. These are new policy initiatives... you plug the loopholes as you go.'[21] In the end, both programmes were guided by a logic of indigenization that created policies of limited success, seemingly designed more to benefit a few well-connected elites than Nigeria as a whole. From these largely failed experiences, Angola and Nigeria moved to embrace a new national content approach—local content.

The Origins of Local Content in Angola and Nigeria

As described above, both Angola and Nigeria underwent significant transformations in the late 1990s and early 2000s. In this section, I describe the events following these transformations that were significant in the modern push for 'local content'. Starting in Angola and moving to Nigeria, we shall see that a combination of dedication from key domestic actors, combined with an external push from Norway's oil for development programme, created the conditions under which a new vision of local content emerged.

In 2001, a technical commission overseeing cooperation between CCIA, MINPET and Sonangol authored a 'Report on the Penetration Strategies of Private Angola Businesses in the National Petroleum Sector'. The report recommended different regimes of protection for Angolan companies, which were eventually adopted in Decree 127/03. It also recommended the creation of a specific fund to help Angolan businesses; the establishment of protocols by which Angolan companies can subcontract the contracts they win; that the multinational companies (on the basis of earned trust) guarantee financing to private Angolan businesses from foreign sources of capital; and that legislation be created to provide support and assistance to private Angolan businesses to help them penetrate the sector.

Since the establishment of Decree No. 127/03, MINPET has entered into a protocol of cooperation with the CCIA for the purposes of fostering dialogue between private Angolan companies, multinationals and the government in terms of local content. The protocol also sets the parameters of the annual review which the two institutions conduct of the goods and services in each regime. Much later, at the end of 2010, CCIA also became responsible for overseeing the *Centro de Apoio Empresarial* (CAE, or *Business Support Centre*), which will be discussed further below.

In 2002, a workshop was organized in Cunene Province under the guidance of MINPET and Sonangol to discuss local content. Following the workshop, an order of the Office of the CEO of Sonangol, dated 28 March 2003, led to the creation of the *Projecto de Desenvolvimento da Participação Nacional* (PDPN, or Project to Develop National Participation in the Oil Industry). A coordinating committee for the PDPN was set up in 2003 by order No. 9/ GAB.MINPET/2005. The committee had an executive director and six sub-groups. Its task was to present MINPET with a plan of actions to be undertaken. The fact that the PDPN was created by Sonangol, yet its coordinating committee was created by MINPET, would later lead to confusion as to who was directing local content efforts through the PDPN.

Following the creation of the coordinating committee, one of its sub-groups commissioned a study to assess the requirements of the oil sector in Angola and the capabilities of Angolan companies to meet these requirements. The study was conducted by the Citizens Development Corps, an organization based in Washington. The work was completed in December 2003. In 2004 the company, which has since been renamed Citizen's Development Solutions, was chosen to implement the Contractor Training Initiative, leading to the creation of CAE.

In Sonangol's analysis, 'The relationship between the ex-PDPN, as an internal entity within Sonangol[,] and the [coordinating committee] created by MINPET was never officially defined.' By 2007, Sonangol had deemed PDPN to have failed; and in May 2008, it shut down PDPN and transferred the programme's functions to the company's Negotiations Directorate. From then on, local content became the responsibility of the Department of Enterprise Development and Promotion (D.NEG/DFE). In an internal presentation by D.NEG/DFE dated January 2010, Sonangol points to several factors to explain the failure of the PDPN. These include:

- Non-existence of a national content master plan with short, medium and long term goals.
- Little collaboration between operating companies and between different sectors (industry, education, etc.) for national content development.
- Unclear definition of Sonangol's role in the management structure of national content.
- Inefficient application of Law No. 14/03.
- Non-existence of mandatory rules for national content and lack of penalties for non-observance.
- Need to update the clauses of the PSAs to ensure implementation of national content procedures.
- Need to include national content parameters in the TOR [terms of reference] of future bid rounds.

- Need for mandatory criteria and tools to measure goods and services provided by Angolan companies.

Moving forward, Sonangol's D.NEG/DFE appears to be engaged in renewed cooperation with the Ministry of Petroleum and the IOCs to implement a new national content strategy and move Angolanization in a new direction. This direction is one that emphasizes the 'dual nature'[22] of local content for development and for elite accumulation, since it gives Sonangol authority to intervene in the oil services sector in new ways and with a new legitimacy.

It is also important to note the role of Norway and the cooperation of the Norwegian Petroleum Directorate in promoting local content in Angola. As a Norwegian diplomat explained, when Norway developed its oil sector, it was US citizens who helped, but everyone had a Norwegian counterpart. Gradually, the need for expatriates was reduced and then eliminated.[23] Jonathon Moses (2010) has argued that Norway's capacity in its petroleum sector was key to its success in building a developmental state. Moses writes that Norway's success was built on strict concession laws and a tradition of state interventionism and planning. Democracy and control, he argues, were at the core of Norway's strategy. In fact, Moses contends, formulating and implementing developmental policies is even more key to an effective developmental state where oil wealth necessitates overcoming the resource curse.

As part of Norway's petroleum cooperation with Angola, agreements between the Norwegian Ministry of Foreign Affairs and the Government of Angola were signed for support of Nok 17 million (1987–1991), Nok 28.5 million (1991–1995), Nok 22 million (2000–2004) and Nok 27 million (2008–2011) (Govender and Skagestad, 2009: 16). The example of Norway's approach to local content has been a clear influence on officials in the DFE.[24] Although local content has not been an explicit focus, according to the Activity Plan for 2010, the most recent agreement has committed Norway to a new local content/Angolanization initiative. Under the initiative, which commenced in 2009, Norwegian and Angola experts will work together on a 'Roadmap for Angola on local content/Angolanization based on the Norwegian and Brazilian experience', while the Norwegian Petroleum Directorate was to arrange a seminar on local content in Luanda in 2010.[25]

* * *

In Nigeria, greater awareness of the limitations of early efforts at national content led to the emergence of a slow rumble among industry insiders. Eventually, the idea took hold that a new approach was needed to increase the benefit to the nation from the petroleum industry. However, backward steps preceded the current push toward Nigerian content. For example, in 1988 many of the guidelines on staff release were suspended, leading to abuse of the expatriate quota system that promoted Nigerianization. This trend continued until 1997, when new regulations regarding utilization of the expatriate quota and new reporting requirements for expatriate labour were announced. These regulations required that all applications for new quotas, renewal of existing quotas and/or additional positions should first be routed through the DPR before final approval by the Ministry of Internal Affairs. However, it was only after the return to civilian rule in 1999 that the local content push began anew.

The 1990s also saw the implementation of a 'Discretionary Allocation Policy' (DAP) to award oil prospecting licences to indigenous entrepreneurs, as well as the 'Marginal Fields Program' (discussed above). By 1992 under the DAP, twenty indigenous companies had been awarded licences. By 1996, the figures had climbed to thirty-eight. Unfortunately, the policy was used primarily for political patronage and elite accumulation and had little impact on national control or national content. Reflecting on the DAP in a 2004 presentation on local content development, then-director of the DPR Macaulay A. Ofurhie conceded, 'Indeed the policy on discretionary award has attracted some justifiable criticisms since it was first implemented, more so, as most of the favoured companies had been unable to muster the required know-how to deliver on the implicit trusts vested on them by the state.'[26]

The legacy of such backward steps is well summed up by Auwal Rafsanjani, Executive Director of the Civil Society Legislative Advocacy Centre (CISLAC):

> Extractive activities in Nigeria have not helped to transform Nigeria, but have instead resulted in corruption, ineffectiveness and lack of development because a lot of people are thinking of other alternative sources of income. They are only thinking of quick money... agriculture has been completely abandoned and has suffered a lot from oil and gas.[27]

By the year 2000, the slow movement for change in the Nigerian oil and gas industry had transformed into a real and concrete will to institute local content policies. As Ernest Nwapa, currently Executive Secretary of the Nigerian Content Development and Monitoring Board (NCDMB), describes: 'For the past 50 years, since oil exploration started at a commercial level in Nigeria, the strategy was just to import goods and services. So, any economy that is based on importing all its goods and services without balancing trade ends up being an impoverished economy.'[28]

The local content push began with a workshop in Abuja in 2001 entitled 'National Workshop on Improvement of Local Content and Indigenous Participation in the Upstream Sector of the Petroleum Industry'. The workshop was organized by the National Petroleum Investment Management Services (NAPIMS), a subsidiary of NNPC. Therefore, the Group General Manager of NAPIMS, M. A. Fiddi, is essentially correct to claim that, in terms of Nigerian content, 'the whole thing started off from NAPIMS'.[29]

The workshop in Abuja also had strong support from the new Obasanjo administration, as evidenced by the participation of the Presidential Advisor on Petroleum and Energy, Dr Rilwanu Lukman. The workshop produced a communiqué with a recommendation for the establishment of a National Committee on Local Content Development (NCLCD). Following approval from the Board of NNPC, the committee was inaugurated in October 2001 under the leadership of NAPIMS. It produced a report in April 2002 highlighting the committee's finding that the Nigerian content of goods and services in the upstream sector of the oil and gas industry in Nigeria was less than 5 per cent, meaning that '95% of the yearly expenditure of about US$8 billion flows out of the country' (NCLCD, 2002: 5).

The committee's report included a definition of local content, strategies for measurement and recommendations. Among the recommendations were targets for aggregate local content value in the oil and gas industry from all the categories of 40 per cent by 2005 and 60 per cent by 2010. The committee also recommended a new local content initiative to restructure the industry and to allow DPR and NAPIMS effectively to monitor and enforce a new Nigerian content policy. The most important NCLCD recommendation was the drafting of legislation for a Nigerian Content Development Bill. The draft bill, included in Volume I of the NCLCD report, placed responsibility on the DPR to ensure compliance and monitor performance.

The DPR was one of many industry stakeholders actively involved in the committee. After the release of the NCLCD report, DPR, for a time, became the principal actor moving forward the local content initiative and the role of NAPIMS was minimized. Under Director Ofurhie, a Nigerian Content Unit was created in the DPR in 2002 as a special unit in the director's office. One of its key actions was to produce a study on local content in Nigeria. The study was commissioned by the Norwegian Agency for Development Cooperation and executed through INTSOK within the context of the Memorandum of Understanding between Norway and Nigeria. It was conducted under the guidance of the Office of the Advisor to the President on Petroleum and

Energy, DPR, NNPC and NAPIMS between August 2002 and April 2003. The study included a review of six oil-producing countries: Brazil, Indonesia, Malaysia, Mexico, Nigeria and Norway. It then analyzed Nigeria in further detail to identify opportunities for local content development and make recommendations. Chief among the recommendations was putting in place a legal framework for local content policy (Heum et al., 2003).

At the same time, local content was also being advanced by a group called SAN at the Lagos Business School, led by Pat Utomi and Fabian Ajogwu, SAN. The two faculty members spearheaded a series of workshops and conferences on how Nigerians could participate more in the oil and gas industry. These workshops involved several well-known professors from the school and major players from the industry. Ajogwu was also a member of the Local Content Development Steering Committee set up to guide local content development and coordinate between the IOCs, NNPC, Netco (another subsidiary of NNPC), DPR and NAPIMS. For him, local content contrasts sharply with indigenization: 'Let me emphasize that from the very beginning we were not looking for nationalization or take over. We were looking at being participants in the oil and gas sector.'[30] Discussions at this committee were important in shaping not only the content, but also the intent of the Nigerian content initiative.

The Nigerian Content Bill drafted by the NCLCD was submitted to the Special Advisor to the President and thereafter submitted to the National Assembly.[31] However, in 2003, prior to the release of the INTSOK study, there was a change in the Obasanjo administration. Edmund Daukoru became the Presidential Advisor on Petroleum and Energy; and F. M. Kupolokun, who was Special Assistant and Advisor to the President, became the Group Managing Director of NNPC. At this point Nigerian content entered a new phase. It would take until April 2010 for a very different Nigerian content bill to be passed into law—one that very much excluded not only NAPIMS, but also the DPR.

According to F. M. Kupolokun, when he moved from Special Advisor to the President to run NNPC in November 2003, local content was a major priority for him: 'I had clear ideas on what I wanted to do.'[32] Kupolokun commissioned two international consulting firms to study local content issues and other successful cases such as Brazil, Norway and Malaysia, which had been previously studied in the INTSOK report. He then created a Nigerian Content Division (NCD) within NNPC and appointed a Group General Manager to head the division: originally Joseph Akande, who was later replaced by Ernest Nwapa. At some point, the targets for Nigerian content were also changed to 45 per cent by 2005 and 70 per cent by 2010; however, neither target was met and Nigerian content now stands at around 35 per cent, according to most NCDMB estimates. If this figure is accurate, it is a major accomplishment, even if it is well below the targets. In 2006, according to Ukiwo, 85 per cent of the US$12 billion annual expenditure in the Nigerian oil industry was being spent outside Nigeria (2008: 79–80, citing Okonji, 2007). The gains through local content mean that billions more of investment is being retained in the Nigerian economy.

Table 2.6: NNPC-NCD Gap Analysis

Sub-Sectors	Capacity Element	Current Available Capacity	Post-Gap Analysis Requirement
Engineering	In-country engineering person-hours	1.5 million	5 million
	Skill discipline engineers [sic]	1,000	3,600
	Engineering companies (500,000 person-hour minimum capacity)	none	5 or 6
Fabrication	Annual tonnage of fabrication including FPSO modules and LNG	25,000MT	150,000MT
	Certified welders/fitters	2,000	10,000
	Integrated fabrication yards (25,000MT–30,000MT min. capacity)	none	6
	Deep sea port and facilities for FPSO integration	none	2
Manufacturing	Annual tonnage of steel pipes	nil	1 million MT
	Annual tonnage of Portland cement	2.23 million MT	11.8 million MT
Shipping and Logistics	50% of annual equity crude for export	no indigenous company	180 million bbls (worth US$900 mil)
	Lighters and medium-sized vessels for coastal services	25	Over 250
	Qualified Nigerian ship captains, crewman and divers	220	over 4000

Source: NNPC-NCD, 2008.

Through the NCD, NNPC released a series of Nigerian content directives. The first set of directives focused on three areas: manufacturing, materials and engineering. The original ten directives were later increased to fifteen and further revised to twenty-three by 2006. Kupolokun and the NCD then ordered more consulting work to be done, including a gap analysis, which resulted in further policies to address the gap in Nigerian content targets on human capacity and fabrication and actually existing capacity (see Table 2.6).[33] As Kupolokun explains, 'It's one thing to say this is what I want; it's another thing whether you have in place the capacity to deliver.'[34]

Meanwhile, the Local Content Development Steering Committee in which Fabian Ajogwu participated quickly identified front-end engineering and design (FEED) as one of the key areas to address. Ajogwu explains: 'FEED was like the Kingdom of Heaven. If you got that, everything else would follow.' This approach came about because FEED had large out-of-country spend, was a key to capacity building and technology transfer and was a necessary step for larger milestones. The committee was also keen on a database of our own human capacity, though this never materialized.[35]

As described by Dauda Anako Maliki, who produced a study on Nigerian content for NNPC under the NNPC Chief Officers' Management Development Programme, there was a 'fresh approach' to Nigerian content after 2005 (Maliki, 2009). A new bill was drafted by the NNPC-NCD under Joseph Akande. Fabian Ajogwu, a regular consultant to the NNPC-NCD, was hired to vet the draft and offer comments. Although the bill passed the Nigerian Senate, it died with the end of the Obasanjo administration. It was revived in 2008 in a new form that called for the creation of the NCDMB instead of entrusting implementation and monitoring to DPR.

A final piece of the puzzle was put in place with the creation of the Nigerian Content Consultative Forum at a series of inaugural meetings in June 2005. The forum contains working sub-committees for the various industry groupings (including fabrication and engineering). By 2007–8, the NNPC-NCD had ordered all the IOCs to form NCDs in their organizations with a manager at the level of General Manager. Despite progress, legislation was stalled in the National Assembly and compliance with NNPC's directives among the IOCs was half-hearted at best. Disagreeing with the notion that the directives were ignored, F. M. Kupolokun admits: 'in a number of cases there was some tension where they just didn't want to do it'. However, the chief executive of a major indigenous oil service company who did not give permission to be quoted on the record, disagrees: 'They've talked the talk, but they haven't walked the walk. There's been no implementation of Nigerian content. The directives issued by the NNPC were not followed by any of the IOCs... The attitude is still "how can we do as little as possible?"[36]

Officials within NNPC have made similar statements. Writing in 2008, Ado Sule Ibrahim, an employee in the NNPC Chief Officers' Management Development Program, argued that until passage of a Nigeria Content Bill, NNPC lacks the power to enforce its Nigeria content directives (Ibrahim, 2008). Writing a study for the same programme in 2010, prior to the passage of the Nigerian Content Act, Joseph Atibi Brown, the Chief Geologist in the Planning Department of the NCD, contended that the law is needed due to the lack of a specific legal framework to support the set objectives: 'The impact of the absence of a legal framework and strategies for NCD has adversely affected the entire oil and gas industry such as youth restiveness in oil and gas producing areas, capital flight, a completely non-existent linkage industries and underdevelopment of oil producing areas and the nation at large' (Brown, 2010: ii).

It is in the context of a renewed effort to promote use of domestic labour and domestic oil service companies (and with assistance from Norway in each case) that local content emerged in both Angola and Nigeria. Local content policies represent one of the most important factors influencing changed possibilities (both positive and negative) for oil extraction in the Gulf of Guinea—and especially for Angola and Nigeria as the region's top oil producers. I will show in the following chapters that although there is justifiable hope that local content will have a significant impact on economic growth, and possibly even socio-economic development, the policies contain the seeds for the same damaging outcomes as affected the historical policies of national content and control in both countries. Therefore it is too early to tell whether or not the local content drive that emerged in each country in the past decade will actually be able to reverse the so-called resource curse and nurture capitalist development through the creation of a new petro-developmental state, or whether it will end up reinforcing poverty and continued underdevelopment.

3

THE PROMISE AND PITFALLS OF DEVELOPMENT THROUGH LOCAL CONTENT

This chapter continues the story of local content developed in Chapter 2 by examining the current state of local content and local content policies in Angola and Nigeria. Treating each country in turn, this chapter will review the current situation, current implementation strategies and potential benefits before turning to an examination of the key concerns with local content in practice. Despite the promise offered by local content and possibility of an emerging petro-developmental state, I will show that local content policies face many of the same pitfalls that have hindered past attempts to promote state-led capitalist development. The pitfalls identified below set the stage for the second half of this book, which will examine the roles of the elite (Chapter 4), indigenous entrepreneurs (Chapter 5) and various civil society actors (Chapter 6) in the creation of petro-developmental states.

Petroleum as an Enclave Sector[1]

Looking back on a cursed history of oil extraction, Pat Utomi, the Nigerian academic and presidential candidate in 2007 and 2011, told me:

> The whole curse of oil phenomenon is not a factor driven by if there is oil there is going to be a resource curse problem. It is driven by lack of elite commitment to a long-term strategy... If there was a leadership elite clever enough to move in that direction, I don't see why oil would have to be a curse. It would be a driver for development.[2]

Utomi's desire to turn oil into a driver for development becomes understandable when reflecting upon the role of petroleum in the Nigeria economy. Crude oil, as discussed above, has become the defining commodity in the economy in terms of revenues, exports and GDP. Utomi argues that the notion of oil as an enclave sector applies particularly well to Nigeria: 'In the main, the oil sector has remained an enclave sector, significantly disconnected from the rest of the Nigerian economy with very little multipliers beyond the rent that accrues to government.'[3] The same can be said for Angola, where even fewer Angolans are employed in the sector despite decades of policies of 'Angolanization'. In fact, the province of Cabinda in Angola is often taken as one of the prime examples of an oil enclave.

The notion of oil as an enclave sector is discussed by James Ferguson, who notes the tendency of capital to 'hop' over 'unusable Africa' and stop only in mineral-rich enclaves. 'Usable Africa' is made up of small, secured and policed enclaves linked not to the territorial national grid, but to transnational networks. For Ferguson, offshore oil extraction is 'the clearest case of extractive enclaving' (2005: 378–80). Foreign companies and foreign workers predominate in extractive enclaves, contributing to the situation where the enclave produces minimal benefit for the host country. While Nigeria has developed significant numbers of engineers and specialists and has a well-developed network of universities, Angola's education levels are amongst the lowest in the world due to decades of war and Portuguese colonial rule. Only a handful of foreign-trained Angolans are therefore able to occupy senior positions in the oil and gas industry.

Although there is far more work to be done, there are Nigerians occupying many senior positions in foreign oil and oil service companies. In Angola, while nationals are moving into more senior non-technical positions of authority, the process is very slow. In both Angola and Nigeria elite cadres of nationals formerly employed by international oil companies and/or the respective national oil companies have developed a high level of knowledge about the industry and have moved to establish their own niches in the sector. This phenomenon is crucial in terms of the potential development of these countries' respective national economies.

In Angola, a national reconstruction project, funded largely by petroleum revenues, began with the end of the civil war in 2002. Nevertheless, Angola remains significantly impoverished. The development impact of the sector has been negligible, despite the large oil revenues flowing into the state. As one civil society leader put it, 'Angola is developing rapidly in terms of the economy, but this is not resulting in a better quality of life for everyone.'[4]

Table 3.1: Employment in the Oil and Oil Services Sector in Angola

	2004	2005	2006	2007	2008	2009
Operators	12,296	13,069	12,834	14,533	14,956	15,399
Service Providers	12,886	14,104	35,984	40,528	49,852	49,278
Total	25,182	27,173	48,818	55.061	64,808	64,677

Source: MINPET, 2010.

In terms of actual numbers of nationals employed in the oil and gas industries in Angola and Nigeria, the statistics are not impressive given the importance of petroleum to the economies of both countries. Even those employed in the industry are not yet satisfied with the progress Angola has made. According to the 2010 report of the Ministry of Petroleum, employment in the sector has risen from 25,182 workers in 2004 to 64,677 in 2009 (see Table 3.1). Of these workers, 23.8 per cent work in MINPET or the operating companies, while 76.2 per cent work in oil service companies (MINPET, 2010). To put these numbers into context, the *Relatório Económico 2009*, an annual statistical report published by the Centre for Scientific Studies and Investigations (CEIC) of the Catholic University of Angola, assumes a 2009 working population of 8,928,215 out of a total population of 18,408,692. Therefore, CEIC estimates that 0.21 per cent of Angolans are employed in oil exploration and production and 0.72 per cent in oil services. In other words, less than 1 per cent of Angolans are employed in oil or oil service activities (CEIC, 2010).

However, the MINPET report makes clear that at least the figures for oil service workers include expatriates. It clearly states that, of the 49,278 workers in the oil service sector in 2009, 5,174 were expatriates. Therefore, even CEIC's estimates may be over-stating current Angolan employment in oil services. Given Mkandawire's warning, mentioned in Chapter 1, that social development is needed for political stability, which in turn is needed for economic growth under a developmental state, more employment opportunities are needed in a sector that has such economic importance to the state and to the economy. One young Angolan who works at a mid-level job in an Angolan oil service company captured the duality of hardship and optimism many Angolans articulate when he said: 'I wouldn't say there is a good quality of life because life here has no quality, but things are getting better.'[5]

In Nigeria, there has been some evidence of more local procurement, reductions of expatriate personnel and appointment of Nigerians to managerial positions (Ukiwo, 2008: 80). However, national employment in the Mining and Quarrying Sector (which includes oil and gas among other activities) is an insignificant 0.15 per cent of the total working population. Even the entire manufacturing sector in Nigeria, which includes some (but not all) activities in the oil service sector, represents less than 2 per cent of the working population (see Table 3.2). As one expatriate working in Nigeria commented to me, 'In Nigeria, extractive industry involves a lot of extraction, but not a lot of industry.'[6]

Table 3.2: Selected Statistics on Employment in Nigeria

	Total Working Population	Total Employed in Mining and Quarrying	Total Employed in Manufacturing
2004	47,993,400	67,142 (0.14%)	836,234 (1.74%)
2005	49,486,362	69,001 (0.14%)	907,877 (1.83%)
2006	52,326,923	72,962 (0.14%)	959,990 (1.83%)
2007	54,030,000	81,045 (0.15%)	821,256 (1.52%)
2008	61,958,542	93,302 (0.15%)	944,324 (1.52%)

Source: NBS, 2009.

The statistics for Angola and Nigeria show that despite great economic significance, the oil and gas industries in both countries have had little significance in terms of direct or indirect employment—a key measure for gauging any positive impact from petroleum resources and a necessary precondition to capitalist development through industrial growth. This analysis conforms to the commonly held academic conviction on the traditional developmental impact of petroleum. To transform into petro-developmental states, more Angolans and Nigerians must gain employment in the oil sector. The year-on-year statistics show some growth of employment, especially in 2008 in the Angolan oil services sector. However the growth in employment, even in the Angolan case, seems much less impressive when population growth is factored in.

Given the new dynamics of change and the new local content push, the notion of oil as an enclave industry may be changing. An indigenized oil service sector in Angola or Nigeria may have significant potential in itself. This potential exists because the service industry requires large numbers of skilled tradespeople and engineers and because local content may have the potential to anchor growth in manufacturing. In this way, it could allow a wider benefit from that growth to spread through the non-oil economy in ways that have already been discussed and will be discussed below in further detail. Moving from an overall economic analysis of the context of oil extraction in Angola and Nigeria today, this chapter will proceed to describe current local content strategies in both countries, their potential impact and the potential concerns with its implementation.

Current Local Content Strategies and Impact: the Angolanization of Labour

As mentioned in Chapter 2, investment in the Angolan oil sector reached almost US\$16.5 billion in 2009 (MINPET, 2010). Capturing more of the capital invested in the sector will lead to significant economic growth and development, particularly if this investment encourages the oil and oil services sectors to serve as an anchor for growth and development of economic activity in related sectors, such as manufacturing and services. It could also create significant employment, a phenomenon not generally associated with petroleum.

The oil service sector is all but ignored by most economic analyses. For example, in Vines, Shaxson and Rimli (2005), the economy is analyzed in three parts: 'the non-oil, non-diamond economy'; 'the oil sector'; and 'the diamond sector'. In the section on the oil economy, there is no mention of oil services. Similarly, in a 2011 United Nations report on industrial development in Africa (UNCTAD, 2011), there is no mention of the potential for development through oil services (which includes manufacturing and heavy industry). Even a recent IMF study on 'The Linkage between the Oil and the Non-oil Sectors' (Klein, 2010) fails to mention oil services.

In Angola, local content has developed along two separate paths. Firstly, Angolanization, which refers primarily to promoting the employment of Angolans in the oil sector, dates back to Decree 20/82 and the early 1980s. Secondly, local content involves the promotion of Angolan companies and Angolan goods and services in the subcontracting of oil services. As noted in Chapter 2, these components were developed in different time periods through different historical contexts and are covered by different legislation. Angolanization remains a project of the Human Resources Department of the Ministry of Petroleum, while procurement of Angolan goods and services is primarily the responsibility of Sonangol. In MINPET, separate departments are concerned with the two components described above. Meanwhile, in Sonangol, the D.NEG/DFE seems entirely concerned with procurement, leaving Angolanization of human resources unaddressed. The current state of local/national content policy is best understood in terms of these two components.

The Ministry of Petroleum has placed a renewed emphasis on Angolanization since the enactment of the new Training Law (Decree 116/08). The ministry has been working, in part through its cooperation agreement with Norway, to strengthen its capacity to monitor the sector and promote its human resources strategy. To do this, the ministry has taken a hard look at its human resources department, which is responsible for tracking Angolanization plans. It has developed a strategic human resources plan for the petroleum industry and is working on its human resources management systems. It has also created a database of qualifications for the sector with the aim of fighting inequalities between Angolans and foreigners in terms of pay and promotions

In terms of Angolanization, pay equality between Angolans and expatriates is perhaps the biggest source of tension within the industry. One Angolan who has worked in the human resources (HR) department of a large multinational OSC complained at great length about pay discrimination. He claimed that companies make false contracts and frankly 'outright lie' to the government now that such discrimination is illegal. They have also taken to providing extra benefits to expatriates outside their Angolan contracts through the company's headquarters. This Angolan complained that his company went so far as to have two HR managers, an Angolan and an expatriate, even though MINPET generally requires the HR management position to be Angolan. This tactic was employed in order to keep sensitive information confidential from the Angolan HR manager. The shadow HR manager doesn't even need to be located in Angola, which makes it impossible for MINPET to monitor. In his words: 'They are involved in a big fraud—making false documents, even for immigration. So it's really incredible what they are involved in here in Angola.'[7]

Enforcing Angolanization in terms of job creation is difficult because there are many ways that companies can mislead MINPET or conceal the extent to which they are resisting the policies. One expatriate manager in an oil service company, whose company filed an Angolanization plan with MINPET that anticipates vast changes to the ratio of Angolans versus expatriates, explained that while the hiring of Angolans is going to take place, the company is also in process of moving most of its expatriate workers to its international company. While locating these employees abroad makes it difficult to get work permits, many workers don't even have to enter Angola to do their work. Companies have also become very adept at getting work permits by creating new positions and titles for expatriates.[8]

The IOCs also mislead and conceal the extent to which they comply with Angolanization policies. The Director of Human Resources for one of the major IOCs, whose company has a reputation for not having made as much progress in terms of Angolanization, pointed out that for the positions that have been Angolanized, there is always autonomy and responsibility. An Angolan herself, she complained that with many of the other operating companies, Angolans are appointed to high positions, but it is actually other people doing the work—either abroad or in Angola. As she related:

> When I go to MINPET, I go by myself and I represent [my company]. I've seen other companies who send people from human resources. The Angolans are accompanied by expats who don't even speak Portuguese! When I go I have autonomy and authority to represent my company.[9]

An interesting source of information is an internal report prepared in 2010 on BP's reputation in Angola amongst staff. Through interviews with a representative sample of 14 per cent of the total staff, the report showed the large-scale dissatisfaction of Angolan employees with Angolanization. The Angolan staff felt as if they weren't included in decision-making as equals and had very divergent views from the expatriate staff on how BP is doing in Angolanization. Roughly 64 per cent of Angolan respondents were dissatisfied with the skills transfer to Angolan staff, and 57 per cent were dissatisfied with the involvement of Angolan staff in decision-making. Although roughly 60 per cent of Angolan staff disagreed with the notion that there is mutual confidence between Angolan and expatriate staff, roughly 75 per cent of expatriates agreed.[10]

Noting that Angolanization of labour in the oil industry is only likely to benefit a small number of Angolans, one civil society leader argued that: 'Angolanization of petroleum must be accompanied by the Angolanization of the benefits of petroleum.'[11] Tellingly, a comment made in the open comments section of the BP survey 'related to the need to invest more in relations with the Ministry of Petroleum and Sonangol and the importance of investing more effectively in local content and Angolanization, including reducing income disparities between Angolan and expatriate staff.' Some of the comments made by Angolans participating in the survey included: 'Angolans are not authorized to make decisions... Angolanization is a front'; and 'In other companies, they didn't just give the job title, they gave authority as well.' The point of discussing the BP survey is not to single out BP. Instead, I would argue that the results are comparable to what would likely be found if any of the other IOCs conducted such a survey.

As a final point, it must be mentioned that the benefits of Angolanization do not reach Angolans on an equal basis or on a basis of merit. Therefore, an additional problem with Angolanization is the question of which Angolans are getting the jobs. In Nigeria, a similar concern exists, with divisions drawn along ethnic lines. In Angola, the major cleavage is race. In an interview with a black Angolan working in one of the big operating companies, the employee, towards the end of the interview, began speaking about inequality in Angola. He argued that those who benefit from Angolanization are often white and mixed Angolans. Sitting in his corporate headquarters, he complained: 'If you go around this office, you will see many more white and mixed people, not black people.'

He estimated that 80–90 per cent of the Angolans working for his company in key positions studied abroad and the majority had lived most of their lives abroad, and in fact were more likely to be recruited from Lisbon than from Angola.[12] This, he said, was 'structural racism'.[13] At a minimum, his concerns point to the need to be asking not only what social class may be benefitting from Angolanization but also suggest that a small elite is benefitting disproportionately. Additionally, his concerns also point to the need to look at the racial and gender dimensions of who accesses the benefits of these policies.

Knowing very well that the law calls for all positions to be Angolanized within five years, a Director of Human Resources at one of the major operating companies candidly stated: 'There are posts that will never be Angolanized and posts where there will never be a foreigner.'[14] When I interviewed two public relations officers at Esso Angola and asked what positions are generally held by expatriates, one interviewee quickly responded that it was positions of leadership and management, noting: 'This is something that will never change.' The officer's colleague quickly jumped in to set the record straight, lest I walk away thinking Esso was planning to ignore Angolan law, stating: 'We don't know if it will never change.'[15]

The above concerns with Angolanization show that despite decades of Angolanization laws, Angola is still unable to promote the development of national labour in the oil industry due to a combination of mismanagement, inaction on the part of IOCs and a political context beyond the government's control. This is a severe limitation on the ability of local content to succeed in promoting economic development, the first aspect of its dual nature. Unfortunately, the situation is even worse when it comes to subcontracting Angolan oil services.

Current Local Content Strategies and Impact: Subcontracting of Oil Services

As mentioned above, subcontracting Angolan companies and Angolan goods and services is a more recent area of focus in Angola. While responsibility for local content was transferred to D.NEG/DFE in 2008, Sonangol's D.PRO and DEC are still actively involved in promoting local content in an enforcement capacity—a responsibility that is shared, at least in theory, with the Office of Inspections in MINPET. However, it is Sonangol that exercises control over the IOCs in its role of approving major contracts.

In 2010, Sonangol made headlines in the international oil industry by rejecting the recommended contractors of the oil company Total, which operates Block 17, due to insufficient local content. As a result, the major contract for the new Clov project is likely to go to the Korean company Daewoo, instead of the Italian contractor Saipem and consortium partner Hyundai Heavy Industries, even though Saipem and partners submitted a lower bid and were Total's pick. Additionally, Sonangol rejected Total's preferred bidders for the subsea umbilical, riser and flowline package and subsea production systems, which were Technip (a French company) and Aker Solutions, and is instead awarding the contract to FMC (a Norwegian company) and Acergy.[16] This example demonstrates Sonangol's power to exercise preference for companies using higher local content.

As mentioned in Chapter 2, D.NEG has also had responsibility for local content development since 2008. This responsibility has been assigned to the Department of Enterprise Development and Promotion (D.NEG/DFE). One of the key Sonangol managers in this department summarized some of what is being planned for a new local content strategy: 'The best way to develop national content in a country like Angola, or even Nigeria, is by project. You must try and optimize the benefit by project and by the PSA, not by a legal framework covering everything... Legislation doesn't optimize local content; it just grants it. It can't enforce, just demand.'[17] The manager made clear that modifications to the provisions of the PSA in future bid rounds, along with amendments to existing PSAs, would be the primary method of implementing the new local content strategy, though he did allow for the possibility of local content legislation. This approach explains why the D. NEG has been the division within Sonangol that has taken over responsibility for local content.

A senior manager in the Ministry of Petroleum confirmed in an interview that MINPET was working with Sonangol on a comprehensive Local Content Plan for the end of 2010. He suggested that this plan could involve legislation, requirements for operators to use more local content, mechanisms for Angolan companies to access credit through the National Bank of Angola (BNA) and increased monitoring.[18] The Sonangol official from D.NEG/DFE also pointed out that legislating use of an electronic marketplace, as has been done in Nigeria, would require a new legal instrument to ensure the safety and security of online transactions.

The CAE, mentioned in Chapter 2, is one of the key institutions in Angola that promotes the development of Angolan oil service companies. Under PDPN, CAE was funded jointly by the operators in Angola, with costs recoverable through the provisions of the PSAs. For convenience, BP held the contract and recovered the costs from other companies operating in Angola on the basis of agreed cost-sharing. Angolan companies could both register or certify with CAE. They then received opportunities to strengthen their capacity to meet the needs of the operators in terms of accounting practices, quality control and other areas of business management. When an operator had a contract on offer, it could contact CAE for a list of Angolan companies that could supply the contract. Impressively, from its opening in 2005 to April 2010, CAE assisted Angolan firms to win 309 contracts worth a total of US$213,540,807, leading to the creation of 4,236 jobs.[19]

In the summer of 2010, CAE had a database of 1,300 clients. However, as an expatriate advisor working for the centre noted: 'Not all of them are legitimate. It's very easy to register with CAE.' Additionally, the advisor noted that most of the services offered by Angolan companies are for 'low-level technical work'.[20] Still, the centre was extremely effective at strengthening the Angolan component of the oil service sector and was praised by all the IOCs. In 2010, when the funding provisions from PDPN expired, BP extended the funding for six additional months while the D.NEG/DFE decided CAE's fate. On the expiry of these six months, a question mark remained over whether the organization will be taken over by Sonangol or discontinued. By 2012, CAE was still in existence and had been fully taken over by Sonangol. CAE is now being run by the Angolan Chamber of Commerce and Industry (CCIA).

For a number of years, CAE seemed to be in competition with TradeJango, a second system for promoting Angolan service companies. Launched by Sonangol in 2005, TradeJango was a company that provides an online e-marketplace for Angolan suppliers to connect with buyers of their goods and services. The company was controlled by Sonangol and managed by Servite, a Brazilian information technology company that owned the remaining 49 per cent of TradeJango. Similar to the NipeX system used in

Nigeria, TradeJango allows IOCs to place tenders for contracts on the website for registered oil service suppliers to bid for. Unlike NipeX, TradeJango was not mandatory. While most of the IOCs use CAE, none were registered with TradeJango. Instead, TradeJango was currently used primarily by subsidiaries of Sonangol and some other government agencies, such as the Ministry of Finance.

A TradeJango employee complained of large-scale 'resistance' to TradeJango from the international operators. TradeJango, he said, is 'waiting for a policy solution'. 'If there was a law to enforce use, maybe that would do the trick... if the proper laws were put in place, usage would increase.'[21] A second TradeJango employee in a later interview denied they are seeking legislation to make TradeJango mandatory. According to him, negotiations have been ongoing with the operators specifically so this can be avoided.[22]

In 2010, there were 18 major buyers and more than 100 active suppliers out of 600–700 registered suppliers.[23] Although they are only available for 2008, statistics for TradeJango were unimpressive. In that year, approximately US$15 million was transacted on TradeJango (see Table 3.3), mostly in very low-end areas of procurement, and the website does not seem to have grown since then. A senior manager at the Ministry of Petroleum confided in 2010 that making the use of TradeJango compulsory was being considered as part of the national content overhaul.[24] However, it now seems that TradeJango has ceased to exist.

Table 3.3: Items Supplied through TradeJango (2008)

Product	Value
Accessories of office supplies	$5,198,226.46
Dossier files	$177,116.04
Staplers and cutters	$229,819.00
Stationery	$7,152,933.35
Office furniture	$2,156,875.00
Total	$14,914,969.85

Source: TradeJango.[25]

CAE and TradeJango were systems put in place to address the problem that the IOCs and international service companies have myriad ways of subverting local content in procurement. The relative ease with which foreign companies can bypass regulations on local content in procurement creates an enormous challenge for Sonangol and MINPET.

One Angolan working as a senior procurement officer for one of the major multinational oil service companies noted that the biggest challenge to buying local is that products and services from Angolan companies are two to three times more expensive. The added expense creates an incentive for companies to import goods that can be found in Angola. However, this Angolan was also very critical of his company and its commitment to national procurement and alleged that even basic services, protected in Regime 1 and reserved for Angolan companies, are being provided by foreigners.

For example, he noted that most offshore catering is done by Portuguese companies, in violation of Decree 127/03. This is a claim that was independently verified by several other interviews. In his department, this Angolan said that he and other nations try to buy Angolan goods, but the expatriate managers do not allow it. Even though he holds the title of Senior Buyer in a department where six of twenty-one buyers are Angolan, he claimed that the Angolans have little say in procurement decisions. Asked to describe the commitment to local content in procurement, the interviewee said: '[My company] doesn't consider it their concern to improve local content. Their concern is to increase profit.'[26]

Operators usually have one or two suppliers worldwide for routine office supplies and can procure these products at large volume discounts. One informant, a knowledgeable journalist who covers the oil and energy sectors in Angola and who had personal experience trying to sell paper to Chevron, used that company as an example for understanding procurement from the IOC perspective. At one point, Chevron received one container per month of paper from Houston. Although paper may seem like an unimportant item, Chevron cannot afford to run out of basic supplies like paper. Because the Angolan market for paper is very poor, prices are double or triple the international price. For Chevron to switch to local suppliers, which it eventually did, was a huge and costly endeavour.[27]

The paper experiment has not been entirely successful for Chevron. An employee of an Angolan company in Cabinda, who works for one of the three to four local companies that now supply paper to Chevron, confided that in August 2010 the company experienced a major paper stock-out. None of the local companies could supply more than a small number of boxes, leaving Chevron in a desperate situation.[28] A Chevron manager denied the incident, but allowed: 'We don't stop. To work with companies here, they need to supply everything we need 24 hours a day.'[29] He was very critical of the Angolan companies' capacity to provide for Chevron's needs. While an effort to switch some procurement is underway, it is not surprising that such efforts are very limited. An expatriate who works for an Angolan company supplying Chevron explained the slow pace of the switch: 'At the end of the day, they won't ever let the most urgent things go to local companies. They are never going to let a local company supply a piece of equipment that could put them out of production for weeks if they don't have it. They're pushing small things to try and satisfy Sonangol.'[30]

Switching procurement involves many new challenges, as a procurement officer for Statoil described. While the company's policy is to use local content whenever doing so doesn't risk its quality/standards, in the Statoil employee's words: 'It's not easy to find quality suppliers.' There is a particular risk in an area such as security, since most Angolan security companies are owned by current high-ranking officers in the armed forces. Statoil gets off-the-record info on ownership in an effort to prevent violation of corruption laws. However, in the employee's words: 'You may find companies with unknown owners. Sometimes we do business with such companies. We know the risks, but we are in this country, so what can we do?'[31] The current state of local/national content shows several weaknesses affecting the potential for economic development. It is by further exploring concerns with local content that the dual nature of local content becomes most apparent.

Concerns with the Implementation of Local Content in Angola

Although the promotion of local content is an important priority and possibly a unique way to foster economic development, its implementation raises several concerns in practice. These concerns will have to be addressed by all the actors involved in order for the benefits of these policies to extend into the economy and into the lives of Angolans and to minimize the tendency for them to increase inequalities of wealth and power.

Primary concerns in Angola include the low level of education and human resources, as well as limited Angolan capacity to offer quality goods and services, given the context of Angola's long history of civil war and conflict. As one Angolan working in the oil sector pointed out: 'There needs to be an intermediate manufacturing sector in Angola, otherwise there cannot be local content.'[32] On the other hand, although there are many obstacles to overcome, it might be said that Angola is developing quickly already.

Rebuilding the Angolan economy is a job that requires coordination of several key groups with very different motivations and priorities. The first such group is the international oil companies. While recognizing the legitimacy of local content policies, IOCs are highly conscious of their own bottom lines. The IOCs walk a fine line due to the power of Sonangol and the clear emphasis that the Angolan government has put on Angolanization. Many aspects of local content involve little to no extra cost to the IOCs. Although IOCs are quick to tout their local content initiatives, they have resisted any change that negatively affects their bottom line or their ability to operate on their own terms. For this reason, they are most wary of the additional risk caused by switching to unproven Angolan companies, hiring Angolans for key management positions (although this resistance often seems rooted in a logic other than economic) and of large-scale change.

It is not surprising, given Sonangol's leverage relative to the IOCs, that operators would want to mobilize and protect their interests. While they are very public supporters of local content, the IOCs are likely to continue fighting local content initiatives that hurt their bottom line or that have even minimal risk of jeopardizing their production. Speaking off the record, a Sonangol employee complained to me that the international operators 'lobby together' to combat policies they oppose.[33] What that employee was referencing were disturbing precedents in Angola of collusion amongst the operators to fight government policies aimed at promoting the use of Angolan goods and services—in particular, financial services.

Angola investigated new financial regulations a few years after the end of the civil war to require foreign companies to use Angolan banks. According to several sources, the IOCs made a coalition to resist the changes. In response to the threat of new financial regulations, the heads of BP, Total, Chevron and ExxonMobil in Angola met together and then began a campaign of voicing their concerns to key officials in the government. At least two of these companies went directly to the President to warn that such requirements would be too detrimental to their overall profitability. Reflecting on the fiasco, an Angolan oil insider concluded: 'The companies colluded together to resist this, but the BNA conducted itself very badly on this subject because the cash call could have happened. Angola lost out and now in the end maybe even the cash call won't happen.'[34]

Fortunately, two years later these fears were proven unfounded when the Angolan government passed a new law on the use of local currency in the oil industry as part of a wider range of 'Kwanzanization' policies. Passed in January 2012, Law 02/12 empowered the Bank of Angola to pass National Bank Order 20/2012, which requires use of the Angolan Kwanza to pay taxes and local contractors in the oil industry in order to boost the Angolan financial sector. Through the new policy, billions of dollars will enter the Angolan financial system each year. The increased use of the Kwanza significantly grows the Angolan banking sector, strengthens the foreign exchange market and gives the government more control over monetary policy than it had under an economy where the US dollar was widely used and a lot of payments for oil contracts and services never even entered the Angolan financial system.

The IOCs are not the only actors whose interests sometimes work against the promotion of local content. With all the power and influence Sonangol commands in Angola come many opportunities for corruption. As described by Soares de Oliveira (2007a), Sonangol is a business success with tentacles that reach into every area of the Angolan economy. The company has formed many joint ventures with multinational oil service companies. These joint ventures assure some measure of Angolan control over the oil service sector.

Figure 3.1: Selected Major Sonangol Joint Ventures in Oil Services

- Angoflex Limitada (Sonangol/Technip)
- Petromar (Sonangol/Saipem)
- Sonadiets (Sonangol/Dietsmann)
- Sonamer (Sonangol/Pride Foramer)
- Sonamet (Sonangol/Acergy/Wapo)
- Sonaserf (Sonangol/Bourbon)
- Sonatide (Sonangol/Tidewater)
- Sonawest (Sonangol/Western Geco/Schlumberger)
- Sonils (Sonangol/Intels)

At the same time, Sonangol's heavy presence in the sector is also a discouragement to other private national investment. Some of Sonangol's joint ventures are successful; however, others have been complete failures. Either way Sonangol's role in approving service contracts for all operators is problematic, given that it operates more than a dozen high-profile joint ventures with multinational oil service companies (see Figure 3.1 for a partial list) and has several subsidiaries providing services to the sector.[35]

Sonangol's influence is now so great that it has begun to attempt to influence which domestic partners are chosen by foreign companies for joint ventures (JVs) when the services they provide fall into Regime 2 of Decree 127/03. In its role of approving contracts over US$100,000 in value, Sonangol exercises a great deal of needed influence. At the same time, the divisions that approve these contracts (D.PRO and DEC) are known for long wait times for approval and poor monitoring and follow-up. An expatriate CAE employee noted that when CAE gets word of a bid, it makes a list of companies and then sends the list to Sonangol. However, he made clear that Sonangol often removes some clients and/or adds others to the list. With sarcasm, he told me: 'No one knows exactly why, but everyone has the same idea.'[36]

Although some Sonangol interventions are legitimate government actions to promote local content, many others feed into the dual nature of local content. The reality faced by many 'up and coming' Angolan businesses is that those who do not have Sonangol protection face added difficulties. One Angolan who works in the procurement department of one of the joint venture companies listed in Figure 3.1 explained that Sonangol had virtually no role in the joint venture, other than to make sure that approvals go smoothly: 'In our case, Sonangol is a [XX] per cent owner in the JV, so we don't have a lot of problems. I think [my company] used this JV just to have access to the Angolan market... It's not a real partnership. I don't think it promotes local content.'[37] In this case, it appears that a multinational OSC chose to partner with Sonangol solely to facilitate the operation in Angola.

Illegitimate interference takes many forms. More than one interviewee relayed stories of Sonangol officials asking for kickbacks in order to approve contracts. One interviewee who works for a multinational OSC was willing to provide a first-hand account of his former company paying kickbacks to Sonangol to get contracts.[38] Several informants allege that Sonangol routinely steers contracts to favoured service providers. This has the effect of deterring some potential entrepreneurs from entering the sector. A former Angolan employee of Chevron whom the company even sent to the US to obtain an MBA commented that he refused to work in the oil services sector because there was 'too much politics'. Now in private business, he explained:

> There is a lot of corruption. To survive you need someone strong to protect you—someone in Sonangol or a general or someone who if someone goes after you, you have someone strong enough to protect you... I've seen people lose contracts because they didn't pay people in Sonangol to protect them. I know I can get a contract. I'm worried about keeping it... If you want to get contracts, you need to give protection to Sonangol—20–30 per cent.[39]

In addition to the problem of corruption within Sonangol, Angolan ownership in Regimes 1 and 2 forces multinational oil service companies to partner with locals (if they do not partner directly with Sonangol). The fact that the legal framework promotes and even requires Angolan ownership in order to participate in the sector is one of the most fundamental ways in which local content operates as a mechanism for elite accumulation in a way similar to the problems of fronting faced by Nigeria during the indigenization era. Noting that the best Angolan partners are active and have money to invest, one journalist who reports on the Angolan energy sector admitted that many foreign firms often end up with 'sleeping partners'.[40]

The Local Content Manager at one large multinational oil service company confided that his company is planning to find Angolan partners and move towards the 51 per cent Angolan model because, although the services it offers are currently in Regime 2 and Regime 3, it believes the services it offers may soon be moved to a more protected regime. He had heard a rumour that many of the services it offers would soon be in Regime 1 of the Decree No. 127/03 system. The manager says that the company wants an active partner and is trying to find one that is not too well-connected (for example, a current minister or friend/family member of one) because then if the political situation changes, it could be damaging to the company. They have come to the realization that 'It's not possible to not have a local partner—they will force you.'[41]

In the manager's words, many foreign companies are making the decision to take partners using the logic that: 'It's better to have half an egg than an empty shell.' At the same time, he related several ways in which a foreign company could get around the need to Angolanize ownership while still retaining day-today management and control over the majority of revenues and profits—even after the company is supposedly 51 per cent owned by Angolans. Firstly, the key staff positions generally remain filled by expatriates. Another possibility, though generally illegal, is to have side agreements on ownership, decision-making or profits. More commonly, the joint venture can subcontract work to the foreign company that will be done abroad, ensuring that more of the profit ends up abroad.[42] These are just some of the ways to skirt local content regulations, suggesting that implementation may be very difficult to control.

Current Local Content Strategies and Impact: the Nigerian Content Act

On 22 April 2010, Goodluck Jonathan in his capacity as Acting President of Nigeria signed the Nigerian Oil and Gas Industry Content Development Act, or Nigerian Content Act (NCA). The NCA is a watershed law that has transformed the potential for Nigerian citizens to benefit from the country's petroleum resources. The NCA gives first consideration for awards of oil blocks, oilfields and oil lifting to 'Nigerian independent operators'; it gives exclusive consideration to Nigerian indigenous service companies that meet certain conditions to bid on land and swamp operating areas; it creates the NCDMB; it requires a Nigerian content plan for all bidding on tenders in the industry; and it lays out a series of regulations designed to domicile manufacturing and services relating to the oil and gas industry in-country.

Taking the definition of the 2002 NCLCD report, the NCA defines Nigerian content as 'the quantum of composite value added to or created in the Nigerian economy by a systematic development of capacity and capabilities through the deliberate utilization of Nigerian human, material resources and services in the Nigerian oil and gas industry'. This definition captures a key difference between today's local content push and previous attempts at indigenization with its focus on the addition of economic value.

Among the NCA's most controversial measures is a stipulation of a maximum of 5 per cent of management positions for expatriate workers and an appendix containing minimum levels of Nigerian content in any project (see Figure 3.2). A second controversial measure is the requirement that IOCs remit 1 per cent of all contract sums to the Board, for the creation of a Nigerian Content Development Fund (NCDF). The fund is not meant to provide operating funds to the NCDMB. Rather, it is for capacity-building initiatives and to help indigenous companies to access capital. Finally, the NCA also gives the NCDMB, which was essentially created out of the NNPC-NCD, authority to hand out hefty penalties—5 per cent of the project sum for each project or cancellation of the project.

Figure 3.2: Selected Minimum Levels of Nigerian Content in the NCA Schedule

Front-end engineering and design	• 90% of person-hours for most activities • 50% of person-hours for LNG projects • 80% of person-hours for deep offshore projects
Fabrication	• 80% volume of terminal/oil movement systems • Generally 50–100% of tonnage for other projects
Materials and procurement	• 45% of high voltage cables; 90% of low voltage cables

	• 60–100% of tonnage for various goods
Services	• 45–100%; either in terms of expenditure or person-hours
Research & Development	• 60–100% of expenditure
Engineering/Information systems	• 55–100% of expenditure
Transportation	• 65–100% of expenditure
Shipping	• 60% of expenditure on domestic coastal carriage of petroleum products • 90% of expenditure on tows and supplies of very large crude carriers
Marine, operations and logistics services	• 30–100%; either in terms of expenditure, person-hours, or numbers of crews
Installation	• 45–100% of person-hours
Inspection/Testing/Certification	• 45–90%; either in terms of man-hours or certifications obtained
Project management/Consulting services	• 45–90%; either in terms of expenditure or person-hours
Modification and maintenance	• 45–90%; either in terms of expenditure, tonnage or volume
Finance	• 100% of general banking services • 70% of monetary intermediation • 50% of amount of loans for credit • 70–100%; either in terms of expenditure or person-hours for other financial services

Source: Nigerian Content Act (2010).

Although the IOCs have complained loudly about the onerous nature of the new reporting requirements, from 2005 to 2009 the IOCs had to submit monthly monitoring reports covering all major projects to the NCD using their templates (Maliki, 2009: 7). Despite a lag of time from when the NCA was signed until the NCDMB was set up and in a position to collect data, by September 2010 the Department of Operations and Projects (formerly the office of planning in the NNPC-NCD) was, according to the head of the department, demanding plans for review and approval from all oil and gas companies for every project and contract.[43] However, according to the Manager of the Monitoring and Evaluation Department, the NCDMB has never issued any fines or penalties under the Act.[44]

Officials have been very careful to distinguish the NCA from Nigerianization of ownership. Discussing the example of Nigeria's indigenization experience, Paul Kennedy writes that the problem with indigenization in Nigeria was that it was opposed by foreign capital, whereas collaboration with Western interest was required for internal political control (Kennedy, 1988: 104–5; citing Osabo, 1978). According to a manager in the NCDMB: 'We are not preaching Nigerianization. Nigerian content is not about Nigerianization. It's about domiciliation; doing it in Nigeria. So if you think that we cannot do this in Nigeria, tell us why and what you think needs to be done to do it in Nigeria.'[45] This is a view often repeated by Nigerian content proponents.

Nigerian officials often explain Nigerian content in terms of 'domiciling' economic activity in Nigeria (even if it is done by foreign firms) to create employment and promote economic activity, instead of 'indigenizing' ownership, as happened in the 1970s. The visions articulated by Nigerian content advocates paint a rosy picture filled with more employment opportunities for Nigerians. Shortly after the passage of the NCA, the Minister of Petroleum, Diezani Alison Madueke, was quoted in a statement released by NNPC saying, 'The Nigerian Content Law has the potential to generate over 30,000 jobs in the next 5 years...'[46] However, there are many concerns surrounding the implementation of Nigerian content. These will be discussed below.

It is easy to be seduced by the vision of Nigerian content in theory. NCDMB Executive Secretary Ernest Nwapa spoke frequently in 2010 of 30,000 new jobs. Two years later, an even more optimistic Nwapa had increased his estimate by a factor of ten, promising that Nigerian content would create 300,000 jobs for Nigerians during the administration of President Jonathan.[47] In discussing the logic of Nigerian content and the link to social and economic development, Nwapa explains:

> ... of all that money that is being spent on oil and gas projects in Nigeria, only 5–7 per cent of it was domiciled in Nigeria up until about 2003. That had a direct impact on the level of development of the national economy, which for the past 30-something years has been moving in the direction of a mono-product economy. The government is making efforts to diversify the economy in culture and other sectors, manufacturing, but oil still stands out as the key revenue driver for the national economy. Foreign exchange and revenue are driven essentially by the oil and gas industry. So the oil and gas industry, which is the mainstay of the Nigerian economy, is not doing enough to retain value in Nigeria so national development cannot thrive. That is the direct linkage.[48]

It is hardly an exaggeration to say that a wide array of stakeholders have embraced local content in Nigeria's oil and gas industry. Arguing that the

NCA will be a great benefit to Nigerian workers, the former National President of the Petroleum and Natural Gas Senior Staff Association of Nigeria (PENGASSAN), Louis Brown Ogbeifun, echoed most of Nigerian labour when he said: 'The recently passed [NCA] is a major breakthrough that the unions have been striving toward for a long time. We see it as something that will reduce unemployment in Nigeria.'[49]

In a rare occurrence, the Lagos Chamber of Commerce and Industry, which strongly opposed indigenization in the 1970s, agrees with labour. In the words of one of its senior economists, 'The benefits are clear. The private sector and the Lagos Chamber of Commerce and Industry support the Nigerian Content Act and encourage businesses to implement it. We believe it will create employment and benefit Nigeria, so we support it and call for it to be fully implemented by the federal government.'[50] The widespread support for Nigerian content marks a key difference between this policy and the policies of indigenization.

A similar vision is also articulated by indigenous oil service companies through the influential Petroleum Technology Association of Nigeria (PETAN), a lobby group for indigenous oil service companies. Shawley Coker, who is Chairman of PETAN and represents the organization on the NCDMB Governing Council, has said: 'We hope that if these policies are well-adhered to, they should have a multiplier effect and create employment.'[51] Additionally, as discussed above, albeit with reservations about some of the regulations, the oil industry also sees the potential benefits. According to the manager in charge of Nigerian content at Shell's joint venture company, the SPDC, Nigerian content also has benefits for relations with Niger Delta communities: 'It's all about empowering people; getting them gainfully employed in productive activities so they are able to send their children to school, improving their economic means of livelihood, making them productive and improving their standard of living. This is what we do and how we contribute to nation-building.'[52] This perspective reflects a strong commitment to Nigerian content, at least among Nigerian managers at IOCs.

According to Nwapa, community empowerment is also a big part of Nigerian content: 'Every operating company now has some kind of community empowerment programme. Most of them are geared toward preparing the ordinary people in these communities to find ways to get involved in the industry and real economic activities in the industry.' Nwapa argues that helping people find ways to be involved in the oil industry is what Nigerian content is about. In his way, the NCA 'goes beyond' notions of corporate social responsibility.[53] As the head of the capacity-building department of the NCDMB, through direct and indirect means, 'Idle hands will now be engaged.'[54]

This 'community empowerment', as eluded to above, is connected in the oil industry's thinking with addressing the demands of people in the Niger Delta. Chukwuma Henry Okolo, who is Vice Chairman and CEO of Dorman Long Engineering, Chairman of the Fabrication group of the Nigerian Content Consultative Forum and Vice Chairman of the Nigerian Economic Summit Group, argues: 'The problem in the Niger Delta is 100 per cent linked to employment creation. I think industry, before government came up with this policy, was less than responsible.'[55] It is also seen as a way to address latent tensions about which Nigerians are employed by the IOCs. Anecdotally, I heard complaints from staff at two different IOCs—Shell and AGIP—that it was Yoruba employees who were promoted into the higher levels of management in their companies.

It is understandable why Shell, rocked by decades of bad public relations related to its operations in the Niger Delta,[56] would want to be seen to be empowering Nigerians. Additionally, portraying Nigerian content as a means of economic empowerment is an understandable priority of the government. However, job creation will only occur if multinational OSCs relocate activities to Nigeria. As Shawley Coker, who worked for several of those companies before starting his own, notes:

> If they will not stop building tankers for Nigeria in South Korea, in the North Sea and way outside the waters of Nigeria on the other side of the ocean, thereby creating over 10,000 jobs for the nationals of those countries, there will be no improvement. They must bring in such factories and plants into Nigeria to help to create employment for our people and help to provide economic freedom and grow some new entrepreneurs after having worked for X/Y/Z multinational for a period of time.[57]

Current Local Content Strategies: the Promise of Nigerian Content

For Nigerian content to succeed, it is the petro-developmental state that must step up to promote policies that both promote economic development and address poverty and social inequality. The NCDMB is very firm in its resolve to ensure that indigenous companies get the contracts. Jobs are given now to companies with higher Nigeria content. All contracts given now have more Nigerian companies involved. As an employee in the NCD of one of the major foreign joint venture companies, responsible for tracking procurement, explained: 'You're seeing more companies that have never been given the opportunity getting jobs now for the first time. Sometimes we're forced to do that.'[58]

The industry as a whole remains sceptical of the ability of indigenous companies to offer goods and services of comparable quality. However, a Nigerian content manager at one of the larger Nigerian indigenous oil service companies explained why, in her view, Nigerian content policies will not affect the quality of products supplied: 'If I can prove they aren't offering acceptable quality, I can go abroad. So that is their incentive to offer quality products and services.'[59]

Although the industry may remain sceptical, the NCDMB believes that it can monitor and enforce compliance with Nigerian content. While this is a large task, the head of the Monitoring and Evaluation Department at the NCDMB believes that ordinary Nigerians working in the industry will help the board enforce policy by anonymously reporting infractions.[60] This view would seem to be supported by one official in the Upstream Monitoring Division of the DPR who said that although Nigerian content is no part of his job description, if he saw something he thought was a breach, he would report it.[61] Many Nigerians working for foreign and domestic companies have expressed similar views.

As Ariweriokuma (2009) notes, deficient capitalization, poor training and managerial ability are often cited as the main reasons for low Nigerian content development. According to the manager of the Capacity Building Department of the NCDMB, three areas of low indigenous capacity are deep offshore activities, human capital and manufacturing.[62] Building deep offshore capacity is a more long-term project, but efforts to improve human capital have already been put in place. As Ibilola Amao, Principal Consultant with Lagos-based Lonadek Oil and Gas Consultants, explains:

> In the last three years, the Nigerian Content vision to transform the oil and gas industry into the economic engine for job creation and national growth by developing in-country capacity and indigenous capabilities has become more widely acceptable as 'value addition.' Human Capital development has also become the most probable means and major consideration that presents itself as a low hanging fruit for achieving any major recordable success. (Amao, 2010)

Human capital development is an ongoing priority for the NCDMB. At the same time, improving manufacturing capacity is also a long-term project. Already, though, some would argue that a great deal of progress has been made. Figure 3.5, taken from a 2008 publication of the NNPC-NCD, shows some of the early achievements. By 2010, many of these achievements have been greatly improved upon, as evidenced by Ernest Nwapa's assertion that engineering 'man-hours' performed in Nigeria are now 'in excess of 3.5 million' (out of a total of roughly 5 million hours per year available).[63]

The NCDMB has made fabrication an important area of emphasis, with their capacity-building department completing a comprehensive fabrication audit. According to the audit, 'Average annual spend for fabrication is estimated at US$1.5 billion. Of this, only about 40 per cent is domiciled in Nigeria. This does not include other sections e.g. engineering, installation where the percentage spend domiciled in Nigeria is much less.' They estimate that in the past, 'while no quantitative estimates had previously been made, it was felt that in country capacity could handle only about 15% of requirements'. However, due to progress in the past few years, the audit conclusion suggests: '[Nigerian fabrication yards] can execute about 40 per cent of the present workload. By a series of specific actions, their capacities and capabilities can be developed over a period of about eight years to undertake 100 per cent of the projected work in specific areas thus exceeding the requirements of the Nigerian Content Policy' (NNPC-NCD 2010: 9).

Figure 3.3: Major Nigerian Content Achievements

Activity	Prior to 2005	2008
Engineering Person-Hours Performed in Nigeria	250,000	3,000,000
International Engineering Companies Working in Nigeria	Nil	2
Fabrication Tonnage in Nigeria	12,000	80,000–100,000
Fabrication Yard Lifting Capacity (Single)	0–100T	500T
Deep-Water Facilities in Nigeria	None	2 in progress
Companies that Fabricate Pressure Vessels in Nigeria	None	Dorman Long, Nigerdock
Companies that Integrate FPSO Units in Nigeria	Not contemplated	Two current bids are based on integration
Companies that Manufacture Pipe in Nigeria	Not feasible	2 pipe mills are interested
Industry Skills Development	No programme	Oil and Gas Human Capacity Development Program has trained 250 engineers
Welders Training Plan	No programme	2,000–3,000 to be trained

| Access to Capital | Interest rate: 24 per cent p.a. | Through the Nigerian Content Support Fund US$350 million is available at a rate of 9 per cent p.a. |
| Well and Drilling Services | Indigenous companies were being edged out by multinationals | Mudlogging and other drilling activities reserved for indigenous companies |

Source: *Nigerian Content Development in Oil and Gas Industry*. Nigerian Content Division, Nigerian National Petroleum Corporation. July 2008 [Powerpoint].

In general, the IOCs have embraced most aspects of Nigerian content and accept its basic principles. However, they have been slow in terms of implementation. The logic of resistance discussed in Turner (1980) still generally applies, though a new reality forces the IOCs publicly to accept and embrace local content. According to the NCDMB fabrication audit: 'There is the paradox that most yards are idle even though it is estimated that there is excess work. Reasons could include the comatose state of the industry in view of the problems in the region. Also some Nigerian companies subcontract the work to overseas yards instead of bracing up to do the work. There is still the added possibility that the IOC's export work for which there is in-country capacity.' (NNPC-NCD, 2010: 24)

The theory of how domiciliation works is well laid out by Okolo:

> Obviously Nigerian Content can be more expensive. Let's say something previously could be done for US$100 million; if you bring it from South Korea or Canada, let's say it would be US$100 million. Because of issues in Nigeria, let's say it's now going to cost you US$120 million. So you if you give me a contract it will be US$120 million instead of $100 million. However, when it is done by a Canadian company or a South Korean company, that US$100 million is out of the country with zero value added. When it's done by Dorman Long or any other company, I will probably import steel products representing US$30–US$40 million, but when you do national economic accounting, what you are going to see is that the balance will be spent as wages, domestic procurement, taxes to government, etc. So there is genuine value-added in terms of GDP. Also, in terms of foreign reserves, only US$30 million left the country.[64]

In Nigeria, as the audit shows, there are a handful of indigenous OSCs involved in manufacturing and fabrication. Two of the most well-known are Dorman Long Engineering and Nigerdock. Both have complained about a lack of work and excess capacity. According to Henry Okolo, 'Most Nigerian companies have been laying off welders and fitters.'[65] Manssour Jarmakani, Executive Director of Nigerdock, agrees that 'yards are going broke'. He complains that 'there's no work'. Without work, he points out, 'Nigeria content will fail very quickly.'[66]

In terms of fostering increased capacity through smaller companies, there are still several hurdles. A good example capturing where Nigeria is at in terms of indigenous manufacturing and fabrication is found in the example of Arco Petroleum. According to Alfred Okoigun, the founder and Managing Director of Arco Petroleum, Nigeria needs to create an enabling environment for manufacturing. Okoigun started Arco thirty years ago. His primary business is representing foreign manufacturers of equipment for the oil and gas sector. He has big plans for moving into equipment manufacturing on his own or in partnership with foreign firms, but has so far been unable to get any manufacturing off the ground due mainly to poor infrastructure. However, the company has been increasingly involved in the repair of machinery that previously could not be repaired in-country.

Okoigun argues that Nigerians must start somewhere. Even if they are simply providing equipment they have purchased from abroad, this is a move in the right direction: 'For now, we're starting from there. Users want to go direct to the source to reduce overhead, but if we carry stock, we're carrying a risk. So that is our contribution. If someone has taken the initiative and risk to do that in Nigeria, they should have an advantage from that.'[67] Okoigun's approach shows that incremental steps towards greater Nigerian content and greater national control of the oil and gas industry are possible through implementation of considered policy prescriptions. However, while wealth previously going abroad would now go to the Nigerian elite, a deeper look would suggest a lesser impact on the bulk of Nigerians, since by his own admission Okoigun relies heavily on expatriate labour.

Arco's example shows the importance of the promotion of indigenous entrepreneurship for the success of Nigerian content. This involves shifting the strategies of Nigerian elites from what David Harvey calls 'accumulation by dispossession' (see Chapter 1) to capitalist accumulation. The shift, according to many Nigerians in the industry, is already occurring from rent-seeking to productive enterprise. According to Fabian Ajogwu: 'I think if we don't truncate what has been started in the next two to three years, we'll see the direct results... a shift to a more capitalistic form of business with emphasis now on participation rather than rent-seeking. You will not be able to sit and collect rent. You will have to now go at it, work it, do it yourself.' Ajogwu also confirms that the shift is already underway: 'I already see my friends getting involved, bringing in rigs. There are all kinds of transactions coming in now... It's already occurring.'[68]

Ajogwu's colleague, Pat Utomi, argues that there may be a generational dimension to the shift as well. According to him, Nigeria needs to follow a model of encouraging and supporting young, 'hungry' engineers and other skilled Nigerians to 'build an enterprise for [themselves] in the interest of the economy':

> What typically happens in Nigeria is that when an opportunity comes, some 'fat cat' who has already learned to live well from previous rent opportunities, jumps in there to extract more rent. He can't do anything, does not develop any skills and just has one or two foreigners working for him and extracting rent... If we want to grow the oil and gas sector, we need to find those Nigerians that worked for Schlumberger, who went off to Bahrain and wherever to work. They are 39 years old. They have all the skills. Create the conditions for them to build a great company... those who extracted yesterday's rent are not going to take the necessary risks.[69]

The preceding section should make clear that the promise of Nigerian content is very real. During my fieldwork, I found that Nigerians from all walks of life are filled with genuine optimism. The optimism, a hope that greater Nigerian participation in the oil and gas industry will bring greater social and economic development, is also optimism about a transformation to a more capitalistic mode of production and development. This optimism is captured by industry insider Austin Avuru: 'There is clearly a very strong drive from Nigerian entrepreneurs not only to invest, but to add value to the industry. I think that in another ten years you are going to see a thriving sector overall controlled by independent, indigenous, small-sized companies.'[70]

There is reason to be proud of the achievements of Nigerian content so far and to be optimistic about the future. Reflecting on what he achieved regarding Nigerian content during his tenure at the helm of NNPC, F. M. Kupolokun noted: 'The major thing now is that you can no longer ignore it. It has become something that everyone now knows—everyone in the industry must think about our goals in terms of local goods and services.'[71] While this is a notable accomplishment, there are many potential pitfalls to be avoided and challenges to be overcome.

Concerns with the Implementation of Local Content in Nigeria

One of Frantz Fanon's most famous essays looks forward to imagine the pitfalls for national consciousness in post-colonial Africa. He could have been

81

writing about the experience of national content when he lamented: 'the national bourgeoisie is not engaged in production, invention, building or labour...' (Fanon, 1965: 120). As we shall see in Chapter 4, the national elite represent significant obstacles to achieving beneficial state outcomes.

The first concern that must be raised about Nigerian content is the familiar concern about fronting. Writing in 1976, M. O. Lolomari comments:

> The average Nigerian is content to serve as a mere agency for foreign companies whether in the field of concession awards or in buying crude oil. He is satisfied with being a silent partner waiting for the dividends to slop, slop, slop into the barrel, or prostituting concessions for the highest foreign bidder. Nigerians potentially of the stature of Rockefeller, Getty, Mattei or Hammer are not yet on the oil horizon. (Lolomari, 1976; cited in Atsegbua, 2004)

As Louis Ogbeifun writes, even some TNCs are forming local companies which they 'sublet to Nigerians' to carry out contracting jobs. Therefore, Ogbeifun passionately writes, 'Nigerians as a people must stop paying lip service to policies that will improve the lot of our nation' (2007: 198–9).

Ogbeifun's concern is echoed by many inside the industry. Speaking to a workshop of the Nigerian Association of Petroleum Explorationists (NAPE), Shawley Coker warned of the need to 'avoid the same pitfalls that derailed the Nigerianization ideals of the Indigenization Decree of 1972'.[72] The concern about local fronting extends to contemporary local content policy in Nigeria. In a 2004 presentation on local content, Macaulay Ofurhie warns about Nigerian fronts[73] and explains how Nigerian content must be different:

> ... there have been reactions from some stake-holding units on the use of companies classifying companies on the basis of ownership. We have also been warned on the possible danger of manipulating the new policy to promote local fronts rather than local content which can stall the current aspirations. The Department is of the view the fear is unfounded. Whereas, the local content seeks to reward local investment and competence, [local fronting] seeks to glorify mediocrity and promote indigenous lackeys. Local content, unlike local fronting, aims at benefiting the larger society, while ensuring legitimate gains on labour and capital, local fronting concentrates on rewarding a tiny and often incompetent segment of the society to the detriment of the larger majority.[74]

The concerns that Ofurhie raised in 2004 are shared by others within the DPR. Speaking about personal concerns with the new law, one senior official in DPR lamented that the problem with Nigerian content is that 'The whole game now is about contracts.' Nigerian content, the official contended, works to make sure that Nigerians get the contracts; but once they get the contract, his concern was that a foreign company would still do the work: 'I'm a

Nigerian, but I can have the backing of, let's say, Canada Inc... I don't have anything, I've never drilled before, but I will bring that rig from Canada with Canadians on it. I will go because I have the contacts, get all the necessary things, bid, have an office in Port Harcourt or Lagos or both and the people can come and do the work.'[75] This concern has also been raised in connection with the role of 'technical partners' in the Marginal Fields Program.

Responding to the suggestion that the oil operators are required to report in great detail on subcontractors, owners of equipment, sources of raw materials, etc., this official brought up some well-known concerns of all DPR officials: the problem of confirming what is in the reports, workplans and submissions of the IOCs, not only in terms of Nigerian content, but in general. For many public officials, there is a widespread sense that what the IOCs report is simply not a reflection of what is actually occurring on the ground: 'But how do you confirm that? ... I told you there is an issue of sincerity. It's not there. How do you validate?'[76] For these reasons, many civil society organizations have demanded that the names of all those who get a contract award be published, along with dates of award and completion. This, one staffer argued, would help to ensure an 'open, transparent process of bidding'. Without that level of transparency, I was told, contracts would be 'dished out as political patronage' under the guise of Nigerian content.[77]

Concerns over Nigerian fronts and political patronage are connected to the pitfall of poor implementation. Shawley Coker has captured the hope that this moment represents for the Nigerian oil and gas industry, but also the recognition of the significant challenges which industry insiders knew awaited them: 'Needless to say, there is a world of difference between the ideals of the Law and the realization of the benefits it seeks to provide and protect. It would take the collective will and effort of the government, operators, service providers, stake-holding institutions, international investors and partners to make the [Nigerian Content Act] work.' According to Coker who, as mentioned above, is also a member of the Governing Council of the NCDMB, 'the firmness with which the provisions of the Law would be driven and defaulters sanctioned by the Board (and relevant institutions) should set a sound regulatory tone for the industry'.[78]

Coker's warning call fits with Alfred Okoigun's reflections on the job that has been done so far:

We've not really done things well. The accountability aspect has not been taken into consideration. For this reason, a few people who get into the government have done well. This is a very discouraging factor to some hard enterprising people. All that being said, there is still much more opportunity than there was in the military regime when you didn't have the freedom to express your opinion.[79]

Still, the most stinging rebuke comes from the dissident DPR official, who questions the very connection between the government's decisiveness in setting targets and their strategy for meeting them: 'There are no definitive plans, but there are targets. They've set targets, but there is no plan, no plan at all!'[80]

Expressing concern about political patronage, Austin Avuru, CEO of Seplat Petroleum, says: 'I still think, even in following the process that has now been established by the government, there are still ways of favouring those who are seeking these opportunities. Once there is an avenue to this kind of favour, there is going to be corruption.' Although he stressed that Nigerian Content was not one of these avenues for favouritism, Avuru allowed that 'Once, in any event, there is authority to approve, then that authority can be applied to dispense favour. Once there is opportunity to dispense favour and there is more than one seeking that favour, there is an opportunity for corruption.'[81]

Voices inside NNPC have also been critical—especially from managers studying the problem for the Management Development Programme. Brown cites the recent LNG projects as evidence than Nigerian content is still low, even in areas where capacity exists such as FEED. For example, in the Nigeria LNG project, 'the Nigeria Content Capacity Development benefit from the project was insignificant compared to the project cost of US$3.6bn' (Brown, 2010: 7; citing Adeyeye, 2009). This point is illustrated in Table 3.4. Even more concerning, in the case of Brass LNG, Nigeria is yet to derive Nigerian content value addition, although over US$1 billion has been spent to date (Brown, 2010: 8; citing *Punch*, 23 April 2009). This lack of progress is because in the most recent LNG projects that Brown analyzed, Brass and Olokola, FEED was being done abroad, contrary to the requirement of the Federal Government Directive on Nigerian Content (Brown, 2010: 7). The best way to address this problem of non-compliance, Brown suggests, is to focus on the need for fines, penalties and contract revocations; and consideration of even more stringent measures such as 'even blacklisting of any defaulting company' (Brown, 2010: 23).

Ibrahim, another NNPC manager in an earlier course, made similar comments about the fabrication of FPSO vessel modules. According to Ibrahim, as expressed in Table 3.5, there is a very low level of fabrication of FPSO topside modules in Nigeria in all the most recent FPSO projects, despite excess fabrication capacity and the required technical competence. Ibrahim writes that NNPC lacks the ability to enforce Nigerian content provisions. Although Ibrahim was writing before the passage of the NCA, and it is too soon after the creation of the NCDMB to judge its success accurately in terms of enforcement, there is reason to suspect that they will face similar challenges with implementing goals and targets that the IOCs are openly opposed to; and this is a major pitfall in thinking about Nigerian content policy.

Table 3.4: Nigeria LNG Project and Nigerian Content Participation

	T1/T2	T3	T4/T5	T6
Project Cost (US$ bn)	3.60	1.80	3.50	2.500
Nigerian Content Value (US$ bn)	0.18	0.09	0.35	0.698

Source: Brown, 2010: 20; citing LNG and Power Presentation to COMDP 055.

Table 3.5: FPSO Topside Modules Fabricated in Nigeria

FPSO Project	Year	FPSO Topside Modules	Modules Fabricated In-country	Percentage of Nigeria Content
Bonga	2002	22,000	0,992	5
Erha	2004	29,000	2,358	8
Agbami	2006	31,000	4,510	15
Akpo	2007	36,471	7,600	21

Source: Ibrahim, 2008: 24; citing NAPIMS Project Documents.

A final potential challenge, which must be discussed in connection with Tables 3.4 and 3.5, is the measurement of Nigerian content. The key question is how to evaluate the level of national content in any given project or activity. This question cuts to the heart of what kind of impact Nigerian content can have and, more importantly, who benefits from it. As of 2014, there are still plenty of ambiguities as to how local content will be measured in Nigeria. Without a system for measurement in place, it is hard to imagine how Nigerian content can be monitored and implemented successfully. Additionally, it will be difficult to ensure that policies promoting growth and development will take precedence over policies promoting national ownership.[82] The ambiguities of measurement and lack of rigour in data collection render a lot of quantitative data suspect—especially data presented by the IOCs and government, who both have an interest in deeming it a success. This difficulty has meant that to date there is very little reliable data on how beneficial local content in oil and gas has been anywhere in the world.[83]

* * *

Poor implementation must also include opportunities lost due to a variety of problems of mismanagement, including the very complex issue of high-level corruption. As a case study, the entry and subsequent exit of the Dutch company Heerema is instructive; it demonstrates not only the large potential for Nigerian content, but also the enormous challenges of shifting an economic structure from rent-seeking patronage to capitalist production. Heerema is one of the largest companies in the world working on design, construction and transportation of offshore facilities for the oil and gas industries, including FPSOs. The company did the topside integration and maintenance of the Bonga FPSO and was convinced at a roadshow in 2005 put on by President Obasanjo to set up in Nigeria and do Bonga's maintenance in-country. Heerema would have set up in Nigeria ahead of the first scheduled maintenance of Bonga in 2011 and was going to create 2,000–4,000 direct jobs and numerous subcontracts, resulting in as many as 10,000 indirect jobs, according to company documents. The company was also going to train the Nigerian Navy as well as pay rent to the Navy in foreign exchange or Nigerian Naira.[84]

Heerema spent a total of US$10 million bringing in staff, paying rent, buying computers and equipment and setting up their in-country presence. Their total planned investment was around US$200 million. They took a 34 hectare lease on a piece of land belonging to the Navy at Ogogoro Island, the farthest island into the Gulf of Guinea off the coast of Lagos. Ultimately, they were unable to get all the permissions they needed and get the government to provide an environment in which they could set up their activities at Ogorogo Island, which was in their opinion the only feasible location for them to set up in the country. They planned to set up a state-of-the-art fabrication yard, with the capability to build constructions of up to 8,000 tonnes per fabrication hall, and with the possibility of maintaining vessels belonging to the Nigerian Navy under special concessions and terms using state-of-the-art technology. Instead, according to an anonymous source involved in Heerema's entry into Nigeria, 'Heerema simply, after many points of frustration, threw in the towel, shut down and went back to Holland.'[85]

As alleged in an editorial in the prominent Lagos daily newspaper *ThisDay*, the reason for Heerema leaving was corruption.[86] As the source mentioned above put it, 'Somebody wanted money somewhere in the government.' The results were tragic. As the source explains, 'Heerema was so huge that Heerema by itself could have taken local content from 6 to 35 per cent.'[87] Heerema's documents similarly speak of boosting overall Nigerian content from 20 to 40 per cent—capability for FPSO integration and Top End Fabrication in Nigeria. Additionally, as anchor tenant on Ogorogo Island, Heerema had already attracted other investors in areas such as galvanizing plants, piping, steel plate and sections, electrical and instrumentation engineering, logistics, a training school/centre, glass reinforced plastic systems and dredging. In addition to its work on Bonga for Shell, which would have been in-country, Heerema had pre-qualified for tenders with Chevron, Total and ExxonMobil before pulling out.

In March 2011 when Bonga was due for maintenance, it was instead taken back to Holland. Oil production was offline for an additional length of time due to the extra transport time. All the money spent was spent in Holland. Instead of Nigerians benefitting, nationals of another country did. The taxes were paid to the Dutch government; Dutch subcontractors got the contracts and jobs; and Heerema, in all likelihood, recouped all their losses in Nigeria in their bills to the operator, which, in turn, will get those costs back from the government of Nigeria. Therefore, as the source explained in late 2010, 'Heerema is only going to weep until March. Because we are stupidly sending back the Bonga to them to fix, they are just going to give us our bill with the cost of our stupidity to us with all that they lost.'[88,89]

While in theory Nigerian content seems to be a rising tide that lifts all boats, in practice different actors have very different interests when it comes to its implementation. Besides fearing poor implementation, patronage and outright corruption, the oil and gas industry fears cases where the public interest is not the same as private, corporate interest. The tension this creates can be seen in how the IOCs discuss Nigerian content.

In a presentation to NAPE, Simbi Wabote of Shell laid out what 'successful implementation' and 'failed implementation' of the government's Nigerian content initiative would look like. Successful implementation would involve government responsiveness, investment in infrastructure and capacity-building, collaboration with industry and 'business friendly regulations'. Conversely, failed implementation would be implementation of the law as passed and a failure to address grey areas in the regulatory structure. While successful implementation is seen as key to Nigeria producing a globally competitive energy service sector, failed implementation would lead to reduced investment, lack of commitment from industry, reduced profitability and stagnation in the Nigerian oil and gas industry.[90] In other words, for both the Nigerian elite and the IOCs, successful implementation of Nigerian content involves policies that promote profit over all other goals and objectives.

Providing a somewhat more nuanced point of view than Utomi's assertion that what is needed is increased entrepreneurship from a new generation of Nigerians, Austin Avuru has suggested that the growth of Nigerian entrepreneurship cannot be explained simply by Nigerians taking skills learned in the industry and starting their own companies. 'Nigerians have been in the business for 50 years, so why didn't it start 40 years ago?' Presumably focusing on the downstream, where more privatization has occurred, Avuru noted that the spirit of investment in Nigeria has been strengthened by government disinvestment from the sector; and it is that which has helped create some wealthy Nigerians and larger companies:

> It is because there is a space now for forming independent businesses that such Nigerians are now engaged when they leave multinationals. You find that in the bulk of these thriving businesses in the oil and gas sector, the people driving them are not necessarily those retiring from the multinationals. They're just entrepreneurs and then they engage those people.[91]

Therefore, what is needed, according to Avuru, is government support for industry. When this takes the form of incentives, tax breaks, or other forms of support, it may be less controversial (though many would question the decision to direct limited resources at the private sector in the first place). However, when promoting a good business climate means privatization and government disinvestment, given Nigeria's long history of political patronage at the expense of the public interest (a history many might say is associated with privatization and neoliberal policy prescriptions worldwide), the benefit to the ordinary Nigerian is less clear.

In areas where the Nigerian content conflicts with what IOCs see as their business interest, there has been a great deal of resistance. As mentioned above, two of the biggest problems with the NCA for IOCs are the minimum levels of Nigerian content in the schedule and the 5 per cent expatriate quota. The resistance has provoked angry responses from Nigerians. Overall, these areas have been the most contentious for Nigerian content.

Louis Brown Ogbeifun's book *The Role of Labour Unions in the Oil and Gas Industry in Nigeria* devotes an entire chapter to 'The Socio-Economic Impact of Expatriate Quota Abuse'. Quota abuse, Ogbeifun shows, leads to job displacement, capital flight and illegal repatriation and other negative outcomes for Nigeria. It also leads to increased production cost (often charged to the Nigerian government through JV accounts or PSC arrangements), reduced national security and a loss of tax revenue (Ogbeifun, 2007: 187–8). Turning to the question of local content, Ogbeifun argues that greater monitoring of the IOCs is required since there are still rigs and drill ships manned entirely by expatriates, in clear violation of long-standing policies about the need for Nigerian understudies (Ogbeifun, 2007: 196).

In August 2010, PENGASSAN formally requested a meeting with President Jonathan to 'discuss strategic issues of critical concern to PENGASSAN'. In their request for an audience, PENGASSAN complained that 'The business as usual process of Expatriate Quota Registration and Renewal still persists and is undermining the Nigerian Content Development Act 2010.'[92] Following up this request, in a speech to the National Executive Council of PENGASSAN a few months after the passage of the NCA, National President Babatunde Ogun argued:

> There is a need to impress on all employers, both multinational, national and indigenous oil and gas companies to comply with the provisions of the Nigerian Content Development Act 2010 that deal with Succession, Capacity and Empowerment Plans, with the reflection of allowable positions specified in percentage for expatriates in management and other positions.[93]

In conversation, Ogun also expressed concern with the accuracy of the reporting on the expatriate quota: 'In Nigeria we have a lot of law, but the government lacks the power to enforce it. The government and NAPIMS like to look at beautiful presentations and then they give in.'[94] For all labour's advocacy on this issue, the NCDMB issued draft guidelines on the expatriate quota in May 2011, not mentioning the 5 per cent. According to the General Secretary of PENGASSAN, the union feelings have not been consulted on the real issues of expatriate abuses, nor have they been consulted on the question of training (another area of local content development that the NCDMB has pursued without consultation with labour).[95]

While concerns about the expatriate quota may seem to be only a small element of Nigerian content, they evoke passionate criticism from advocates of human capacity development and Nigerians working in the industry and inside the IOCs, as well as from labour. Ibilola Amao, the consultant whose company focuses on Nigerian human capacity development, takes exception to the resistance to Nigerianization:

> I think if you sign a contract—a JV or PSC contract—and you agree to engage in succession planning, technology transfer and human capacity development, you shouldn't have a problem with that clause [the retention of a maximum of 5 per cent expatriate staff]. So that must be an act of insincerity. I don't think there is any oil company that has been operating in Nigeria for less than 10 years, so this is nothing new. The PSC and JV contracts have succession planning in them, have Nigerianization in them. Five per cent is good enough. If they intended to abide by the JV or PSC contract they signed in the first place. It all boils down to sincerity.[96]

The over-reliance on expatriate labour has a chilling effect on the ability of Nigeria to push national content and national control. As a Nigerian working for an indigenous oil service company noted:

If they're not here, they have the technology. You can't learn it. You need the train- ing from people like that. People like that need to remain in the system to train Nigerians. The question is how long they should stay. That should be determined by what they give out... You can teach someone something for many years without them getting anything unless you teach them with the sincerity of your heart.[97]

An official in the NCDMB, also fed up with resistance to Nigerian content from the IOCs, complained:

The IOCs are not willing to cooperate. They still don't see us as partners. They think we are coming to deny them something and they are not complying with most of the directives. When we say stop bringing in threaded pipes into Nigeria because we have companies that can do the threading, they are still bringing in threaded pipes. By so doing, they are killing companies in Nigeria that are doing this job.[98]

Even senior Nigerian managers, as in the following example of a manager at NAOC who asked not to be identified, often have cause to complain about this highly divisive issue:

The other day I saw a white guy that had been sent back to Italy and replaced with a Nigerian, but he had come back for another job. Every day we see new white faces. Do you really think there aren't any black people that can do that job? There are so many unemployed graduates in Nigeria. That is my opinion. I could get fired for saying this to you, but I see new white faces every day doing jobs that black people could be doing.[99]

While these issues are important barriers, the fact remains that the IOCs have no choice if they wish to remain in Nigeria but participate in Nigerian content as the government and regulating bodies define it. Less than full com- mitment risks the success of the initiative. As Henry Okolo put it, 'Nigerian content is a national strategic imperative and it must be achieved, so people should stop looking for excuses why it won't work and start thinking how it will work.'[100]

Turning finally to the area of manufacturing, fabrication and indigenous industry, there are several pitfalls to discuss. The first challenge mentioned by most indigenous companies in exploration and production or service provi- sion is access to capital. Although there is now a Nigerian Content Develop- ment Fund, access to capital at competitive international rates is still limited. On the E&P side, Egbert Imomoh also argues that the biggest limitation on the growth of indigenous producers is the problem of accessing capital. For this reason, he set up Afren plc in London with UK-based investors, allowing Afren to bring capital into Nigeria. He then launched a Nigerian indigenous company, First Hydrocarbon Nigeria, which is 45 per cent owned by Afren and 55 per cent by Nigerian investors.[101]

Besides difficulties in accessing capital, a problem that should be addressed in part by the creation of the NCDF, indigenous companies face serious difficulties from a lack of acceptance by the international oil and gas industry. According to Coker, one of the biggest challenges of indigenous companies is 'being accepted by the TNCs as competent to do work for them'. He comments further: 'even though when you worked for the multinationals you could do the work for them—and some of us ran their departments. Now the fact that we are on our own suddenly makes it impossible.'[102]

Coker's stated belief is that resistance to Nigerian content is often rooted outside the logic of business interest:

> Some IOCs don't want the economy of the host country to thrive so they can continue to operate as in the past. Some people don't want countries to get independence and economic freedom. Also, racism still exists in the industry... Sometimes it's expected that we cannot perform. You are already judged to have failed before you knock on the door, which boils down to just acceptability—finding it difficult to accept a local company.[103]

Coker's accusation is repeated by Henry Okolo, who explicitly links the difficulties faced by many indigenous companies to racism: 'The issue we are going to have to confront in Nigerian content... is that there are preconceptions and racism in Nigerian content discussions.'[104]

Both Dorman Long and Nigerdock executives have expressed frustration at the preconceptions and structural obstacles their companies face in expanding into new areas of fabrication—particularly FPSO integration. Commenting on the difficulties in building capacity in these areas, Okolo contends: 'From the date of the award of a contract to the date the FPSO hull arrives in Nigeria is about three years. So if you ask me if we can get a location ready to receive the FPSO hull in three years, I will tell you we can do it in less than that.' He goes on to point out, 'Nobody builds idle capacity. If you tell me today and you'll sign a piece of paper that in twelve months' time I'm going to have this work and you'll make a financial commitment, I'll put the capacity in place.'[105] Okolo's competitor, Jarmakani of Nigerdock, confirms that if he knew he had an FPSO integration contract, he would make the needed investments; however, 'the mindset is to focus on reasons you can't do something'. 'They say they need guaranteed investment to build the facilities, but the government says build the facilities and then you'll get the contracts. It's a chicken and egg problem.'[106]

Others however are not swayed by the complaints of Nigerdock and Dorman Long, arguing that focusing Nigerian content on these companies obscures the real pitfalls. According to a public official in the petroleum sector who wished to remain anonymous, there are larger issues in manufacturing and industry:

> Nigerdock, Dorman Long, they are just welders. They weld. They import the metal sheet. They only do the bending and welding—all of them. So the actual impact, if I have to go to India or China to buy metal sheets to do a pressure vessel, what is the value addition? ... When they go to buy steel, we drain the foreign reserves and then ship it out to do the integration... You can pay more to learn the technology but we are not paying for the technology because Dorman Long and Nigerdock, they are not doing something special. Nothing. Just welding and bending. What are they doing? They don't produce anything! They just bend and weld![107]

The real challenge, he argues, is for Nigeria to produce steel and metal sheets: 'It's in the best interest of Nigeria to develop the steel industry to migrate us from the Stone Age to the iron age. You can't talk local content when you are in the Stone Age... The common nail cannot even be wholly produced here in Nigeria and you are talking about Nigerian content!'[108]

Although perhaps FEED is where the greatest Nigerian content gains have been made, there are also problems with the implementation of local content policy in this area. A Nigerian employee in the Nigerian Content Division of Total E&P Nigeria explained that by moving to a frame agreement for engineering services, the company has been able to benefit from policies to promote Nigerian content. Under the frame agreement it has a call-up service instead of having to go through the contracting process all the time, which increases efficiency. However, there is still an issue with the length of contracts for engineering and vessels.[109]

As the Total manager explained, Nigerian OSCs are forming and then are unable to be successful because they can only receive a maximum of three years of guaranteed work under this model (contract maximums are two years plus an option for one additional year). In order to get credit and establish a successful company, especially for vessel-building, longer-term contracts are necessary, which is why Total has pushed for five-year contracts with options for two additional years. Unfortunately, there has been resistance to this from NNPC, which has been extremely detrimental to the success of Nigerian manufacturing and engineering.[110] Total's push for longer-term frame agreements for engineering services demonstrates that it sees sufficient national capacity in FEED to rely on domestic OSCs, which in turn demonstrates the success these Nigerian companies have had in building themselves into providers of valuable, quality services.

* * *

Alfred Okoigun captures the limitations faced by many Nigerians interested in manufacturing: 'Serious manufacturing cannot be done with generators... I'd love to go into manufacturing. That is my desire but the government has not sufficiently addressed the challenges.'[111,112] The concern about power can be added to the several other manufacturing challenges. From his position within the NNPC hierarchy, Maliki lists four main challenges in meeting Nigerian content targets: non-passage of the Nigerian Content bill [since addressed with its passage in 2010], effects of the Niger Delta crisis, a lack of experienced engineers in NNPC-NCD and the fact that 'Ajaokuta Steel Company and Aladga Steel Plant are still dormant due to policy inconsistency and declining foreign investment in the steel industry' (2009: ii). According to NNPC, 54 per cent of the US$12 billion spent in the Nigerian oil and gas industry is on procurement (NNPC-NCD, 2008). Within the 54 per cent of total spend on procurement, 25 per cent is on steel products (Maliki, 2009).

Table 3.6: Nigerian Content Five-year Projected Forecast (2006–2010)

	In-country demand	In-country availability
Engineering man-hours	6,000,000	3,500,000
Number of engineers	3125	1823
Fabrication tonnage (metric tonnes)	150,000	100,000
Pipe manufacturing (metric tonnes)	4,391,708	200,000

Source: Maliki, 2009: 17; citing GMD, NNPC presentation, 2009.

As Table 3.6 (adapted from Maliki's study) shows, heavy manufacturing is the area in which national content has made the fewest advances. Obviously, as Maliki points out, the low availability of capacity for pipe manufacturing is due to non-availability of steel. The fact that the Ajaokuta Steel Company's blast furnace has not been started for over 23 years due to inconsistent government policy and lack of foreign investors is compounded by the fact that the Warri–Ajaokuta rail system has not been built (Maliki, 2009: 20–21). In an internal presentation on the state of Nigerian content, a manager in the NCD of one of the JV companies described Ajaokuta more evocatively: 'It's moribund. If you saw it you would weep.'[113]

The preceding sections have reviewed the current state of local content in Angola and Nigeria, as well as both the promise and pitfalls in implementation. However, due to the dual nature of local content introduced in Chapter 2, even the most successful implementation of local content in terms of promoting economic growth and development may still result not in a petro-developmental state, but in greater underdevelopment. To understand how this may occur and what stands in the way of the sustainable and democratic petro-developmental state, I will move in Chapter 4 to an analysis of elite accumulation in Angola and Nigeria.

4

ELITE ACCUMULATION AND POTENTIAL CLASS TRANSFORMATION IN ANGOLA AND NIGERIA

As mentioned in earlier chapters, the emergence of local content policies in Angola and Nigeria coincides with and feeds into several important shifts currently underway in these countries. Shifts in strategies of elite accumulation from methods more akin to rent-seeking are leading more of the elite to engage in capitalist accumulation. However, I have found that while local content is becoming an increasingly important mechanism of elite accumulation, the adoption of local content policies can also be viewed as part of a wider and more fundamental transformation in the political–economic structures of Angola and Nigeria in which capitalist production may be able to replace the rentier economy.

This transformation is an important consequence of the push for capitalist production focused on the addition of economic value. The emergence of a more authentically capitalist bourgeoisie, as opposed to the sort of comprador bourgeoisie associated with peripheral capitalism and capitalist social relations under a petro-developmental state, is likely to spur economic growth and industrial development. At the same time, it will also undoubtedly have numerous impacts on class relations and the distribution of wealth and power, potentially fostering new dynamics of underdevelopment. While Chapter 5 will provide case study evidence of a shift in social relations of production and Chapter 6 will explore the role of various forms of agency in shaping the eventual outcome of the transformations that are the focus of this book, this chapter will explore the evidence of a shift in elite strategies of accumulation, before proceeding to analyze the ways in which such a shift may enable the emergence of a petro-developmental state.

In what follows, I argue that a mutually reinforcing dynamic is being created in which local content encourages the formation of an indigenous capitalist class. This class, in turn, sees local content and the petro-developmental state as being in its own interest and seeks to increase the implantation of policies of state protectionism for indigenous capitalists. These changes may finally bring about the kind of real capitalist transformation that has so far eluded countries in the Gulf of Guinea.

Already suffering the worst aspects of dispossession, uneven development and environmental degradation from its peripheral association with global capitalism, it may be the case that capitalist production and capitalist social relations, implemented or at least supported from above by large segments of the domestic elite, offer Gulf of Guinea states their best hope of also benefitting from the positives of capitalist development. At the same time, the dynamics of power in Angola and Nigeria have a strong class nature. The outcomes in terms of who benefits from local content and to what extent local content can produce a sustainable and democratic petro-developmental state are therefore best prefaced with a discussion of the agents that implement or at least offer tacit support for local content policy: the Angolan and Nigerian elite.

Elite Accumulation in Angola: a Historical Approach[1]

Beginning in the mid-1980s, the ruling MPLA underwent a transition culminating in 1990 with the decision by the Central Committee to end the one-party system and formally abandon Marxism–Leninism and embrace economic liberalization. Ferriera (1995) argues that Angola's petroleum '*nomenklatura*' was not quick to embrace such fundamental change. Rather, the politics of rentierism and the elite's ability to pillage the state allowed them to resist change until it became inevitable.

For Ferreira, these events ushered in a period of transition over 1991–2 during which the *nomenklatura* adapted to the market economy and economic liberalization. By 1993–4, this 'reconversion' was complete and the *nomenklatura* had successfully adapted without significantly altering their source of wealth, which remained petroleum rents. As one Angolan NGO activist told me, 'Lenin's disciples have become neoliberals!'[2] The transformation was done through a shift in accumulation strategies to embrace privatization. Ferreira concludes:

The economic reconversion of the *nomenklatura* is today almost complete: on the ideological and political front, the acceptance of the functioning of a democracy (with limitations) proved not incompatible with the maintenance of its social and economic status. Authoritarianism was not the only possible guarantee of their privileged situation; a market economy proved similarly compatible with the preservation of their privileges. (1995: 18, author's translation)

In what has become perhaps the definitive statement on the political economy of Angola into the post-war transition, Hodges describes a system where 'The rent from oil is used primarily to satisfy elite interests and finance means of retaining power, through expenditure of security and patronage, rather than to promote social and economic development' (2004: 203). In this system, patronage flows directly from the top and the president uses all the powers of his office to reward loyalty in symbiotic patron-client relationships.

There is a large degree of uniformity in the picture painted of the Angolan elite. In their 2005 *Drivers of Change* report, Vines, Shaxson and Rimli write: 'Angola's economy is strongly controlled by a presidency that wields power through personalized networks which, as in many African and other countries, can be more important than the ministries and other formal institutions' (2005: 7). Hodges argues that corruption is endemic throughout the public administration and even takes on some of the language of Marxist political economy when he says that corruption at higher levels is 'part of the process of "primitive accumulation" by the politically connected elites' (2004: 83). One of my informants described this process by explaining that in Angola things are the reverse of the West in that 'first you go into politics, then you get rich'.[3]

Both Hodges (2004) and Kibble (2006) have referred to the notion of a 'Bermuda Triangle' operating in Angola—a complex relationship between the presidency, Sonangol and the central bank, bypassing the Ministry of Finance and creating a 'black hole' for the country's oil revenues. Complementing all these analyses, the elite[4] are described by David Sogge as 'a constellation of politician-rentiers, petroleum sector technocrats and military officials' (2006: 8), while Chabal (2008) argues that Angola is governed by a system of 'presidential neo-patrimonialism'.

Hodges (2004) describes several strategies of direct and indirect elite accumulation used in Angola in the post-Marxist–Leninist period. Indirect appropriation occurs through manipulation of exchange rate policy, interest rates and access to credit. For example, until 1999, the government used privileged access to the administratively-set official exchange rate to enrich the elite and transfer state resources to individual beneficiaries. Ferreira (1995) also describes the privileged ability of those close to the president to import goods from abroad for sale on the black market as a key method of elite accumulation.

More direct methods of elite accumulation described by Hodges include privatization and land reform, as well as base looting of state coffers. Much of this privatization occurred without proper valuations of the assets or competitive bidding.[5] Meanwhile, as Hodges notes, many army officers and state officials acquired farms and other businesses as political favours, often for nominal sums or no payment at all, under a large land privatization programme that began in the early 1990s.

Over time, the transition to the market economy has made restrictions on competition and the Angolanization of the economy increasingly important strategies of elite accumulation. At the same, Hodges notes, the elite's incorporation into domestic and international circuits of capital has become increasingly important to their enrichment—particularly as aforementioned strategies, such as the exchange rate policy and allocation of credit, waned. Central to the new strategy is the climate of oligopolistic or monopolistic market conditions created by import procedures, other forms of administrative favouritism and harassment of businesses by the *Polícia Económica*.

Sonangol plays a central role as a vehicle for presidential patronage, particularly in terms of access to business opportunities. It enables the president to distribute oil revenues and other benefits before those revenues find their way into the state treasury. In a study of Sonangol, Soares de Oliveira writes: 'In short, the Sonangol Group has been not only the manager of the *Futungo*'s phantom revenue flows, but also the enabler of elite rentierism across important non-oil dimensions of the domestic economy, simultaneously guaranteeing that all profitable business opportunities are arbitrated by state rulers via the company' (2007a: 608–9).

Writing a few years after his initial study of Angolan political economy, Hodges (2008) is able to assess the impact of the end of the civil war and confirms that increasingly the elite are relying on their previously accumulated wealth and preferential access to the state to benefit from the new market system. In effect, the patronage system has moved into a phase where some wealthy Angolans who benefited from earlier phases of accumulation (and privatization) can now take advantage of their ties to the presidency to benefit from the government's policy of Angolanization. To do this, they participate directly in the oil industry through the establishment of service companies.

Hodges found that Sonangol, in turn, pressures oil operators to contract to these companies.

At the same time, Hodges writes that kick-backs on government contracts and the straight diversion of state resources to private individuals and companies continue to be important mechanisms of surplus appropriation, made possible by the general opaqueness of public finances and the secrecy of oil-guaranteed loans. Taken together, the literature on Angola does reveal several periods of political-economic change and a process of increasing complexity in strategies of elite accumulation founded on presidential patronage and abetted by Sonangol. This background sets the stage for discussing the current transformations underway within the Angolan elite.

Towards the Reinvention of the Angolan Elite

Following from my theoretical approach as discussed in Chapter 1, Angola has hitherto been only peripherally capitalist, though it has been interpenetrated by international capital, because it has always featured predominantly non-capitalist social relations of production. If the Angolan elite are shifting slowly to embrace a capitalist social structure and the capitalist mode of production, this would represent a transformation not only in strategies of elite accumulation, but in the elite themselves; from a rentier elite to a real bourgeoisie. Of course, it may be a very long time before social relations in Angola are predominantly or even primarily capitalistic in nature. Nevertheless, the important point is whether or not a significant shift may be occurring or about to occur.

Scholarship on the accumulation strategies of the Angolan elite reveals a remarkable capacity on behalf of the elite to adapt and reinvent themselves as necessary to suit changed geopolitical realities. Today, as the elite reinvent themselves, they may be seeing greater value in increased international legitimacy and the credibility such legitimacy gives them to participate in capitalist accumulation.[6] At the same time, as Angola becomes more important economically and strategically to the West and to China, there may be greater desire to grant that legitimacy despite lingering remnants of the unsavoury past.

Speaking about the possibility of primitive accumulation leading to capitalism and the makings of an *haute bourgeoisie*, Soares de Oliveira writes: 'Reality could not possibly be more different.' He goes on to say definitively: 'Elites are focused on "rent seeking, not economic activity"' (2007b: 140; citing Rose-

Ackerman, 1999). However, this analysis is premised on the assumption that other sources of income 'cannot compete with oil rents' (2007b: 141). It is precisely on this point that the antinomies of the hypothesized transition will play out. In a 2012 interview, respected Angolan economist Alves da Rocha is quoted as predicting exactly the kind of transition Soares de Oliveira dismisses: 'It is known that the oil sector in these countries has been used to create a national bourgeoisie... It is a bourgeoisie created on the basis of favours by the state and not on merit.'[7] The power dynamics involved in creating this bourgeoisie are indeed extremely important. I will therefore return to them at the end of this chapter.

In terms of the creation of an indigenous or 'real' bourgeoisie, much will depend on just how altered the political economic context is, not just due to the end of the war in 2002, but because of a completely different geopolitical moment in the Gulf of Guinea as a whole. Soares de Oliveira writes that 'the elite is not a "class" with a constant notion of where "its" interest lies...' (2007b: 133). However, history has shown a powerful tendency for the elites to gain consciousness (as a class). Capitalist accumulation is preferable to dependence on political patronage. Therefore, the elite are likely to make a capitalist transition when they are able to do so and, in particular, when it becomes possible to profit more from capitalist accumulation than from rent-seeking activities. The site of the new strategy of accumulation is within the oil industry and, more immediately, within the oil service sector. It is therefore this sector that will be examined in Chapter 5 in order to perceive the beginnings of a shift in social relations of production in Angola as well as in Nigeria.

The Economic Theory behind Local Content Initiatives: Evidence from Nigeria[8]

In Nigeria, the NCA was adopted in a unique moment of opportunity for Nigeria and the Nigerian oil and gas industry. Nigerian content development is a movement to transform the structure of the Nigerian economy to promote greater national content and national control for the purposes of economic development and security. In the Nigerian case, there is more direct evidence of a set of policies crafted by individuals espousing economic liberalism and trickle-down economics. Therefore, Nigeria lends itself more to a study of the ideology and economic principles underpinning the promotion of Nigerian content.

The elite-led and organized nature of Nigerian content and the very conscious and traceable steps the elite took to craft a system that suits their own interest are very instructive in understanding Nigerian content as a new strategy of accumulation. Describing how the new law will encourage Nigerians to enter the oil and gas industry, Ernest Nwapa said:

> When it was just a policy, you still have people investing with one leg in, one leg out. Now that there is a law, and you see that the Board is very very serious with implementing it, people are more aggressive with their investments... The number of people building vessels, the number of people investing in small and medium-sized rigs, those equipment used in the industry like barges, etc. A lot of Nigerians are getting into that.[9]

In the NCA, any clause that offers a benefit to an indigenous company has to be understood in the context of promoting Nigerian ownership. For example, Article 3 offers certain privileges to 'Nigerian independent operators' (3.1) and 'Nigerian indigenous service companies', though these terms are not defined anywhere in the law. While there are undoubtedly benefits to the country from promoting national companies, such benefits only accrue through these companies' engagement in productive economic activity. To ensure the promotion of productive activity, the NCDMB will have to evaluate the contribution of Nigerian companies and decide how much weight ownership should have in the measurement of Nigerian content. Although draft forms and procedures for the measurement of Nigerian content exist, it is still too early to know how Nigerian content will be evaluated by the NCDMB in practice.

It cannot be denied that Nigerian content promotes a shift from foreign ownership to indigenization. Proponents of Nigerian content speak at great length about the potential benefits of domiciling economic activity in Nigeria, regardless of the national origins of the investors. However, the NCA as it was written and Nigerian content as conceived by those who developed its policies are understood to promote indigenization. Acknowledging the aspects of Nigerian content that promote indigenization of ownership, Henry Okolo argues that while shareholders benefit, employees benefit the most: 'It's a win-win for all segments of Nigerian society, but the ultimate winner is employment creation.'[10] In explaining the thinking that went into the development of the NCA, Fabian Ajogwu, explains:

> Capital has no heart and it's not patriotic. It only sees returns on investments and minimum economic environments that guarantee the returns... For local content to work, we need to present that Nigerian with returns on investments and a minimum economic environment which he would otherwise have rushed to Norway to find. There's no need to be emotional about it. It's just the truth. But with more

opportunities for participation here locally with a regulatory framework supporting it, you have better chances of getting the elite involved—and they are already doing so.[11]

A Nigerian content manager at one of the major IOCs argues that indigenization was not 'in the same vein as Nigeria content', since it was about transferring ownership of existing companies to Nigerians. Nigerian content, he contends, is about making things happen in Nigeria, domiciling work in Nigeria, encouraging project management and procurement in Nigeria and promoting the growth of small and medium enterprises.[12] As Ernest Nwapa puts it, 'We're not saying that international companies cannot operate in the sector. All we're saying is "come and do it here".'[13]

While it represents a significant departure from indigenization towards embracing the tenets of orthodox neoliberalism, this view is shared by Ajogwu:

> I am also of the school of thought that local content should be about empowering the country and its people. It's not about seizing or nationalizing assets in the sector. I'm also of the school of thought that local content can only be achieved in an environment that is capitalistic in outlook but with guided regulation... If you want a Nigerian to be involved, he should be able to find his equity. If the country so desires, it can set up a fund to assist him, but he should pay for his joint stock. This school of thought that I belong to also sees that what is important is not that a significant percentage of Nigerians—3, 4, or 5 per cent of Nigerians—gain ownership of assets in the sector, but that the composite value to the economy should increase to the benefit of Nigerians and the Nigerian economy. So that was really what the policy debate was about.[14]

When pressed about the theoretical considerations that went into discussions around the creation of the NCA to explain exactly how the policies benefit the larger Nigerian population, Ajogwu, who later consulted for NNPC on the draft legislation, describes a fairly orthodox neoliberal perspective:

> If you increase Nigerian content, you will have more activities that hitherto happened in Houston or Holland now happening here. It will create indirect jobs for subcontractors, raw materials and so on. So you can see the trickle-down factor. Even if you don't transfer technology, just doing something you would have done in the US in Nigeria itself enhances the economy and the trickle-down effect... The emphasis on local content is also economic redistribution. I'm not talking about socialist redistribution. I'm talking about economic in the sense that more players will come through competition and through competition the wealth clusters may redistribute. They may shift. I'm not saying take from Peter to give to Paul. I'm saying Paul suddenly outcompetes Peter and becomes better than him.[15]

Discussing the potential impact of local content policies on the distribution of wealth in Nigeria, Edmund Daukoru, who held senior positions, including Minister, through the key years of local content formulation, made very similar comments:

> Definitely it will not worsen inequality. Whether it will improve on the current situation, I don't know. But one thing is sure; not everybody is a manager of resources or is even willing to be a manager of resources. Some people will always have to work for other people. If Nigerians have the capacity to be the employer of labour in the sector, there is already in my view trickle-down taking place. If that means we are enriching some Nigerians at the expense of others, that will always be the natural way. Not everybody will be a wealthy man. But let those wealthy people be Nigerians and they will then employ their own kind.[16]

This approach to national content and national control is significantly more acceptable to foreign governments and international oil companies. Simbi Wabote gave a presentation to NAPE while he was General Manager of Nigerian Content at Shell Nigeria that reviewed successful models of implementation of local content in Norway and Brazil. He is seen as one of the leading proponents of Nigerian content. For Wabote, what is important is 'transparent implementation of [the] Act and predictable enforcement'. For this reason, Wabote argues that instead of the policies of the indigenization era, which attacked foreign participation in Nigeria's economy, Nigerian content must 'provide regulations that encourage the participation of foreign companies in critical categories'. He calls this the 'open door approach' (Wabote, 2010).

Asking not to be identified, one US diplomat in Nigeria confirmed that the US is very accepting of local content and believes that Nigerians should grow and protect their indigenous oil sector. This statement is contrasted by the vigour with which the US embassy originally fought Nigerian content. However, the diplomat argued that local content is not an issue for IOCs because 'they will find a way around it'.[17] This ambiguity in terms of understanding the potential impact of Nigerian content suggests a need to delve deeper into the promises and pitfalls of Nigerian content, as envisaged in the NCA.

Nigerian content development is a movement to transform the structure of the Nigerian economy to promote greater national content and national control in the oil and gas industry by promoting indigenous participation and domiciling goods and service provision in-country; however, it is also a movement to entrench the Nigerian elite and strengthen their dominant position to the detriment of overall economic and social development. In describing the potential gain to the average Nigerian, Ajogwu argued that in the domiciling of work in Nigeria, 'even the poor farmer's wife could gain by serving in the canteen. It's a beautiful way of empowering the economy.' Ajogwu gave the example of the large oil and gas consulting firm Mackenzie, which had set up in Nigeria a few weeks prior. These movements of companies into the country, he argued, would add to the economy through paying rent, paying taxes, hiring local workers who would pay income taxes, etc. 'It's capitalistic because we're not going in a socialist way to take over companies.' Ajogwu explained: 'We want people to be entrepreneurial and to seize opportunities when they see them. What Africa needs is jobs, not aid.'[18]

The shift described so far, already underway and bolstered by Nigerian content, is a shift in strategies of elite accumulation and in economic structure. However, it is less clear that it is a shift in who benefits from oil and gas or from the Nigerian economic structure in general. The Nigerian Content Manager of one of the large indigenous service companies argues: 'Those who benefited in the past by doing things that were not in the interest of the country will not benefit now. If the law is implemented the right way, those elite would have to shift strategies from activities that are bad for the country to activities that are good for it.'[19] This quote raises an important question: will it be a new elite, an old one, or the ordinary Nigerian that benefits from Nigerian content?

Those who currently benefit from Nigeria's oil and gas are largely the political elite and their close associates who collect rent and patronage. As Pat Utomi says, whether by including crude oil lifting rights or other small aspects of the business, allocation of oil blocks which are then resold to foreigners, extraction of rents by the political class in collaboration with the managers of the NNPC, or other means, 'the leaders of Nigeria are very good at extracting rents for their friends'.[20] Egbert Imomoh confirms: 'They just play the role of collecting the rent and spending the rent.'[21]

These and countless other statements confirm what a government official in the petroleum sector candidly argued:

> The people who are really enjoying the oil wealth in Nigeria are the political class and the technocrats. Oil finances the budget almost 100 per cent—both the recurrent and capital budgets. Who manages the budget? Who passes this budget into law? It's politicians. They can't pass it until they know the budget is geared toward their own interest. The technocrats implement the budget as passed. In the implementation, because of non-sincerity, they gear it toward them. That's it. It's simple. The ordinary Nigerian has little benefit.[22]

Ibilola Amao is perhaps most blunt, arguing that 'Nigerians are more interested in buying and selling, importing, doing nothing, making money from their beds; some of them', clarifying that 'By lazy I mean lazy in their thinking and orientation, not work ethic.'[23] However, Henry Okolo makes it clear that 'There is no rent-seeking in Nigerian content. It's hard work.'[24] Okolo's statement confirms that Nigerian content actually represents a shift in elite strategies of accumulation, if not in who benefits from it.

Ernest Nwapa also says he is seeing this shift already taking place and acknowledges that it has an effect not only on domiciliation of activities in Nigeria, but also on ownership:

> There is a requirement for Nigerians to own facilities in Nigeria... So a lot of Nigerians who would rather go buy property abroad are now seeing opportunities to buy shares in the assets and equipment that are used in the industry because of the requirement of the law that says that 50 per cent of the equipment must be owned by the Nigerian subsidiary and the transformation to that model of ownership is driven by Nigerians buying shares in those assets. So, automatically, what we are seeing is that many Nigerian partners are already in discussions on how to remodel the ownership structure of their companies.[25]

The shift is universally acknowledged by those in the industry. F. M. Kupolokun, former GMD of NNPC and now a high-powered industry consultant, argues that the shift is occurring in part because it is indeed becoming harder to profit illicitly from the oil sector due to the efforts of the Economic and Financial Crimes Commission (EFCC) and Independent Corrupt Practices and Other Related Offenses Commission (ICPC):

> With the coming of both the EFCC and ICPC, there is this thing... nobody wants to go to jail. So the mere fact that you know that the EFCC may be peeping over your shoulder and if you do the wrong thing you can find yourself in jail, and you are seeing examples of people that EFCC has put in jail, they will need to be more cautious. If you are criminally-minded then not only will you be more cautious. You will then change your ways. Either you will resist doing it or you will look for different styles of doing such a thing.[26]

Austin Avuru argues that while transparency has increased in Nigeria, 'corruption has remained the same'. If, as Avuru contends, 'even though there have been improvements in transparency, they may not be commensurate with a drop in corruption,'[27] the main shift so far may have been in terms of how the elite accumulate, instead of to whom the benefits of the industry accrue. If this finding holds true, as I believe it does, then despite the coincidence of elite interest with the promotion of local content, the success of local content in creating a sustainable and democratic petro-developmental state still relies on political struggles, which I will argue in Chapter 6 takes place on the terrain of civil society.

Nigerian Content and Class Relations

In Nigeria (as well as in Angola) the dynamics of power that are playing themselves out with reference to local content can be primarily understood as dynamics of class. Speaking about the unequal distribution of wealth in Nigeria, one civil society activist argued that the fastest growing categories in Nigeria are the 'super rich and super poor'. The dynamics of this change, he explained, are that 'Those who were rich are now super rich. Those who were poor remain poor.'[28] The fact of growing economic inequality suggests that the future for the ordinary citizen under Nigerian content may not be significantly brighter. In discussing who may benefit from Nigerian content, F. M. Kupolokun suggests that 'What can be done in the community should be done in the community so that people will have work to do.' However, he goes on to say:

> We want to give jobs to people at the community level, but there's a limit to what they can chew, what they can digest and what they can bite. If you want to design a refinery, you are not going to give it to someone in the local community... you give to each layer what is appropriate for the layer to do. If the elite is most appropriate to do a particular job, then they get the job.[29]

What does this mean in practice for Nigerian content? Kupolokun says: 'Each person should do what is appropriate and therefore 80–90 per cent in terms of spend will go to the elite, naturally. The only difference is we are saying the elite should not be a white face like you anymore. Let it be a black one like mine. Let it be the Nigerian elite!'[30] However, Kupolokun argued that the benefits of Nigerian content will trickle down to ordinary citizens. He explains:

> If I am to do a design or to manufacture a jacket or a platform in Port Harcourt—I am the elite owning the fabrication yard—I will make a profit. But, the woman selling rice, selling food, will also have enough to sell because there are many people here who by 12 p.m. will want to break and have lunch. Whereas in the past, such a platform would be manufactured somewhere else—in Spain or in Portugal—they will tow it all the way to Nigeria and in two weeks they will install it and that's all. Build it in Nigeria and I am saying that the woman running the restaurant nearby will have more business to do.[31]

Ernest Nwapa agrees. He sees clusters springing up from each new development in Nigeria. This will create direct employment opportunities and indirect impacts: catering, clothing for workers, rents to communities, haircuts, hotel rooms, etc. 'It will percolate down; trickle down to lower levels', he argues.[32] These are the same arguments for business-friendly policies that so often come from those highly placed in the industry, whatever their nationality.

Paradoxically, Nwapa claims that Nigerian content may have a positive effect on income distribution. 'Today, the upper income levels are probably doing okay in the oil and gas industry... We have Nigerians in high-paying jobs in the industry. Not enough of that activity is felt by the masses. That won't happen unless you do something drastic.' What he is saying is that since the spread between rich and poor is currently high, Nigerian content is a way of bridging that gap precisely because the service side is not as discriminatory as upstream and 'manufacturing will employ a lot more people in the lower income bracket and in terms of numbers participating, you will have a signifi-cant realignment of the ratio'.[33]

The fact is that Nigerian content is too new for anyone to express much more than an opinion about its effects. However, a look at the history of national content in Nigeria, the ideology behind the current Nigerian content push and the shifts already observed by industry insiders suggests that unless more is done, the primary beneficiaries will be the same Nigerian elites who have benefited from rent-seeking and patronage and are now using Nigerian content to transform themselves into capitalists in order to maintain their privileged role.

At a forum on the upcoming Petroleum Industry Bill, Simon Amadubogha, a lawyer and activist based in Port Harcourt who also lectures at the Niger Delta University in Bayelsa, gave a presentation in which he asked: 'Who are those Nigerians who will take over the Nigerian oil industry? Those who have political power today. Those who are controlling the industry today to the detriment of the Niger Delta. Those people are creating laws that will make them powerful by controlling the oil industry' (Amaduobogha, 2010). Indeed, this assertion seems like a safe bet. However, what remains to be seen is whether or not there may in fact be a space in which individual actors as well as groups can work to ensure that more of Nigerian content's promise is fulfilled and its pitfalls avoided.

Economic Growth and Growing Social Inequality: Evidence from Angola

The primary evidence used to determine economic growth is data related to GDP. As mentioned in Chapter 1, Angola and Nigeria have been among the world's fastest growing nations in terms of GDP growth over the past decade. Although this statistic (and GDP growth rates in general) become less impressive when one examines where Angola was a decade ago, the trend is still important in creating conditions under which a transition could take place. Despite some differences, key estimates and projections for GDP growth in Angola show a return to healthy economic growth, if not the spectacular expansion of 2005–8 (see Table 4.1). After 2008, Angola underwent two years of low growth due to the impact of the global financial crisis. However, GDP growth was slowly rebounding until the oil price shock of 2014.

Table 4.1: Real GDP Growth in Angola (Per cent)

2004	2005	2006	2007	2008
11.2	20.6	18.6	21.1	13.4

Source: EIU, 2010.

More telling perhaps are the data obtained from the National Agency for Private Investment (ANIP), which show steady increases in new private investment by Angolans and foreigners over 2005–9. The data are sufficient to show large increases in both domestic and foreign private investment over the past five years (once adjusted for a large spike in construction and in transportation, storage and communication in 2005).

Table 4.2: Private Investment: Angolan vs. Foreign (thousands of US$)

	2005	2006	2007	2008	2009
Angolan Private Investment	$738,771	$332,787	$447,303	$417,079	$679,404
Foreign Private Investment	$2,475,255	$498,802	$882,236	$803,510	$1,162,668
Total	$3,214,026	$831,589	$1,329,539	$1,220,589	$1,842,072

Source: ANIP.

The data from ANIP exclude most oil investment, since this investment is made under the terms of the PSAs and also exclude all public investment (including private investment from China under the loan arrangements with China Exim Bank). Some new sectoral investment in the oil service sector is captured in the data (see Table 4.3), although a large portion of this investment also occurs through the PSAs. In the raw data provided by ANIP, some investment in the category of Business Services is specifically tagged as being related to the oil industry. This category of data is captured in Table 4.4. The figures represent only a small portion of new investment in oil services; however they do show a significant increase in both foreign and domestic investment in oil services.

Table 4.3: Private Investment in Angola by Sector (thousands of US$)

	2005	2006	2007	2008	2009
Agriculture, Forestry and Fisheries	$18,805	$30,665	$57,223	$28,116	$375,711
Real Estate and Business Services	$41,819	$42,703	$61,987	$97,064	$146,890
Construction	$2,225,500	$255,527	$207,008	$261,026	$345,355
Education, Health, Social Services and other	$4,023	$24,554	$44,817	$10,490	$16,697
Extractive Industry	$64,961	$85,772	$11,289	$32,918	$22,527
Hotels and Restaurants	$5,370	$100,701	$21,213	$26,796	$14,191
Manufacturing	$156,298	$185,858	$734,497	$675,115	$838,885
Electricity, Gas and Water	$292	$0	$120,200	$0	$2,916
Retail	$49,240	$35,554	$42,343	$43,924	$54,555
Transportation, Storage and Communication	$647,718	$70,255	$28,962	$45,140	$24,345
Total	$3,214,026	$831,589	$1,329,539	$1,220,589	$1,842,072

Source: ANIP.

Having established that Angola has experienced high growth and significant new investment, I want once again to underline the ways in which local content can strengthen social inequalities. When asked who benefits from oil revenues in Angola, a former Angolan Minister of Finance from the Marxist era said: 'It is a small minority that is benefitting from the oil. Maybe ten per cent, maybe only one per cent is benefitting. The rest are not.'[34] This is precisely what civil society activists are fighting against when they call for greater redistribution. A civil society participant in Angola confided that it is difficult to influence the government on redistribution of wealth. 'You can have dialogue,' he said, 'but it is not easy to make change. Things are more difficult today,' he said, 'because of the government's power and oil wealth.'[35]

Table 4.4: Private Investment in Business Services related to the Oil Services Sector in Angola (thousands of US$)

	2005	2006	2007	2008	2009
Angolan Private Investment	$111	$100	$2,650	$2,951	$4,300
Foreign Private Investment	$13,392	$4,566	$6,338	$15,489	$18,078
Total	$13,503	$4,666	$8,988	$18,440	$22,378

Source: ANIP.

A very senior civil society leader described the Angolan elite in terms of several concentric circles of influence around the president. The inner circle is the president's immediate family, and the circle after that are those who invest capital on behalf of the president. Following that at a wider radius are several circles of politicians, military and police officials, bureaucrats, appointees and others who depend on the president.[36] As discussed above, this structure allows the president, through his circles of influence, to exert a great deal of control over who benefits from Angolanization. At the same time, it allows him to ensure that his personal position, as well as that of his party and its elites, is strengthened by moves to promote Angolan participation in the oil industry. The various concerns that have been raised about local/national content suggest the need for a complete rethinking of how to understand issues of race, class and power in Angolan society and their relation to questions of political economy and economic development. Ultimately, it is Angolan civil society that must determine how best to grapple with political-economic issues such as those surrounding local content and the struggle for economic and social development.

Taken together, the data show strong growth in the economy and in investment by both Angolans and foreign investors. However, in the context of Angola (and also Nigeria), quantitative evidence is only useful to complement what must be shown qualitatively. Therefore, a series of interviews with key informants are used to show a dynamic and increasingly favourable landscape for the development of capitalist social relations centred on the oil industry.

The Angolan Elite and Angolan Development

As Evans reminds us, the East Asian 'national project' was successful because of the 'embeddedness', or connection of the state to the national elite. Evans writes: 'The essential complement to this broad ideological connection was a dense set of concrete interpersonal ties that enabled specific agencies and enterprises to construct joint projects at the sectoral level.' He goes on to argue that embeddedness involves 'Maintaining dense ties to entrepreneurial elites while avoiding capture and being able to discipline them' (Evans, 2008: 7). The East Asian project worked, he argues, because of class conditions.

In the case of East Asia, the local industrial elites were weak economically and politically and transnational capital was largely absent from the domestic process of accumulation. These factors allowed construction of embeddedness. Some of these factors will be returned to in Chapter 6 when we investigate the role of civil society in the creation of the petro-developmental state. For now, the question to be addressed is whether the elites are likely to help or hinder the emergence of a petro-developmental state.

In Angola, although the elite undergo a transformation towards embracing more capitalist forms of accumulation and the promotion of economic growth, they stand in the way of meaningful economic and social development in important ways. While they may pursue policies that lead to overall economic growth, they will also grow their own power and influence with an overall goal of controlling every aspect of Angolan society and using their new control to accumulate even greater wealth. As in Nigeria, there is little evidence to suggest that they will pursue any developmental policy that does not provide them with a direct benefit; and while they may endorse local content policies if they are in their own interest, they will also go to great lengths to exert control over the benefits of these policies.

What then is the motivating factor in Angola's development project, and what motivates the Angolan elite? Do class conditions and the specific system of accumulation create a likelihood that development can take hold—not as a result of benevolence, but because of the alignment of class interests? The Angolan development strategy is very capital-intensive and relies on heavy investment. According to one informant, an expatriate development specialist, there is a theoretical belief that employment will trickle down from investment in large-scale projects: 'It's very much a trickle-down theory.' But in fact, as he rightly points out, these models have been demonstrated to be not successful. In fact, he argues, 'New projects don't create economic benefits really.

They are great boons for contractors, but I think they have a negative impact on the country.'[37]

The nature of doing business in Angola makes finding Angolan business people extremely difficult. I was therefore well into the second month of research before I was able to break through and arrange series of interviews with Angolan businessmen in the oil and oil services sector. In an early interview, the owner of an Angolan oil services company told me:

> In most countries you see that people that have their own companies, their own businesses, don't mind saying what they have, how many companies they have—if they have a company, how many workers they have, how much they sell, how much they do. Here in Angola you don't see anyone telling you that they have a group of companies—how many workers they have, how much taxes they pay. Nobody will tell you that. People tend to do everything very secretly.[38]

Since 1990, a particular group of Angolans—generally those with a background in Sonangol—have started up oil exploration and production companies as well as companies providing services to the IOCs operating in Angola. However, as one such businessman confided to me, Angolan businessmen generally make their money from trading/export–import businesses and also domestic trading (i.e. buying in Luanda, selling to the provinces).

Based on his own ethnographic research into the business climate in Angola, Metz (2011) refers to two separate spaces in Angola's market economy: the 'privileged market economy' (for elite and state-owned firms) and 'restrained market economy' (for small, medium and micro enterprises). Given this dynamic, it is not surprising that in 2008 the World Bank ranked Angola 168th in the world in terms of ease of doing business.

According to an economic reporter for one of Angola's independent newspapers, 'In Angola, corruption functions by the connection between politics and business.'[39] The first Angolan businessman I interviewed described a particularly inhospitable climate for Angolan entrepreneurs: to supply to the government one must currently be in the government. It is a climate in which it is impossible to compete fairly and in which there is little freedom to enter the market without the right connections.

This particular businessman also made a comparison I heard more than once during my interviews: 'To understand capitalist development in Angola today, you have to see how Europe was two centuries ago... The big families control everything. In Portugal until 1975 that was the case. Few people could really enter into big businesses. Angola is still doing that. It is still trying to create an aristocracy... to have only a few big families, a few big businesses that can support the economy.'[40]

Obviously, the validity of comparing emerging capitalism in Angola to its emergence in Europe is of limited value given the vast differences in historical context. However, this comparison does show that the emergence of capitalism, far from the rosy picture painted by some enthusiasts, is a messy process. The above-mentioned member of the elite put it well when he admitted: 'We are the sons of rich fathers. We are behaving terribly—like spoiled kids.'[41] While one cannot look at the unregulated nature of economic activity in Angola and compare it to Great Britain during the industrial revolution, what must be established is whether or not Angolans are beginning to take capital, invest it in factors of production and produce outputs of higher value that allow them to make profit.

To establish whether or not there is movement towards capitalist production, it is necessary to determine whether there is any sign that wealthy Angolans are investing more of their money in Angola (whether or not this money was illicitly accumulated). The quantitative data from ANIP hint at such movement, but cannot present a satisfying case alone. Soares de Oliveira (2007b) has clearly documented a tendency for the elite to move rents from oil abroad, as have many other authors. However, one prominent Angolan economist responded: 'I am convinced this will change in ten years. Angolans will become more interested in investing in our economy rather than investing abroad... We do already have rich people who put their money in agriculture, construction and manufacturing.'[42]

Confirming the idea that Angola has entered a new moment for both domestic and foreign private investment, I interviewed a European lawyer who represents some of the most senior members of the president's inner circle, including family members and members of the cabinet. This lawyer helps his Angolan clients invest in Europe and also works with wealthy Europeans and European investment groups looking to invest in Angola. The lawyer confirmed that the view of investment in Angola by both his European and Angolan clients is shifting: 'It's no longer a place where you go to get a fast buck out of the country. Now people go to Angola for the long term.'[43]

A move by the Angolan elite to invest more at home was also confirmed by other Angolans in the oil sector. When asked if there has been more investment by Angolans in the Angolan economy, Carlos Amaral, one of the best-known Angolans in the oil industry, said: 'I believe yes. After the 2002 stabilization, you can see many more Angolans participating directly in the economy... I wouldn't be able to tell you the numbers, but when I go around Angola, and I travel a lot, there is much more entrepreneurship going on.'[44] This statement is generally representative of what most Angolans I spoke with observed.

Some of the sectors in which there has been local growth, according to Amaral, include insurance and banking. However, Amaral noted that some of this was by imposition and that this growth has occurred despite limitations in the way the system is set up to allow for such investment. Similar to other interviewees, and mirroring Metz's description of the business climate in Angola as 'savage capitalism', Amaral described this emerging entrepreneurship as 'a very wild kind of capitalism', arguing 'We need more rules, but these rules can't be created on day zero. They have to be created and also implemented. They need to be known around the country—not just in Luanda.'[45]

* * *

At the beginning of this chapter, it was noted that the new strategies of the Angolan elite have involved abusing their official positions for new business opportunities. In fact, it is more accurate to say that an official position in government or membership in a small circle of elites is required to have the opportunity to go into business. As the anti-corruption crusader Rafael Marques de Morais puts it, 'Angola's top state officials ignore the distinction between public and private property and turn themselves into the country's top entrepreneurs' (2012a). In a separate article, Marques describes exactly how this system works:

> The President has established a special task force within the intelligence services, which selects, distributes and oversees business opportunities for certain political and social figures, reward loyalists, co-opt dissenters, enrich certain families and ensure a vertical and tight control of the patronage system to maintain the status quo. The task force, according to an insider, also creates companies and selects their shareholders; with the President having the final decision regarding the shareholders, it also has had the job of compiling dossiers for blackmailing those who dissent, on corruption grounds. Furthermore, most of the relevant foreign investments in the country are made through joint ventures with companies owned by the presidential family and the ruling elite, which helps to secure international support and complicity through corruption. (2012b: 6–7)

Marques, who contributed regularly to *Seminario Angolense* until he was dismissed in June 2010 by the newspaper's new owners (see Chapter 6), has been at the forefront of exposing official corruption in Angola through his website *Maka Angola*.[46] In the summer of 2010, he made an enormous splash by revealing that General Kopelipa (see Chapter 6), Manuel Vicente (then CEO Sonangol EP) and General Leopoldino Fragoso do Nascimento were the owners of Nazaki Oil and Gáz, which had been awarded stakes in Blocks 9/09 and 21/09, operated by the US company Cobalt International Energy

(Marques de Morais, 2010). Cobalt, backed by Goldman Sachs and a partnership between the Carlyle Group and Riverstone Holdings, was subsequently put under investigation in the US by the Securities and Exchange Commission, which handles civil cases, and the Department of Justice, which handles criminal cases.[47,48]

At issue in the Cobalt case is whether the company is in violation of the US Foreign Corrupt Practices Act (FCPA), which makes it illegal for US citizens or companies to conduct business with foreign officials. In a statement, Cobalt claimed: 'We are fully co-operating with the SEC and DoJ investigations, have conducted an extensive investigation into these allegations and believe that our activities in Angola have complied with all laws, including the [foreign corrupt practices act].'[49] However, Burgis also quotes Georges Rebelo Chicoti, Angola's foreign minister, as telling an audience at London's Chatham House think-tank that while Angolan energy companies needed to gain experience, foreign groups 'are not obliged' to take designated local partners. This is an important point, since my own research indicates that other IOCs also have local partners owned by Angolan officials.[50]

In 2012 the Angolan government changed strategy with regard to the Cobalt case. Vicente, who is now Angola's vice president, has admitted co-ownership of Nazaki and claimed his business dealings to be entirely lawful. As Ana Silva (2012) describes: 'With the confidence of a man above the law, Vicente suggested that if Cobalt's dealings with him and his associates were to create further problems, the company should abandon its interests in Angola.' If Vicente's casual disregard for foreign anti-corruption law was not troubling enough, Vicente went on to criticize foreign companies that perform due diligence checks. 'People who come to work with Angola and associate with Angolans very often, and practically to the point of becoming common practice, want to do "due diligence" on the Angolans. This trend should be flipped on its head. The resources are Angola's, and we are the ones who should be doing "due diligence" on the people coming here—not the other way around' (quoted in Silva, 2012).

Most IOCs are listed on the New York Stock Exchange, making them subject to the FCPA. The United Kingdom, European Union and Norway all have similar laws against business dealings with foreign officials. Even more IOCs are investors (but not operators) in oil blocks that have local partners which may be owned by government officials. According to a senior manager of the Norwegian company Statoil, the company made inquiries about the ownership of its partner investors in Angola but 'does not believe' the response it received.

The manager maintained however that block awards are at the discretion of Sonangol and that Statoil cannot control who is made their partner. Therefore, he argues, 'We don't have business with the other companies I mentioned. We are both just investors.' He went on to tell me that Statoil's policy if it were an operator would be that all Angolan companies should be public or their owners should be known, since this is required for due diligence.[51,52]

As noted in the Introduction, both Angola and Nigeria are viewed in a new light by the West. No longer the model cases of 'resource curse', both countries are seen today more as 'emerging economies'; while Africa as a whole is beginning to be seen more as an exciting and attractive new region for investors with tremendous potential—particularly in the natural resources sector. Marxist debates about the general desirability or necessity of capitalist transformation in Africa go back several decades. What effect local content policies may have on rent-seeking behaviour, to what extent they produce structural change in the wider Angolan and Nigerian economies and to what extent they may impact the general population or the predominant mode of production in those countries can only be speculation at this stage of the game.

While the effects of local content polices will play out in unknown domestic and geopolitical contexts, the Angolan and Nigerian petroleum elite have made an organized and concerted effort to design and implement these policies in such a way as to maximize their benefit in terms of power and wealth. If a more capitalistic economy emerges from these policies, it will be because those elites have made a conscious effort to embrace new strategies of accumulation based on the production of value. For a successful petro-developmental state to emerge under these conditions, economic growth will have to be accompanied by forces that push the government and the elite towards developmentalism. These factors can be structural (e.g. increased power for workers due to growing industrial employment) or they can be agent-driven (from below). The point of this chapter has not been to label the changes underway in Angola and Nigeria as 'good' or 'bad', but to acknowledge them, gather evidence of their existence, understand how they operate, and attempt, in this moment in which they are occurring, to delineate the limits of the possible outcomes that may emerge. This project will continue in Chapters 5 and 6.

5

HOW COMPANIES ARE IMPLEMENTING LOCAL
CONTENT IN ANGOLA AND NIGERIA

In addition to providing detailed studies of the promises and pitfalls of local content in Angola and Nigeria, I attempt in this chapter to provide preliminary evidence in support of the hypothesis that major capitalist transformations are underway in both countries. There are concrete limitations when it comes to collecting any kind of social science data in Angola and Nigeria. This is particularly true of data related to strategies of elite accumulation, class relations and major structural change. Due to these limitations, I decided that the most effective way to collect data on whether or not any kind of transformation is occurring in strategies of elite accumulation and to detect change or potential change in modes of production would be to paint a picture of the sector through case studies. Below, I consider the ten Angolan and ten Nigerian businesses that I profiled for this study.

Overall, the evidence of movement towards domestic capitalist accumulation through the production of value through secondary economic activity in oil exploration and production (as opposed to accumulation through rent-seeking) is mixed. As one informant warned, there is a world of difference between greater investment and greater *productive* investment. Additionally, while the cases below show some level of dynamism and a clear desire to engage in capitalist accumulation, the process is still at a very early stage, with many companies expressing little more than an intention to change their business model.

While many indigenous companies do seem to be operating on a business model premised on realizing profit through the production of value, examples persist of companies set up by Angolans and Nigerians with little interest in moving beyond rent-seeking behaviour. The state controls the land and the resources underneath its territory. Beblawi spoke of the *kafil* or 'rentier mentality' (see Chapter 3) of the local elite who seek to profit from favourable business dealings with the state or to profit from policies put in place by the state *without* making a valuable contribution. However, where local companies are engaged in or actively seeking to engage in the production process, they are mixing labour into that process and accumulating capital in a capitalist manner. If this happens on a large enough scale, it begins to alter the social relations of production.

During my time in Angola and Nigeria, I prepared case studies of three oil exploration and production companies and seven oil service companies in each country. In Angola, the final two OSCs are currently foreign-owned, but are nevertheless useful cases for understanding the operation of Angolanization; while in Nigeria all cases are Nigerian-owned companies. In the Angola cases, an inability to conduct business openly is common for all but two of the cases, which are thought to have high-level protection from Sonangol.

The companies face similar difficulties in finding qualified Angolans to fill positions, and many struggle to be profitable given the high cost of importing materials into Angola. In Nigeria, all of the cases demonstrate a high level of technical know-how and greater use of Nigerian labour. However, Nigerian oil service companies face many obstacles, from the bias of IOCs to the limitations of Nigeria's infrastructure when trying to break into new areas of service provision. In this chapter, I will proceed by taking up the cases one by one before concluding with some analysis of the cases.

Case Studies of Emergent Capitalism in the Angolan Oil Industry[1]

Beginning with the exploration and production companies, there are few locally-owned companies in the E&P business in Angola, all of which are quite small. In total, there are only a few companies with current production in Angola that I believe are majority Angolan-owned (other than Sonangol). They are Somoil, Initial Oil & Gas, Falcon Oil, Poliedro, Kotoil, Alper Oil and Nazaki Oil and Gáz. Companies in E&P (both those with and those without current production) generally fall under one of two categories. The first group are looking to build their knowledge, experience and capacity to be able to undertake more activities themselves. Such companies are actively seeking to make a profit from working in the sector and operating small ventures—generally onshore or in shallow water since this is much less capital-intensive. There are only one or two private domestic E&P companies in Angola that would fall into this category.

The second group are companies set up by powerful members of the elite without experience in the oil sector (as opposed to the companies attempting to build capacity, which are set up by powerful members of the elite with a background in the sector). As discussed at the end of Chapter 4 with reference to Nazaki Oil and Gáz, these Angolans are looking to profit from small holdings in deep offshore blocks operated by others whom they accessed through their political connections and hope to profit from the rents accruing. There are over a dozen such companies in Angola, though many are now dormant. Most are very opaque. They are, as one informant quipped, little more than bank accounts. In truth, not only have these companies been unproductive, they have also largely been unprofitable because the people running them lack appreciation of the complexity and volatility of the international oil industry.

Given the lack of publicly available information, it was initially very difficult to learn anything about the ownership of these companies. However, by the end of my research I had gathered some information about the ownership of most of them. In most cases, I could not get enough information to verify or prove what one or two sources were telling me. Nevertheless, I feel that the information I collected on ownership has offered me a glimpse into ownership patterns and political connections in the Angolan domestic oil and gas industry. Additionally, the case studies show that while there may be some potential for local content to promote greater national participation in the oil services sector, there has been very little actual value production to date.

Some information has come into the public domain through courageous investigations that suggest the owners of particular companies were close associates of the president, current members of the civil or military arms of government, or current Sonangol officials. As case studies, there is little to say about the companies that are just bank accounts in the name of a general or cabinet member close to the president. For the government of Angola, these local 'front' companies can generate negative publicity and sometimes great embarrassment when their ownership is revealed. Given their general lack of returns to their owners, it seems unlikely that such companies will persist. Additionally, the international oil industry is concerned that such companies tend not to pay their share of costs or participate in block management meetings. Of greater importance to the IOCs, association with illicit companies connected to current government officials creates a risk of prosecution for violations of anti-corruption legislation in many Western countries.

Figure 5.1: Case Studies: Angola

Case	Ownership	Activities	Description
1	Angolan	E&P	Company active and currently producing a small quantity of oil
2	Angolan	E&P	Company active and currently producing a small quantity of oil
3	Angolan	E&P	Active, but with no current production
4	Angolan	Services	Active in a variety of services through different Angolan companies with separate Angolan investors and foreign joint venture partners
5	Angolan	Services	Active in oil and gas (through foreign joint ventures), real estate and investments
6	Majority Angolan	Services	Joint venture with a foreign company. Active in procurement of goods and services to oil sector
7	Angolan	Services	Active in a variety of services through foreign joint ventures
8	Angolan	Services	Active in a variety of services through foreign joint ventures
9	Foreign	Services	Active in a range of services through joint ventures
10	Foreign	Services	Active in a few specialized services; seeking a new joint venture partner

Company 1 was set up by a highly knowledgeable and skilled Angolan engineer with a background in government, Sonangol and the IOCs.[2] Intending to become a successful entrepreneur and make profit out of oil operations in Angola, he devotes himself to the business full time. Acting as CEO, its founder nevertheless has a minority interest in the company. It is probably the only private Angolan E&P company that is serious about being successful from a business standpoint. Although the company and its CEO are well known, the company does not have a website nor has its contact information been made public.

The greatest difficulty the company faces is access to capital. According to the company's CEO, '[My company] is not going well. We are up to our necks. Oil production is a game for foreign companies. These conditions have to be adapted for us to survive.'[3] The problem, according to him, is that his company has to grow on its profits. Not only does it not have great access to capital, but it pays the same taxes and signature bonuses as foreign companies. However, unlike foreign companies, it cannot deduct costs in any other jurisdiction (office expenses, interest on loans, etc.) from its Angolan taxes. In his interview, the CEO stated his belief that Angolan companies must get preferential terms in order to survive and that promoting Angolan E&P companies should be a government priority. This desire became a reality shortly thereafter with the passage of Decree 3/12 of 2012, which offers tax incentives for private and public Angolan oil companies.

Company 1's staff is mostly Angolan, with several engineers who have experience in multinational companies. According to one senior engineer, there are few opportunities for Angolans in the upper management of IOCs. For this reason, he chose to move to Company 1. He complained that the major international operators are biased against Angolan companies and do not trust them. The senior engineer has actually begun registering his own company, which will offer supply boats and provide some semi-skilled services such as reservoir engineering and production logging in order to take advantage of new policies promoting local content.[4] The conduct of Company 1 and the other entrepreneurial activities of its highly qualified and professional staff show the dynamism and potential for Angolans to contribute meaningfully to the oil sector if given better opportunities to do so.

Company 2 enjoys much more direct support from the government and Sonangol. It is widely known in the industry that the company was set up by a former Minister of Petroleum, although formal ownership on paper rests with a variety of Angolans. According to two separate sources I interviewed, ownership may currently include high-ranking officials in the Ministry of Petroleum. Although the former minister is not involved in day-to-day operations, at the time the company won its first concessions, he was still in charge at the ministry. This fact would expose several major IOCs to anti-corruption charges in Europe and North America if it could ever be proven publicly that he or any of the senior officials in his ministry were behind the company.

The full ownership of the company is not publicly known and is said to be spread among numerous high-ranking Angolan officials. Company 2's contact information is more publicly available than most companies in Angola.

Although it is well supported by Sonangol (some informants claimed that it has received special concessions and loans from Sonangol), it is being managed in a professional way by individuals with the necessary experience and technical backgrounds and seems to be interested in business success. The motivation for this interest may largely be to show the industry that a private Angolan E&P company can be well-managed and successful. It seemed to me that several of the employees in their head office were foreigners, although I was unable to confirm details with senior management, despite several requests for an interview and visits to their offices.

The company has also experienced problems raising capital and competing as equals with the multinationals and has therefore advocated preferred treatment for Angolan companies. An Angolan oil insider told me that he saw nothing wrong with the fact that the company was protected and receiving special treatment from Sonangol in Sonangol's role as concessionaire. The real disgrace, he argued, is that this is done 'under the table' and without admitting it. The insider argued that there is a mentality in Angola that prevents Sonangol and the government from offering support and favourable conditions to all Angolan oil companies in a transparent fashion.[5] While Company 2 is another professional and reputable Angolan oil company, this case also demonstrates how the promotion of indigenous companies in the oil sector has not been separated from the opaque and questionable accumulation strategies of the Angolan elite.

Company 3 was set up by a group of Angolans, all former senior officials in Sonangol or the Ministry of Petroleum. There is some evidence that one of the members of the ownership group may be a current Sonangol director, but I cannot confirm this myself. The company has invested in a small share of a few offshore blocks, but according to the company's director has not yet seen a return. The ownership of the company is not public, nor is the company's contact information easily available. The director of the company, who is also its largest shareholder, told me that he felt pressured by the government and Sonangol to invest in these blocks because they want more Angolan E&P companies participating in the sector. He claims to have had no interest in forming an E&P company because he knows enough about the industry to know the difficulties in making them profitable. Instead, he had wanted to concentrate exclusively on oil services.[6]

Without state pressure, this group of knowledgeable and experienced Angolans would not have chosen to invest in offshore oil. Their reluctance demonstrates the complexities and lack of benefit for Angolan companies involved in offshore oil extraction. Angolans with technical and business experience do not want to invest in the upstream sector, while wealthy but inexperienced rent-seeking members of the Angolan elite are losing money on their upstream investments. These insights suggest that the focus of local content efforts should be on promoting Angolanization of the workforce and more Angolan content in procurement of goods and services. It is in the oil service sector that companies engage in economic activity that generates value through production, instead of just extracting it. In doing so, an economy dominated by the oil and gas industry can still move away from the harmful consequences of rentierism.

Company 4 is the first of the seven case studies of oil service companies. There are some key differences between Angolan E&P companies and OSCs. For example, obtaining capital is also an issue for oil service companies in Angola (especially ones offering highly technical or complex services or services based on proprietary technology). However, the problems faced by Angolan E&P companies do not affect oil services to the same extent because E&P—even onshore extraction—is significantly more capital-intensive. On the whole, it is also much more possible to earn a healthy profit from oil services, particularly if your company is well-connected.

Company 4 is a group of mostly successful Angolan oil service companies controlled by an Angolan businessman and former Sonangol official. He started each company with different Angolan investors, capitalizing on his unique set of experience, training and connections (in both politics and industry). The investors are all well-off individual Angolans. None of the various company offices have published contact information. The founder of the companies observes: 'Most of the people have been involved in training, more than anything else. Probably it is the biggest business in this country. Producing is something different.'[7] In terms of Angolan businesses currently producing goods and services of value in the oil services sector, he correctly identifies his company as one of a select few.

The individual behind Company 4 has been operating several of his businesses for many years and has an excellent reputation in the industry. With the recent local content push, he has found many new opportunities for joint ventures with foreign firms. In these arrangements he offers a valuable contribution as an active partner. He has been successful in the hostile business climate of Angola because he offers quality specialized services for which there is little or no domestic competition, allowing him to gain preferential treatment under the terms of the PSAs and Decree No. 127/03 (see Chapter 2).

Unfortunately as he attempts to expand he is meeting with resistance from Sonangol, indicating he has fallen somewhat out of favour. Sonangol even tried to block one of his new joint ventures and force the multinational he was working with to choose a different Angolan partner.

The individual behind Company 4 tries to employ mostly Angolans in his companies. Driving this is a philosophy that: 'The oil sector should not be an island that takes everything from outside and puts everything outside.'[8] Due to his contacts with the IOCs, he meets their staff and if he identifies a particularly bright or capable person, he might try to hire them away. This practice illustrates the shortage of skilled engineers in Angola. In 2010, this individual was part of a group of senior experienced Angolans trying to form a new company to offer integrated services to oil operators. In this way, along with a core of Angolans with high-level experience in the industry, many of whom left Sonangol around the same time at the close of the 1980s, he is continuing to push new boundaries and be a successful capitalist. Since 2010 these plans have fallen through. This is perhaps due to interference from Sonangol.

By contrast, Company 5 was the case that to me exemplified the worst aspects of the Angolan business climate. The company is an Angolan enterprise with three core businesses: real estate, oil and gas and investments (including commercial businesses and agricultural projects). Most prominently, the company is a joint venture partner in the agreement between Sonangol and a major multinational oil service company. Its role in oil and gas, however, is simply to facilitate joint ventures (as a broker) and take a share of the JV company. As one of the executive directors of the company made clear, they do not really even work directly in oil and gas. When I pointed out to the executive director that all three of its areas of business—real estate, oil and gas and investments—involve activities in which the company is earning rent instead of engaging in production, he laughed and then agreed, without responding further.[9]

It is an open secret that Company 5 is favoured by Sonangol among potential JV brokers and local partners, which is why foreign companies looking for an easy entry into Angola seek it out. The company's executive director frankly admitted that Sonangol often tells multinational companies wanting to enter Angola to contact his company because it is trusted.[10] Acknowledging its good relationship, the executive director was deliberately vague in explaining how he maintained these good ties, at one point laughing when pressed and saying I had asked a very difficult question. When I was in Angola I heard rumours that Manuel Vicente, then the CEO of Sonangol, was behind the company.

Since then, I have been able to confirm that the main owner at the time was Vicente's son-in-law, Mirco de Jesus Martins. Mirco Martins is a well-known businessman who represents Vicente in various business interests. He used to work for BP and also has business ties to General Kopelipa (see Chapter 6) and José Filomeno dos Santos, the president's son.[11]

Another concern is that the majority of the company's employees are foreigners (although the company should not in theory be able to get so many work permits). According to the executive director, who is Angolan, most of the staff comprise Indians, Brazilians, Portuguese and some other west Europeans. Their activities involve monitoring the company's investments and other administrative tasks. In his words, 'We don't have Angolan people with the background to work with us.' The director went on to say that he thought most Angolans were lazy and didn't want to work.[12]

Despite all the criticisms, what is notable about this case is the lengths the company takes to appear professional and reputable, as demonstrated by its office, its very well designed website and its sleek promotional material. Its office address and contact information are available online, along with a summary of its major activities. It seems that this company is a new version of a company following an old model of business in Angola. The company takes advantage of personal relationships with state officials to find business opportunities where it does not have to make any meaningful contribution other than to act as a front, and is therefore not moving towards any kind of value production as opposed to rent-seeking.

Company 6 is an Angolan company in a JV with a foreign oil service company. There are three major shareholders. The international company is a minority shareholder, while the Angolan managing director and a former Angolan Minister of Commerce hold the remaining equity. The address and contact information of the Angolan company are listed on the website of the international company. The Angolan company has one contract—a purchasing contract from Chevron worth US$2 million per month. An employee of the company admitted that he thought the company was set up solely to take advantage of the opportunity of the one contract—probably identified by the minister when he was still in office.[13]

Another important aspect of this case is the operation of the purchasing contract, which shows several of the limitations of enforced local content. Chevron used to source certain supplies and equipment directly from US-based suppliers. Now the Angolan partner, Company 6, puts in these orders and the shipments go straight from the supplier in the US to Chevron.

The company then pays the bill and is reimbursed from the purchasing contract. As a company employee said, 'essentially we're paper pushers'.[14]

Despite the nature of the company and Chevron's questionable involvement in its creation, Company 6 has plans to build its own warehouses and stock the materials Chevron is likely to need, becoming more of an actual supplier and making a genuine (if not significant) economic contribution. It would obviously need to employ people to run the warehouse; however, these are likely to be the same people Chevron currently employs (at higher wages) to run its warehouses.[15] No one I spoke to at Company 6 knew of any plans to build factories in Angola to produce any of the materials currently imported from the US. Therefore overall the case is one that demonstrates the limits of forcing IOCs and multinationals to achieve local content by setting up local companies to import goods.

Company 7 is founded by an Angolan former Chevron employee. The founder, who was sent by Chevron to study business in the US, is very keen to build a successful company offering important services to the industry. Although the company is starting to be well-known in the sector, it does not have publicly available contact information.

The company began mostly by offering training services in areas like health and safety, fire prevention, etc. It later moved into the provision of labour, which is still its largest business. Most recently, it has moved into facility engineering and services, scaffolding, metallic construction, electrical work, mechanical work, drilling, well bore clean-out, fishing, testing and parts supply. Over the last few years, it has expanded to all the major port cities in the country. Company 7 works in partnership with a few large multinational companies. According to the operations manager, the company's goal is to build into more of a conglomerate, working in agriculture, manufacturing and other technical/engineering areas.[16] This goal shows that they are taking steps towards the goal of producing and creating value.

The operations manager admitted that connections and contacts are critical for success in Angola, but argued that 'you also need the know-how'. His point was that 'Once people discover you, you will make lots of money.' The most important thing for getting started is 'to be known by Sonangol and the operators'.[17] The company's founder and CEO admitted that local content is very political: 'You have a company. You may have talent and abilities, but if you don't have anyone inside Sonangol or inside the government, you won't have contracts... so you need to create strong links.' Even if an operator may want to use a particular company, he said, without the contacts in Sonangol that company will likely lose the contract. He complained: 'Other companies just go into the business and try and do something that is not contributing much to the growth of the economy.'[18]

The company has struggled with the unfair business climate in Angola. Not possessing 'protection' within Sonangol, the company's CEO described how he had been working on a partnership with a foreign scaffolding company until someone at Sonangol decided the partnership should not be with Company 7 and forced the multinational involved to partner with a different, newly-created company.[19] Nevertheless the company has vigorously pursued new contracts, particularly contracts to work in partnership with multinational oil service companies that hold larger service contracts with the international operators. This strategy has allowed it to expand and, to some extent, prosper. This fact demonstrates that there is some room for a private Angolan company offering services needed by the IOCs to make money without strong Sonangol connections, though it is not clear to me that the company has sworn off the kinds of payments that are so common in all areas of the Angolan economy (see Lopes, 2006; Hodges, 2004).

The next case similarly demonstrates a positive trend in Angolan oil services. Company 8 is an Angolan company, though it works in a few different joint ventures. It is a fairly large group, conducting business in Europe and the Americas. The company's aim is to present itself externally as highly professional, similar to any Western corporation. It has a well-designed website with a lot of information as well as a series of policy documents setting out policies on human resources, the company code of conduct, health and safety and environmental policies and an Angolanization policy, along with its contact information.

Although Company 8's promotional material is impressive, a mid-level official in the company admitted that the services they provide to the oil industry are mostly in catering and personal protection equipment, although the plan is to expand into engineering and upstream activities. He also confirmed that although no one on the company's board currently works for Sonangol or the Ministry of Petroleum, most of them used to and entered the sector through those connections.[20]

The company's most important joint ventures are in catering and protection equipment. For the supply of personal protection equipment, Company 8 works with a Brazilian company. All the equipment is manufactured in Brazil by this partner and imported. However, with the support of the Brazilian company, the Angolan company is building a factory in Angola to manufacture the same equipment. Company 8 supplies services to a couple of operators and also to some of the multinational oil service companies as a subcontractor. In this way, they are expanding and offering increasingly valuable services to the industry.

Company 9 is a large, well-known multinational OSC involved in a wide range of services. Some of the services it provides are highly specialized and technical, while others are less technology-intensive, such as dredging and leasing vessels. The company operates two separate joint ventures in Angola. The older of the two has been in place more than a decade. The joint venture company, which is considered an Angolan company, also has operations in Nigeria, Ghana and a few other African countries. It has one of the most detailed websites of any multinational operating in Angola—offering a full company profile, organogram and policies on Angolanization and Health, Safety, Environment and Quality.

According to the expatriate managing director, it would be very hard to work in Angola without a joint venture because Sonangol has a list of all the companies that provide a service. Sonangol's preference is to find a company that is 100 per cent Angolan, but if it cannot, it prefers to find a joint venture company to ensure some level of local content. On the subject of integrating Angolans into the workforce, the MD says 'I would like to do that.' He believes that in time there will only need to be one or two people representing the foreign partner to the JV in key positions like financial manager, which he describes as 'very delicate'. Ultimately, he believes that while people are resourceful at evading the labour and immigration laws, they will have to Angolanize because Sonangol and MINPET have every company's organogram and will force companies to change their human resources practices.[21]

Company 9 has had some successes in Angolanizing labour, although the company's MD expressed great frustration with Angola's system of immigration control, which he says is deeply flawed. The company has an Angolan HR manager, which the MD says is very important, and he is seeking an Angolan Chief Accountant but is having difficulty finding a qualified candidate. The MD claims that because his company has been getting more spot work than long-term contracts in the last few years, he has had less ability to train Angolans for skilled positions due to the uncertainty. In terms of procurement, the company has a foreign-based procurement officer and gets most equipment from abroad because no one in Angola makes the equipment they need. Things like office supplies are sourced locally.[22]

Company 9 has a long list of successful contracts it has carried out in Angola, and appears to be making an effort to provide quality services for the industry and to invest in Angola. However, the area of its business that it is least comfortable with is its relationship to its Angolan partner. The company's success in Angola is heavily dependent on the local partner, who is responsible for finding contracts, and the company relies on his contacts in the government and in Sonangol. For the foreign partner, a major concern is that the company may fail at any time if the Angolan partner loses stature or falls out of favour in Angola. According to the expatriate MD, this can make things 'very messy'. The company does seek out clients and participates in tenders. However, the MD admits that after the tender process begins, the partner must step in to 'follow the process' and help them get the contracts. The MD would not be more specific on what kind of help was involved in getting the contracts.[23]

Finally, company 10 is also a multinational OSC that has been in Angola over a decade. In contrast with company 9, this company has almost no presence on the internet. It has operated with a minority Angolan partner for some time, but was now seeking other Angolan investors to make the Angolan subsidiary majority Angolan-owned. Currently, the Angolan company is more of a branch office. Contracts are held by the international company and the Angolan branch simply subcontracts to provide the services. However, the company is moving towards creating a local company that uses local staff to provide local services. In this model, the relationship would be reversed. The local company would hold the contract and the international company would subcontract its expertise.

According to an expatriate manager of the company, the new approach has been taken 'only because of legislation and enforcement' and because 'laws are now being enforced that are on the books'. These laws, from labour and immigration law to procurement regulations, may have existed previously, but it is only now that the government has signalled a desire to enforce them. In the words of this manager, 'It is clear to us that Angola is going to change—thumbscrews are being tightened.' What this means, especially in terms of Angolanization policy, is that the company will have to train more Angolan labour. The manager, whose job includes responsibility for local content, admits that in the past decade the company could easily have trained Angolans from scratch—they could have taken them from high school, sent them on training all over the world and made them active employees by now. While he admits 'that's real long-term planning', it is only now that his company sees the incentives to do this.[24]

Although these case studies provide evidence for and against a change in methods of production and strategies of accumulation, taken together, these cases offer evidence that a shift towards capitalist social relations may be underway. As the shift described above continues, it is likely that more and more Angolans will begin to view value production as more profitable than rent-seeking. Although there were intentions among some large and some small companies to engage in increased manufacturing and value production, there remains a great deal of rent-seeking, along with many companies and individuals engaging in questionable behaviour. Over time, if this shift is actually occurring, more Angolan companies will become more involved in new areas of the oil service sector, employing more Angolan labour—both skilled and unskilled. What is important about this shift is that it can occur on the basis of economic growth alone and could, along with external factors, such as the changing geopolitical realities, eventually translate to social development as well through shifting power dynamics and class relations.

In the cases above, the state is noticeably absent from the discussion. The conditions for Angolan companies to be successful in the oil service industry have been created by the state through local content regulations. However, in order to 'nurture' capitalist development more action may be required. Angolan E&P companies require state subsidies to compete with large multi-nationals, while small and medium-sized non-state oil service companies may actually be at a disadvantage by having to compete with Sonangol and its many subsidiaries and joint venture companies. A state agency with the resources and expertise to look at the activities of individual oil service companies could help them expand and pursue their own growth strategies to meet the industry's needs in a way that CAE, with its limited focus on basic capacity-building, cannot. However, not only does Sonangol's local content division not have the resources or expertise necessary to examine the sector at that level, it is in some ways a conflict of interest for Sonangol to be responsible for the development of independent oil service companies given its presence in the sector.

The cases also show, perhaps even more clearly, that more Angolans are taking seriously the possibility of running successful businesses by offering quality services to the oil sector. Even those hoping to continue accumulating rent from the oil industry are recognizing the need for international legitimacy. For this reason, many are preparing to offer higher quality value-added products and services in order to continue accumulating wealth instead of using their wealth for conspicuous consumption and/or moving it abroad. On the other hand, the cases also demonstrate the 'dual nature' of local content in Angola, described in Chapter 3. Where local content is used as a cover for the domestic elite to engage in accumulation by dispossession, the production of value is likely to suffer. The transformations occurring in the Angolan oil and oil service sectors offer the possibility (though not by any means the certainty) of producing positive change in the everyday lives of large numbers of people. Interestingly, a very similar dynamic of change can be found in Nigeria.

Case Studies of the Indigenous Companies in Nigerian Oil and Gas Industry[25]

In order to demonstrate that the shift away from rentierism and towards capitalist accumulation may also be underway in Nigeria, this section will profile ten Nigerian companies, both E&P companies and OSCs. As Table 5.2 shows, there are numerous Nigerian E&P companies already active in the Nigerian oil and gas industry. The first company is Sahara Energy Field Ltd (SEFL), which is part of the Sahara Group.[26] Sahara Energy Resource Ltd was founded in Nigeria in 1996 as an oil trading company by the current MD, Tonye Cole, and his friends Tope Shonubi and Ade Odunsi. In 2007, the separate divisions of the company were spun off into four separate companies, including SEFL.

As a private company, there is little information publicly available about the Sahara Group. SEFL has a stake in four oil blocks, including one onshore block in which it owns 100 per cent of the lease and three deep offshore blocks. It also has a majority stake in the Tsekelewu marginal field and a small stake in Block 5 of the Nigeria–São Tomé Joint Development Zone. The company is looking for other upstream opportunities in the Gulf of Guinea region. Unfortunately, although the company has held marginal fields for a number of years, it has been slow to bring any of its fields into production.

According to a top manager at Sahara, the company employs 300 staff members in Nigeria and 600 worldwide. Out of the Nigeria staff, a senior manager claims that only five employees in Nigeria are expatriates.[27] However, the company's website puts total staff strength at only 450. If accurate, the expatriate ratio is likely the lowest amongst oil companies in Nigeria and demonstrates the possibilities for running an exploration and production company in Nigeria without reliance on expatriate labour.

Sahara Energy is a large, successful and professional E&P company that has expanded from a small Nigerian company to have offices and projects in neighbouring African countries, as well as in Europe, Asia and South America. However, the group continues to rely and profit chiefly from the skills and connections of Tonye Cole. It has expanded from modest beginnings trading excess fuel oil from the Port Harcourt and Warri refineries into a large conglomerate involved in storage, trade, retail and marketing of petroleum products, as well as aviation, marine services, engineering, construction, procurement, operation of power plants, liquefied natural gas and even agriculture. Although the company seems the epitome of an organization contributing value and employment to the Nigerian economy, according to a top manager it does not have an official policy on Nigerianization or Nigeria content. Instead 'we just do it', because Nigerian content is 'part of the company culture'.[28] This is surprising given Cole's outspoken support of Nigerian content initiatives and emphasis on corporate social responsibility.

Table 5.1: Indigenous Nigerian E&P Companies with Current Production[29]
(Daily Production as of 31 August 2012 in Barrels of Oil Per Day)

Company Name	Operated Production	Equity Production	Gross Production
NPDC	87,000	102,350	124,350
Seplat	42,000	18,900	42,000
Conoil	25,000	25,000	25,000
Pan Ocean	8,000	3,200	8,000
Moni Pulo	4,200	4,200	4,200
Allied Energy	3,000	3,000	3,000
Amni Petroleum	3,000	5,000	20,000
NDPR	2,500	2,500	2,500
Platform	2,100	2,100	2,100
Brittania U	2,300	2,300	2,300
Shebah	2,000	800	2,000
Walter Smith	2,000	2,000	2,000
Energia	1,600	1,600	1,600
Dubri	200	200	200
Sapetro	0	26,250	175,000
Famfa	0	25,000	250,000
Niger Delta Western	0	9,000	20,000
Midwestern	0	5,640	13,000
First Hydrocarbon(FHN)	0	4,950	11,000
Oando Energy Resources	0	4,500	19,600
Suntrust	0	2,340	13,000
Express Petroleum	0	1,200	2,000
Atlas Petroleum	0	600	1,000
Oriental Energy	0	0	40,000

Source: AOGR, 2012.

Figure 5.2: Case Studies: Nigeria

Company	Description	Area of Activity
Sahara Group/Sahara Energy Field	Large Nigerian oil company with operations in Europe and several African countries	Upstream exploration and production
First Hydrocarbon Nigeria	Majority Nigerian-owned oil company	Upstream exploration and production
Seplat Petroleum	Incorporated joint venture between two Nigerian oil companies and a French oil company	Upstream exploration and production
Africa Oilfield Services	Majority Nigerian-owned oil service company. Originally a foreign-owned oil service company	Fishing, well intervention, wireline, drilling, machining, fabrication and other services
Intels Nigeria	Large Nigerian integrated logistics company. Part of Orlean Invest	Oilfield logistics, support base operator, free zone operator
Dorman Long Engineering	Large Nigerian company involved in oil and gas, telecommunications and power. Originally a British company established in Nigeria in 1949	Fabrication, galvanizing, engineering, construction, materials supply, procurement and asset management
Nigerdock	Large Nigerian oil service company. Part of the Jagal Group of companies	Oil and gas construction, major marine services, shipbuilding and repair, oilfield logistics, free zone operator
Arco Petrochemical Engineering	Nigerian oil service company	Engineering, logistics and procurement company
Ciscon Services	Nigerian oil service company	Various well completion services
(Anonymous)	Nigerian subsidiary of a multinational company	Engineering, procurement and construction company

The second case study company is First Hydrocarbon Nigeria (FHN).[30] FHN was founded in 2009 by Egbert Imomoh, a former Shell executive who is also Chairman of Afren plc.[31] Afren was set up in 2004 to take advantage of discovered but undeveloped oilfields in Africa and is listed on the main board of the London Stock Exchange. Imomoh helped found Afren with Ethelbert Cooper and other UK-based investors to overcome what he calls 'the biggest limitation on the growth of indigenous producers'—access to capital.[32] In 2009 Imomoh helped launch FHN, which is 45 per cent owned by Afren and 55 per cent by Nigerian investors, including two Nigerian banks. The company has plans to list on the Nigerian Stock Exchange.

As a Nigerian independent oil company, FHN is well positioned to benefit from the Nigerian government's policy of increasing indigenous participation in the upstream sector. The company acquired a 45 per cent stake in an onshore oil block owned by Shell Production and Development Company of Nigeria and was able to secure international financing through Afren plc, which acts as technical partner to FHN on the block.[33] Afren is also technical partner to two other smaller Nigerian oil companies—Oriental Resources and Amni Petroleum. The company has exploration interests in Ghana, Nigeria, Côte d'Ivoire, Congo Brazzaville, the Nigeria–São Tomé Joint Development Zone, Kenya, Ethiopia, Madagascar and Seychelles and current production in the range of 15,000–20,000 barrels of oil per day (bpd).

Imomoh notes that for Nigerian investors, 'people need to understand the industry better... It is risky and the gestation period can be relatively long. If people are used to the mentality of importation, buying and selling, then telling them to tie their money down for 3–4 years with no income or dividends and significant risk, they will need to be educated.' However, he has noticed a shift and greater willingness of the Nigerian elites to invest in the upstream sector. 'I would expect that with time we will see those kinds of funds, wherever they come from, flow into the sector.' Moreover, he suggests that this shift has already occurred. 'It has started in the Nigerian banks. The banks themselves a few years ago would not touch the industry. Most of the banks now all have energy desks and many of them are beginning to loan money.'[34]

In a sense, Afren and FHN are adding value to the Nigerian economy since their joint business strategy, in the words of Imomoh, is to take underperforming assets and increase their value. As Imomoh explains: 'We will work quickly. Because we are small, decision-making processes are very tightened and short. We can work these assets and bring them into production very quickly.' The company benefits greatly from Imomoh's expertise and his connections in Shell Nigeria (where he rose to the position of Deputy MD) and in London (where he was a Senior Corporate Advisor for Shell International before his retirement). When asked of his plans to expand in Nigeria, Imomoh said: 'We set up here because so much of Africa's oil is here, so we wanted to be here. We believe there is an abundance of fields in Nigeria. So if we are here we believe we can get assets... If more assets come up, we can acquire them.'[35] However, Afren and FHN work strictly in the upstream sector. If they continue to invest in Nigeria, they may generate a great deal of wealth for themselves and for the government of Nigeria, but are unlikely to expand beyond exploration and production or employ significant numbers of Nigerians.

In the case of Imomoh, it is important to note that although he is uniquely positioned to compete for former Shell assets and benefit from the push to indigenize onshore oil blocks in the Niger Delta, Imomoh carries a great deal of baggage from his time working for Shell Nigeria. Far from representing a new group of young Nigerian entrepreneurs, Imomoh's name is linked to some of the country's most shameful cases of human rights abuse. Imomoh was General Manager of Shell Eastern Division, with responsibility for Ogoniland at the time when Ken Saro-Wiwa was executed by the military government. He later led Shell's efforts in 1997 to return to Ogoni. In October 1993, shortly after being promoted to General Manager, Imomoh wrote to the military governor of Rivers State to request military assistance for Shell's operations in Ogoni, though he later denied under oath that Shell had been involved in human rights abuses in the Delta. Roughly 2,000 Ogoni were killed, 30,000 made homeless and countless others tortured and raped during the Ogoni campaign of 1993–4 (Rowell, Marriott and Stockman, 2005: 88–9).[36]

The final E&P company to be profiled is Seplat Petroleum,[37] which is an incorporated joint venture formed in 2009 by two Nigerian oil companies (Shebah E&P and Platform Petroleum) and a French oil company called Maurel and Prom. Seplat was formed to acquire a 45 per cent stake in three onshore oil blocks from SPDC, as part of Shell's continuing divestment from onshore Niger Delta production. The company is also rumoured to be interested in several other oil blocks onshore in the Niger Delta that Shell is considering divesting. The CEO of Seplat, Austin Avuru, was the MD of Platform Petroleum and a well-known figure in the Nigerian oil and gas business. Platform has produced over 2 million barrels of crude oil, generating over US$175 million in total wealth, including US$8 million in retained profit (of which US$3.4 million was returned to shareholders.[38] Explaining the creation of Seplat, Avuru notes: 'Access to capital is very limited for indigenous companies. It's an uphill task for an indigenous Nigerian company to access funds in Europe and the US. There are challenges there and the Nigerian banking system, which ought to understand us better, I wouldn't give them a lot of credit.'[39]

Seplat has current production of about 57,000 barrels of oil per day (AOGR, 2012). Avuru says that he expects that the NCA will encourage more indigenous participation and a stronger Nigerian oil sector. His advice for indigenous companies is to be smaller and more compact so they can be proactive and nearer to the communities. 'They will have good relations not because they are indigenous, but because they are smaller and more proactive.'[40] Platform was an integrated oil company (a company working in both the upstream and downstream sectors) and was also moving into midstream operations by building a gas plant. However, according to Avuru, Seplat is more strictly an exploration and production company. While this suggests there are now increased opportunities for Nigerians to make money in petroleum exploration and production, it also suggests the limited effect these new opportunities may have on the Nigerian economy overall—especially given that one-third of Seplat's top management and one-third of its Board are expatriate. Although Seplat's website claims that 'there has been a remarkable positive multiplier effect on the local economy through Seplat's acquisition', it doesn't provide any information to back up the statement.

Few Nigerian E&P companies seem to be translating their success into diversified sectors of the economy. As in Angola, many Nigerian E&P companies exist to benefit from patronage and the extraction of economic rent only. However, there are more serious Nigerian oil companies with the expertise and the backing to succeed in business. Despite this fact, few companies other than Sahara seem interested in integrating oil extraction with other economic activities.

As in Angola, the real potential of Nigerian content lies in the oil services sector. The first case study in this sector is a company called Africa Oilfield Services Limited (AOS),[41] an oilfield service company established in 1981. The company has technical agreements with various international companies to supply specialized equipment and services to oil companies operating in Nigeria. Recently, it has also begun expanding into Ghana, though it continues to manage operations out of its Nigeria offices.

Originally a foreign-owned company, AOS brought in Nigerians to take ownership of the company. According to a top manager at the company, the new board and change in ownership structure occurred roughly ten years ago. Roughly five years ago, the company began to Nigerianize top management positions. As he explains, 'AOS was owned by a non-Nigerian. We were partly a foreign company, so we needed to form an alliance with a Nigerian company because jobs that AOS used to get were not going to come to us any more.'[42]

The company now has one of the most advanced Nigerian content policies in the industry, which commits it to '[develop] the Nigerian economy in maximizing engineering expertise, technical knowledge and transfer of technology'.[43] The policy tracks the percentage of Nigerian labour at various levels of the company (see Table 5.2) and commits them to minimum percentages of Nigerian content in various aspects of its operations and to specific goals for use of local suppliers.

In 2010, AOS pioneered the Nigerian assembly of drill bits—a machining and fabrication service that was previously only available abroad—in order to facilitate the company's technology transfer and training and development goals.[44] The company also commits in its Nigerian content policy to 'reinvest 75 per cent of profits connected with this contract in the further development of our portfolio of services in supporting the Nigerian oil and gas industry'.

AOS has clearly made major strides on Nigerian content and impressive efforts to reduce the reliance on expatriates. Understandably, some remaining expatriate managers are concerned with this direction. Arguing that local content 'amounts to nationalization', one expatriate working for AOS commented: 'Although they push local content, quality and cost make it difficult because you get inferior quality [from indigenous companies] at inflated cost.' The statement seems a bit incongruent with Nigerian local content policy, which makes it clear that preference is only given in cases where goods and services meet the necessary quality standards. On the other hand, due to the customs regime and duties, there is a high cost for imports in terms of money and time to import, which is often behind the company's realization that, in the words of the expatriate informant, 'you often just have to find the best you can locally'.[45]

Table 5.2: Nigerian and Expatriate Labour at Africa Oilfield Services

Employee Group	Per cent Nigerian	Per cent Expatriate
Top Management	67%	33%
Middle Management	65%	35%
Senior Staff	100%	0%
Junior Staff	100%	0%
Labour Contract Staff	100%	0%

Source: AOS Nigerian Content Policy [internal document].

An additional concern for local manufacturing is that the larger oil service companies can access a pool of equipment that is moved around globally, which is significantly more cost-effective. However, while they articulate many disadvantages faced by local oil service companies, both expatriate and Nigerian managers at AOS recognize the reality of the situation, which is, as the expatriate manager admitted, that eventually indigenous companies will dominate oil services. This is especially true for standard industry services like the rental of drill pipe and handling equipment. It is telling that a Nigerian mid-level manager I spoke to was more optimistic than his boss about Nigerian content policy, arguing that Nigerian content will benefit the country by creating a middle class of people who are educated and who will remain in Nigeria, which he believes 'has got to have an effect on the rest of the economy'.[46]

The second case study of an oil service company is Intels Nigeria Ltd,[47] a large Nigerian company that runs an oil support base/transit and supply base providing over 25 different services. The company is based at the Onne Oil and Gas Free Zone near Port Harcourt, which it owns and operates. The majority stake in the company is owned by a company called Orlean Invest Holdings, which owns several companies in Nigeria and abroad, including the engineering and building company Prodeco. Orlean Invest is controlled by an Italian businessman named Gabriel Volpi. Volpi, who acts as chairman, also holds Nigerian citizenship. However, the holding company is registered in Panama (USS, 2010: 175, 188–9). The former vice president of Nigeria, Atiku Abubakar, is also a shareholder in Orlean Invest, having traded in his 16 per cent share in Intels for shares in the parent company. Mr Volpi, who is also MD of Intels, is also mentioned in a US Senate sub-committee on investigations report on foreign corruption, which includes a case study of Atiku; and both men have been named by a Nigerian newspaper as having links to organized crime in Italy.[48]

All of the holding company's investments are managed by Orlean Invest West Africa Ltd (OIWA), which operates a large compound on the outskirts of Port Harcourt. A top manager at OIWA estimates that the company is worth more than US$800 million and is roughly 70 per cent Nigerian-owned, including Volpi's and Atiku's shares. He said that in all there are about forty companies owned by Orlean Invest. Intels, which Atiku helped found in the 1980s, is by far the largest. Not only does it run the Onne Oil and Gas Free Zone and many oil facilities around the country, but it also operates oil terminals and oil services zones at ports in Angola, Equatorial Guinea, Gabon and São Tomé and Principe. The same manager, an expatriate, estimates that Intels employs roughly 15,000 people, while Prodeco employs about 5,000. The number of expatriates working at Intels is fairly low given the total staff—perhaps only 150—while the percentages are higher at Prodeco and at the OIWA head office.[49]

A senior Nigerian manager at OIWA explained that reducing the reliance on expatriates makes business sense: 'Expats, they come and they go. So we need to integrate Nigerians.' However, an official at Intels in their newly formed Nigerian content department argues that 'The government must create the enabling environment for companies to be able to get this done... If government isn't supporting the Act, I don't believe companies themselves will be able to follow it.'[50]

At Intels, the company has moved slowly to embrace Nigerian content. A Nigerian content department was only created around the same time as passage of the NCA, and the Nigerian content policy of the company was unavailable to me when I visited because it had not yet been approved by management. Although they are moving to set up at least one manufacturing plant—for coated pipes—the company seems unsure how they will meet the Nigerian content requirements in the NCA. The company is certainly a successful, world-class operation that makes valuable contributions to the Nigerian economy. The Intels/Orlean Invest case does illustrate some of the less reputable and opaque aspects of the industry and the continued presence of mixed methods of accumulation. However, the case also demonstrates the possibility of rent-seeking companies also embracing both capitalist logic and capitalist social relations of production while continuing to benefit from access to the state (which is not inconsistent with the logic of capitalism).

The third case is the large Nigerian engineering and fabrication company Dorman Long Engineering.[51] As its CEO Henry Okolo relates, Dorman Long was actually a British company founded in Nigeria in 1949, eleven years prior to independence. Nigerian ownership began with the indigenization period of the 1970s. By the late 1980s, the company was 100 per cent Nigerian-owned. According to Okolo, there are currently about 250 large and small shareholders in the company, though there are plans to list the company on the Nigerian Stock Exchange. As a large, well-established company, it has significant private equity investment and access to a large pool of local bank facilities, which gives it a significant advantage over newer companies.[52]

The company has four core business areas: fabrication (steel structures, marine, FPSO topsides), asset management (operations, logistics and maintenance of oil and gas facilities), galvanizing and protective coating for steel, and supply chain solutions (operation of joint ventures with various multinational oil service companies for materials supply). Largely through its procurement business, it has also expanded into Dubai. One of the company's main goals—also an important Nigerian content objective of the NCDMB—is to achieve topside integration of an FPSO in Nigeria. This was discussed in Chapter 3.

Okolo has been one of the biggest proponents of Nigerian content. His company's advertisements proudly display a Nigerian flag and the words 'Nigerian content'. He has also spoken out against what he calls 'preconceptions and racism in Nigerian content discussions', though he argues that this is more of an issue with some IOCs than with others. He therefore has called for strict enforcement and litigation when necessary to 'defend the Nigerian economy'.[53]

Despite the difficulties in getting sufficient work from the IOCs, Dorman Long has been involved in numerous high-profile projects and has shown an ability to do work that multinationals could not do. One of Okolo's proudest achievements was the work his company did on the Shell Sea Eagle FPSO in the offshore East Area (EA) field in shallow water off Bayelsa State. EA platform was one of MEND's first targets in 2006 and has been repeatedly attacked since. The field is capable of yielding 115,000 bpd. As he tells it, Halliburton was forced to abandon the job due to militancy. Dorman Long came in and trained 100 people from the Niger Delta to work as welders and painters on the project, using funding from Shell to bring in painters and welders from the UK to do the training.

Okolo argues that Shell has saved millions by being able to switch to Nigerian labour on the EA field and also for the management of the Bonga FPSO. He boasts: 'There was not one day of disruption and we brought back the facility to production in record time.'[54] He is also proud that Dorman Long is looking to expand and compete for contracts in Equatorial Guinea and throughout the region—further proof of its commitment to capitalist development and growth.

The fourth case, Nigerdock,[55] is often mentioned in the same breath as Dorman Long, as the second major Nigerian fabrication company, although like Intels it is also a logistics company and operator of an oil and gas free zone. Nigerdock is part of the Jagal Group, a massive conglomerate involved in oil and gas as well as pharmaceuticals and household products. The group has been in Nigeria for over forty years and involved in oil and gas for over twenty years. In addition to Nigerdock, the group owns Skillbase (a deepwater logistics and service base) and is involved in several joint ventures with multinational oil service companies.

Nigerdock has four stand-alone divisions: offshore fabrication, pressure vessels, shipyard and training centre. Like Dorman Long, Nigerdock's advertising proudly displays a Nigerian flag and announces its support for Nigerian content. The company has invested US$250 million since 2003 on the Snake

Island facility to make it one of the most advanced shipbuilding facilities in the world and the largest shipyard in West Africa. According to the Executive Director, Manssour Jarmakani, 'We're the only Nigerian company that can do FPSO topside integration. Anyone who tells you different is fooling you.' He goes on to say: 'People say we don't have the certification and equipment for FPSO integration, but if I knew I had an FPSO integration contract, I'd invest and do it in two months—no problem. The mindset however is to focus on reasons you can't do something.'[56]

Nigerdock is a large company, employing roughly 1,200 people. FPSO integration is a major priority for the company. A senior manager at Jagal Group explained: 'We want to integrate an FPSO in Nigeria. That is our target, that is our plan, and we are going to do it!' The manager went on to say that they fully expect to do this within a few years and are already in a tendering process to integrate an FPSO in Nigeria. As with Dorman Long, the obstacles to this were discussed in Chapter 3. However, despite criticisms of what they have accomplished so far, there can be little doubt about these companies' genuine desire to add value to the Nigerian economy.

The fifth case study company is also one that has been referred to in Chapter 3—Arco Petroleum.[57] As mentioned, Arco was created over thirty years ago and would like to move into manufacturing but lacks the required resources or infrastructure in terms of transportation networks and capacity of the system for generating and delivering electricity in Nigeria. Okoigun's company has done much to promote Nigerian content. Now worth roughly US$50 million, Arco was started on a loan of US$5,500. The company currently employs roughly 400 people, though Okoigun admits he has been forced to rely heavily on expatriate expertise. Arco was one of the early champions of the Warri industrial park, from which it does much of its engineering and logistics work.

Okoigun has a strategy of how to begin manufacturing items he currently imports: 'I'd start with simple components—gaskets, common spares used in compressors, pumps and valves. These are things I'd love to go into.' However, as discussed in Chapter 3, the lack of basic infrastructure has largely deterred him so far.[58] The Arco case highlights the need for the Nigerian state, if it wants to promote economic development through the upstream oil sector, to invest in the infrastructure that makes it possible for value to be added in Nigeria and by Nigerians. With such intervention, the Arco case in particular highlights the readiness of local capitalists to invest in manufacturing and to benefit from capitalist accumulation.

The sixth case is Ciscon Nigeria Ltd,[59] managed by Shawley Coker. The company was founded in 1986 by Coker and three others and currently has around 300 employees. It has offices in Lagos, Port Harcourt, Warri and Houston. Although he has been very successful, Coker believes the two major impediments to the growth of indigenous oil service companies are capital and being accepted by the IOCs and multinational oil service companies. In terms of capital, Coker notes: 'Most of the international companies get their equipment with a loan from a bank for 3–4 per cent, whereas in Nigeria we have to take money at a much higher rate than our foreign counterparts. If we have to borrow money at 19 per cent and we have to buy the equipment from the same company that sells to multinationals, where do you start?' These comments, mirrored by many other indigenous oil service companies, underline the need for the NCDF.[60]

He also notes that not only is oil service equipment capital-intensive, but when delivering to Nigerian companies they require payment in full before they will ship the equipment. Even then, if proprietary technology is involved that requires their personnel to be sent to Nigeria, they may not be willing to go to Nigeria 'due to one fear or another'. If the equipment does get sent, Nigerian companies must pay full duties, while multinationals often bring in equipment under temporary importation licences and may pay as little as 1 per cent of the duty. Coker's comments add to the argument for why the Nigerian state should better protect, invest and subsidize this industry to nurture capitalist development.

Like many indigenous companies, Ciscon has no formal Nigerian content policy. This oversight may limit the benefits to the rest of the economy from any growth, though Coker argues that Nigerian content simply comes naturally to Nigerian entrepreneurs. Although Coker worries about the extra hurdles which indigenous companies face, naturally given his dual roles as Ciscon's MD and Chairman of PETAN, he is optimistic about Nigerian content and expects to see an impact in the next few years from the passage of the NCA. 'Nobody accepts change overnight... They have made free money over the years. Having made such free money over the years, if someone says no you cannot make your business in those old-fashioned methods, I'm sure you'll kick against it. It's no different. Change is always a problem.'[61]

The final case study company is a Nigerian company set up by a European engineering, procurement and construction company in 2009. The MD would only speak to me on condition that I didn't name his company because he was new to the country and his company has experienced difficulties in

Nigeria before. The multinational company previously operated a Nigerian subsidiary which contracted for one of the IOCs, but encountered difficulties due to new Nigerian content regulations and pressure from a Nigerian oil workers' union. The new company has been set up as an intermediary and subcontracts its work to the European subsidiary. A majority share of the new company is owned by Nigerian investors. According to the expatriate MD of the company, all the technical know-how comes from Europe, but the company wants to bring in qualified Nigerians to ensure that some knowledge transfer is happening.[62]

The new company has made an effort to demonstrate its commitment to Nigerian content. It has prepared a policy to be included in bids for tenders that states its commitment to the NCA and adoption of NCA regulations. If it makes a serious attempt to adopt the new regulations, the local content will undoubtedly have an economic effect; however, it is unclear whether this will happen or whether the company has been formed as a front to circumvent Nigerian content by including a few wealthy Nigerians. The company's MD argues that while Nigerianization is proceeding, 'it is not often you can't find someone' [with the necessary skills]. However, he says, it is much easier to meet the human resources requirements than it is to meet the materials requirements of the NCA.[63] In the end, it may be that he is not trying very hard.

* * *

The above case studies show that, although Nigerian content is too new for anyone to express much more than an opinion about its effects, several Nigerian companies are using Nigerian content to produce value for the Nigerian economy. Along with the Angolan case studies, they also show that, while there are very real concerns, there is also potential room for an expansion of capitalist accumulation in Angola and Nigeria—especially with an effective and state-led policy approach. In the Nigerian case, investment has been limited in recent years due to the uncertainty created by the long-stalled Petroleum Industry Bill (PIB). This uncertainty and drop in new investment has set back Nigerian content development. Quantitatively, these cases cannot demonstrate that a shift is occurring in strategies of elite accumulation, or that a transformation is underway in the upstream oil and gas industry towards more capitalist social relations of production. However, qualitatively, the cases do represent evidence that such a shift may be occurring and is a possible outcome of wider oil industry reform.

The case study evidence from both countries also suggests that there may be different varieties or types of indigenous accumulation or that the companies described may best be thought of as operating on a continuum between pure capitalist accumulation and pure accumulation by dispossession. Following from this notion, the transformation being analyzed herein would be both an increase in the number of indigenous companies and the amount of indigenous economic activity *and* a movement along this continuum towards more capitalist behaviour. However, it is important to note that many companies display mixed methods of accumulation. While they have an incentive to engage in capitalist production, they continue to have an incentive to engage in rent-seeking and other forms of accumulation by dispossession (which, as discussed in Chapter 1, does not disappear even in advanced capitalist economies, it simply becomes more sophisticated).

A look at the history of national content (particularly in Nigeria), the ideology behind the current local content push and the shifts already observed by industry insiders suggests that unless more is done, the primary beneficiaries will not be the Angolan and Nigerian people. Nigerians face two unattractive outcomes. While indigenization benefits the Nigerian elite and allows widespread rent-seeking and patronage, domiciliation exposes the country and the industry to the effects of neoliberal globalization (which also primarily benefits the elite of Nigeria, as well as foreign interests). Given the closed nature of the Angolan state, Angolans are largely unaware of the issue of local content and its location at the centre of questions of oil, development and elite accumulation.

To chart a course that allows these countries' resource wealth to reach the majority of their people and make oil work is no easy task. By way of conclusion, it is necessary to consider what the shift might mean for Angola and Nigeria, since it must be local agency that works for the best outcome within the limits of the possible. At this crucial moment, local content policies are still being implemented and even formed. In order to understand those limits and the potential to struggle for the best possible outcome, Chapter 6 will proceed to analyze the activities and motivations of various non-governmental organizations, activists, labour unions and communities in oil-producing areas to protect their livelihoods and influence and participate in decision-making about petroleum resources and how best to deal with them.

6

CIVIL SOCIETY, SOCIAL MOVEMENTS AND LOCAL CONTENT IN HOST COMMUNITIES

Civil society is the terrain upon which struggles over state and society are resolved. On this terrain, questions of how to use petroleum resources and who will benefit the most from their extraction will be resolved. To date, the dominant classes in Angola and Nigeria have had a great deal of power to influence these decisions. Their enrichment has occurred at the expense of economic and social development for the vast majority. The dynamics of change already discussed have so altered the current moment for oil extraction in the Gulf of Guinea that elite calculations have been changed. The elite now think and act differently when it comes to maximizing their own benefit from petroleum resources. This change will produce new potential for capitalist economic development and may even produce positive social change.

So far, this book has explored the compelling evidence that Angola and Nigeria are experiencing top-down implementation of what I call the 'petro-developmental state'. However, civil society is made up of various organizations, groups with varying degrees of formed and unformed interests, social classes and actors of all sorts. Even though much of the current transformation in both the state and social relations of production are top-down, the eventual outcome of the transformation may still be influenced by various actors on the terrain of civil society.

While the state is understood as the key actor in the implementation of petro-developmentalism, it is made up of bureaucrats and politicians who respond to developments on the battleground of civil society with some degree of autonomy from any one particular group or set of interests. While the developmental state may promote economic development by favouring certain fractions of capital to create comparative advantage, Evans (1995) makes it clear that relative autonomy is required for the state to implement policy successfully. It is the task of this chapter to bring in some (though by no means all) of the other key actors in Angolan and Nigerian civil society and begin to think about their power to influence social change with reference to petro-development. I have argued that there are numerous potential pitfalls on the road to successful implementation of the petro-developmental state. Similarly, there are numerous potential pitfalls to civil society actors contributing to positive social change.

Stakeholder Agency and Civil Society

It is impossible to do justice to the vigorous debates in recent years about the term 'civil society' in the social sciences. However, a few words about the concept as I employ it and its importance for discussing the developmental state are needed before proceeding. In his review of eight countries in SSA, Jimi Adesina writes: 'The retreat of state from social delivery (healthcare, education, human security, etc.) undermined the relevance and the legitimacy of the state in the eyes of its citizens' (2007: 30). Echoing Mkandawire and Chang, the purpose of Adesina's piece is to show the connection between social policy and development concerns. His work also shows the link between the retrenchment of state capacity for social provisioning and the tide of crisis in statehood. In effect, the contributions of Evans (2008), Mkandawire (2010) and others to the theory of the developmental state are that to be successful, not only must today's African developmental state be democratic, it must also include civil society participation in meaningful ways.

As Howell and Pearce (2001) note, the term 'civil society' is often understood in a narrow sense to refer only to non-governmental organizations (NGOs). However, as Julie Hearn (2001) reminds us, civil society can also be viewed in a Gramscian sense as a battleground in which various powerful actors intervene in order to influence political and developmental outcomes. Civil society is a contested concept. For the purposes of this study, it is understood in a broad sense to refer to a terrain on which various groups (including well-organized interest groups, amorphous groups such as 'youth', social classes and various institutions) with both formed and unformed interests struggle to see those interests realized.

As we have seen, the idea of wealth 'trickling down' to the general populace, in this case through national ownership and participation in the oil sector (indigenization), is a purported and obviously fallacious goal of elite-led local content. The preceding chapters have shown that economic growth is possible under global neoliberalism for the oil-producing countries of the Gulf of Guinea. Given the nature of the current moment of neoliberal austerity, it is also possible that without intervention, local content will end up encouraging national ownership for the benefit of the elite while falling short of its goal to increase economic activity and job creation through 'knock-on effects' from the oil industry. These observations suggest a role for other civil society actors and organizations in deciding how to implement local content. Even if local content and the larger transformations discussed in this study are implemented from above, civil society can help shape who benefits from local content. Such participation could help ensure the long-term stability and success of the petro-developmental state.

Despite the obvious promise of domiciling services in Angola and Nigeria in order to capture industry spend (as opposed to indigenizing services in terms of ownership), local content is absent from the policy documents and advocacy strategies of most of the domestic or international organizations advocating social change or improved policies for economic development and/or social justice. Evans suggests links between civil society and his concept of embedded autonomy:

> In order to be able to create effective state-society linkages, the state must facilitate the organization of counterparts in 'civil society'. The 20th century development state's interaction with industry gave industrial elites a reason to become a more collectively coherent class. The 21st century developmental state must do the same for a much broader cross-section of society. It won't be easy. 'Civil society' is a complicated beast, full of conflicting particular interests and rife with individuals and organizations claiming to represent the general interest (2008: 16).

At first Evans' assertion may seem confusing, given the relatively minor that role civil society played in the emergence of the East Asian developmental states. However, Evans argues:

> The centrality of dense connections to civil society and the construction of democratically deliberative institutions would at first seem to make the 21st century developmental state the political antithesis of the 20th century version. A closer look suggests that the classic 20th century developmental states have already begun to change the character of their embeddedness (2008: 17).

As evidence, he suggests that Taiwan and South Korea are already shedding authoritarian traditions and allowing more public deliberation on policy priorities.

Civil society in Angola and Nigeria face somewhat different yet equally large challenges in pushing for social change and greater benefit from the country's petroleum wealth. In Nigeria, national civil society organizations (CSOs) remain focused largely on conflict and environmental degradation. Such groups do retain an interest in wider petroleum industry restructuring through the PIB insofar as it may result in strengthened language on transparency, accountability and environmental protection. They are also focused on a 10 per cent derivation for communities that host oil production or oil infrastructure such as pipelines. Unfortunately, neither country has seen active civil society engagement with the push for local content.

The avoidance of Nigerian content may result from a mistaken belief that it is too late to influence the outcome of a particular law such as the NCA once it has already been passed. It may also be because it is far easier to measure the tangible outcomes of a campaign to influence the content of a bill still under consideration (like the PIB) than it is to measure the outcomes of a campaign to influence the implementation of a bill that has already become law. From a growing insurgency in the north to renewed militant activity in the Niger Delta, there are so many issues to occupy foreign and domestic actors that Nigerian content seems to be slipping through the cracks despite the hype that surrounded the passage of the NCA.

In Angola, civil society organizations independent of the state did not exist during the Marxist–Leninist period. The government is mistrustful of organizations beyond its control. Therefore, journalists, labour unions, activists, the church and non-governmental organizations (foreign and domestic) are denied basic freedoms. They operate in a context where direct criticism of the government, and particularly the president, is met with severe consequences (from harassment and threats to imprisonment and murder in extreme cases). Although many CSOs have worked within the limits of the system to promote better use of the country's petroleum resources, once again local content is largely absent from the work that most organizations are doing. In many cases there is a complete lack of knowledge of the concept. This oversight can only be understood in the context of the culture of secrecy that makes information about the petroleum industry—even the laws governing it—largely opaque and allows the elite to exert extremely high levels of control over state apparatuses and systems of accumulation. Instead, Angolan CSOs are concerned largely with the amount of government spending on social services and other issues surrounding the allocation of petroleum rents.

In the sections that follow, I will discuss the role that some civil society actors have played in oil extraction and the challenges they face in contributing to influencing policy decisions and policy implementation around issues of oil and economic and/or social development. I will then look at four civil society trends with an ability to influence oil policy and developmental outcomes in positive and negative ways: the role of multinational corporations through corporate social responsibility (CSR), the role of labour unions as particularly powerful membership-based organizations, the role of communities at the sites of oil extraction and the role of new social movements in Angola and Nigeria.

The Role of Civil Society in Oil Extraction

In this section, I will introduce several aspects of how civil society intervenes or attempts to intervene in questions of oil extraction and development, and will explore the challenges that actors and groups face in influencing how petroleum resources are used and who benefits from them. Looking first at Angola and then at Nigeria, I will examine some of what is being done, what is not being done and what constraints exist for pursuing change through social action. Although civil society organizations in the two countries face different realities and restrictions, ultimately there is little room to expect bottom-up transformation in either case.

Civil Society Organizations, Political Parties and the Media in Angola

In Angola, civil society organizations, political parties and the media are all severely limited by the state from contributing to decision-making and even to discussions about questions of oil and development. The embedded power relations are such that these organizations face severe state repression and dirty tricks. The lack of transparency in Angola also limits the effectiveness of political organizing and action. Therefore while transparency is often seen as a foreign demand, in Angola local CSOs clamour for what they call 'substantive transparency'. This means transparency from government but also from international oil companies.

CSOs concerned with poverty alleviation and development are often the first groups one would think should be meaningfully engaged on issues of petroleum resources. Amundsen and Abreu (2006) list six types of CSOs that are important in Angola: national NGOs, international NGOs, faith-based organizations, the media, trade unions and professional organizations and organizational networks. While in some ways a vibrant civil society does exist, Vines, Shaxson and Rimli note: 'Angola still lacks a social contract that would enable civil society organisations to hold government or service providers accountable' (2005: 24). While civil society in Angola has taken great strides since the end of the civil war in 2002, its ability to influence government policy remains limited. Orre writes:

> Despite the political liberalisation that has taken place in the capital, where growth of a critical civil society has developed to a certain extent… the life of individual members of the opposition party militants in general and the UNITA party politicians in particular, have remained as complicated as they were shortly after the peace agreement. (2010: 127; citing Andrade, 2009; Amundsen and Abreu, 2006; Marques Guedes, 2005)

The need for continued support to civil society organizations is paramount because 'inefficiency and unproductiveness of political parties means that, in many situations, the onus of contesting burning issues and defending the poor and marginalised sectors (the majority) of the population falls on civil society organisations' (Orre, 2010: 360; citing Andrade, 2009).

Christine Messiant's work on the José Eduardo dos Santos Foundation (FESA) shows how attempts have been made to bring CSOs in Angola under the MPLA. In fact, Messiant describes a coordinated effort by the MPLA to set up multiple government-organized non-governmental organizations or 'GONGOs', as well as its own new social movements such as the Movimento Espontâneo to rival international and domestic organizations and the church (2008: 113). Carrying on the traditions and structures established during the Marxist period, the MPLA also retains control over several important mass organizations. These include the Organização da Mulher Angolana (Organization of Angolan Women) and Organização dos Pioneiros Agostinho Neto (Agostinho Neto Organization of Pioneers), itself organized by the youth movement of the MPLA, the Juventude do Movimento Popular de Libertação de Angola.

Only a few of Angola's independent CSOs work on issues of oil and development, due to the sensitive nature of the work. For the most part, their work is limited to research and advocacy on the allocation of revenues from oil extraction. One of the oldest NGOs in Angola is Acção para o Desenvolvimento Rural e Ambiental (ADRA), established in 1990 to work on poverty alleviation and sustainable rural development.[1] The organization has moved from issues of food security, land and microcredit into education promotion as well as limited advocacy work on social services in the state budget and the management of petroleum resources. ADRA has offices and projects throughout Angola, making it by far the largest NGO in the country and has contacts at all levels of government.[2]

One of the only other comparable NGOs in Angola is Development Workshop (DW). Both ADRA and DW remain conscious of the limits they operate within and attempt to work towards social change without appearing to threaten the government. There are a few well-known cases of NGOs in Angola that crossed the line and were targeted by the MPLA. For example, SOS Habitat and Associação Justiça, Paz e Democracia (AJPD) are two organizations that challenged the government and have suffered as a result.[3] A prominent NGO leader therefore admitted to me that many CSOs chose to criticize the regime using 'safe words'. Making an analogy that perhaps doesn't translate well into English, she commented that it is better to be an 'activist chicken' than an 'activist pig' because the chicken does not have to die to make an omelette.[4] This analogy does underline the weighty considerations that both activists and NGO practitioners have to weigh when deciding how to promote social change.

For ADRA, analyses and critiques of the state budget are a new activity undertaken as part of its *Petróleo para Bem Comum* ('Oil for Development') project. The project, funded by the government of Norway and executed with Norwegian partner organizations, monitors the national budget in terms of how revenue is allocated and used. According to the project proposal, the goal of the project is to 'analyze the opportunities and possibilities to support civil society actors in Angola and ways to involve them and encourage them to play a key role in the state budget process in the areas of education, health and agriculture'.[5] The project is notable in that it promotes greater awareness of the budget process, calls for greater inclusion and includes funds to lobby members of the National Assembly.

Working with Observatório Político e Social de Angola (OPSA), ADRA produced an analysis of the 2011 budget which shows that education and health spending dropped in 2011 compared to 2010 while defence spending rose slightly (ADRA and OPSA, 2010). The report was launched just ahead of the National Assembly's consideration of the 2011 budget and provided to several key legislators; it argues that the state should spend more on social services and less on defence. It also notes that Angola is still well behind the rest of the region in terms of expenditure on health and education as a percentage of total government expenditure. Therefore, it recommends redistribution of spending to direct more funds to the priority areas of health, education and agriculture.

According to ADRA's coordinator of the Oil for Development project, education, healthcare and agriculture make up less than defence in the state budget.[6] ADRA's general director laments the lack of consultation with civil society organizations about the budget: 'We passed our opinion to the National Assembly, but the government doesn't have a lot of dialogue on the budget. This is a big problem. There is not dialogue between the government and society.'[7] A senior member of ADRA's Board of Directors who has worked to promote social change in Angola for decades also notes: 'It is very difficult to influence the government on redistribution. You can have dialogue, but it's not easy to make change.' He went on to say that one of the key differences between past decades and today is the government's unchallenged power and greater oil wealth, which reinforces the need for an independent middle class and strong civil society organizations.[8] Unfortunately, this normative prescription seems unlikely to be filled any time soon.

As noted in Chapter 2, oil revenue makes up roughly 80 per cent of the revenues of the government of Angola. Plataforma Mulheres em Acção (PMA), one of the only other CSOs working on the state budget, is one of the largest and, in fact, one of the only active gender advocacy organizations in Angola. PMA is a coalition of 29 member organizations working on gender issues in Angola. As their 2010 Semi-annual Report makes clear, PMA has decided to concentrate its activities on 'transformative leadership and gender mainstreaming in the general budget of the state' (PMA, 2010). The organization has also identified education, health and agriculture as priority areas of the budget due to their impact on women.[9]

The elite have what one gender and development consultant calls 'a lack of understanding about the role of civil society'. In her opinion, it does not help that gender advocacy in Angola is weak compared to other African countries. According to her, even PMA needs to spend more time on educating themselves about gender budgeting. As she describes, they did one workshop and 'now consider themselves specialists'. This has led her to call civil society in Angola 'a bit amateurish'.[10] The work that ADRA, OPSA and PMA do on the state's allocation of oil revenues through the national budget is important work, as is the work that ADRA, DW and other organizations do on budgeting at provincial and municipal levels. Unfortunately, the organizations still have only limited capacity to do this work and are heavily dependent on technical assistance and capacity-building from foreign NGOs. They also have to be cautious to ensure that their work is not seen as too critical by the government, lest they provoke a backlash.

There are no Angolan CSOs that actively work on any issues of oil policy, taxation, tracking payments from IOCs to the government, monitoring of the state oil company, monitoring of IOCs, Angolanization or local content. Although I found occasional references to research that an NGO might have done in the past on oil and development, I could not actually get access to the work. For example, I was not allowed access to a study that one NGO did on the impact of the Angola LNG plant in Soyo because it was commissioned by Angola LNG. The same NGO also worked on a project funded by the British government entitled 'Oil-Affected Communities', which looked at communities in Angola, Nigeria, Alaska and the United Kingdom. However, no one in the organization could locate the study for me, despite several requests.

* * *

There is a second aspect of NGO activity that is connected to questions of natural resource management. For NGOs in Angola—both foreign and domestic—decentralization has been a priority issue in recent years. According to the general director of ADRA, decentralization is necessary to foster democracy and participation in the democratic process. It also is a necessary precondition to local communities having greater control over resource extraction in their territories and playing an active role in the distribution of revenues. However, both institutions and provincial and local governments lack the capacity in terms of human resources and finances to govern effectively. As ADRA's director notes, the administration of the country is very centralized. Over 80 per cent of the state budget is for the central government and there is very little space for provincial or municipal authorities.[11]

The first law to establish the modern state structure of provinces, municipalities and communes (local government in rural areas) was passed in 1999, updated in 2007 and more recently superseded by a new law. With respect to natural resources, there is very little official role for local or provincial government and absolutely no control over resource extraction or the revenues that such extractive industry provides to the state. Instead, development priorities and projects are set in Luanda with little or no consultation.

In theory, the central government has committed to return 10 per cent of revenues from natural resources to the provincial jurisdiction they came from; but in practice, according to multiple sources, this has not occurred with much regularity. An official in the provincial government of Cabinda told me off the record that the province does receive funds from petroleum extraction, which amounted to roughly US$72 million in 2009 and was used to build schools, hospitals and roads.[12] However, an OSISA report confirms that only a very small portion of the 10 per cent promised is being delivered to Cabinda (OSISA, 2013: 32).

In order to advocate for decentralization and local empowerment, many of the most prominent NGOs in Angola began meeting monthly to coordinate their efforts—especially with regard to lobbying the government.[13] Efforts in 2010 were focused on building stronger cooperation with the Ministério da Administração do Território (MAT), the ministry responsible for local government and decentralization, and with the *IV Comissão*, one of nine commissions of the National Assembly which deals with local power and governance issues. The central government has a history of occasionally transferring limit responsibilities (while retaining overall control), but not, as another activist involved in questions of decentralization noted, transferring the knowledge or capacity necessary for the programmes to succeed.[14] It is safe to say that political centralization in Angola is a significant barrier to citizen engagement and empowerment broadly speaking, and also a barrier to feelings of ownership, usefulness and legitimacy for resource extraction.

* * *

Political opposition parties are another organized group in civil society that could be playing a role in promoting wiser management of petroleum resources. In liberal democratic theory, opposition parties play an important role in multiparty democracy by checking the power of the governing party, adding the perspectives of other citizens and groups, providing oversight and promoting alternative policies. Although a competitive political system is unlikely to produce substantial social change, the cases of Norway and Brazil do suggest that multiparty politics could promote better policy that more effectively addresses the specific challenges faced by resource-rich economies. It could also help balance relations of power and relations between social classes. Whether or not opposition political parties could have an impact on the state and the state bureaucracy, greater political debate could at least open discussions about policy related to the oil industry and bring important discussions about oil and development into the public sphere.

In Angola, as one civil society leader explained, multiparty politics are fairly new and democracy is more formal than substantive. While the economy is developing rapidly, this economic development is not resulting in a higher quality of life for many, due to a development model that disregards the importance of redistribution of wealth—a key government responsibility in a resource dependent economy.[15] Instead, the MPLA has very effectively suppressed opposition parties through co-option and by virtue of its total control over the state—particularly its resource wealth and its monopoly on coercive force. The suppression of any and all political opposition belies the MPLA's approach to maintaining power and ensuring it will act as gatekeeper in all spheres of accumulation and all opportunities for wealth creation. This position ensures that MPLA loyalists occupy not only all positions of political power, but also all positions of economic power.

Just as NGOs face state repression, so too do opposition political parties. The major opposition party in Angola, UNITA, entered into a 'Government of Unity and National Reconciliation' (GURN) during 1997–2008. Many of my informants were careful to note that both government and opposition politicians must be understood as members of the elite. While UNITA was excluded following the 2008 elections, its senior figures have continued to benefit, as they had since 2002, from business opportunities and other incentives designed to ensure their loyalty. Although they have been increasingly vocal on certain issues, such as changes to the constitution, changes to electoral law and the independence of the electoral commission, these can be understood as issues affecting the party's ability to occupy some formal positions and thus ensure continued relevance and access to state largesse.

In the 2008 election, the MPLA increased its hold on the National Assembly. Changes to the electoral laws following the election led to the dissolution of most political parties in Angola for failing to win a sufficient portion of the vote. For this reason, in 2010 the Bloco Democrático (BD) was formed, mainly out of members of the dissolved Frente para a Democracia em Angola (FpD). The BD is a party of mostly academics and disaffected elites who have left the MPLA. Speaking about the changes to the electoral law of Angola (*Lei Eleitoral*) in 2010, a senior member of the BD and one of the former leaders of the FpD noted: 'Although laws are changed to make things more democratic, all the changes end up making things less democratic. We are a multiparty democracy, but power is very concentrated.' Calling the 2008 elections a 'big fraud' in which 'the spirit of democracy was not upheld' due to the lack of presidential and local elections, this politician concluded that laws from 1992 'are being revised for the worse' and new laws are being created 'to concentrate power and wealth'. Therefore, 'Right now, things are going down again toward authoritarianism.'[16] As noted in Chapter 1, authoritarianism, while functional to a certain point, can ultimately lead to crisis unless the developmental state can transition to more democratic values and more equal power relations between competing interests.

In Angola, opposition parties are unable to provoke any meaningful discussion about policy and decision-making in Sonangol or the Ministry of

Petroleum. They have limited ability to contribute to debate around new petroleum-related legislation and would lack the capacity to contribute meaningfully even if they were allowed to. The decision to pursue local content policy through Sonangol, while understandable for many reasons described in Chapter 3, prevents parties in the legislature from having any say on local content either. Even if Angola's political opposition was willing and able to discuss questions of oil and development and wanted to bring more information into the public sphere, it would have limited options to do so given the MPLA's control over the media and obstructiveness when it comes to questions of transparency and freedom of information.

* * *

In many ways, freedom of the press is much better in Angola now than it was in 2002. By 2010, as a prominent civil society activist observed, there were several notable independent newspapers, *Rádio Ecclesia* was broadcasting to more Angolans than ever before and many materials were published that were critical of the government. This activist told me he had been interviewed by the state newspaper *Jornal de Angola* the week before I spoke to him and was able to say things that were critical of the government with no consequences for him.[17] However, in May 2010 a prominent economist was fired from his job as a consultant to the Ministry of Planning after giving an interview to a Brazilian newspaper in which he gave a less optimistic assessment of the economy using lower estimates of economic growth.[18]

In June 2010, independent media in Angola once again came under attack when *A Capital*, *Seminario Angolense* and a 40 per cent stake in *Novo Jornal* were bought by a previously unknown company called 'Media Investments'. Although no one knows who bought the papers, which were three of the main independent newspapers in the country, a variety of informants I spoke with claimed that Media Investments is owned by MPLA insiders. As one prominent civil society leader told me, 'In Angola, when no one knows, everyone knows.'[19] The MPLA's takeover of the independent and especially the critical media in the country not only displays their growing ability to exert control; it also displays the MPLA's desire to take control of multiple points of non-oil accumulation.

One of the major figures in the remaking of the Angolan media is General Manuel Helder Vieira Dias Júnior (Kopelipa). Kopelipa is the head of the military house of the government and former head of the Gabinete de Reconstrução Nacional (GRN), a body set up to oversee the government's loan arrangements with China. General Kopelipa, who is one of the most powerful men in the country, owns several businesses including the *Media Nova* group, which owns *TV Zimbo*, *Rádio Mais*, an advertising company and a printing house.[20] While many other groups have been trying to get a licence for a television station for several years, only *TV Zimbo* has been able to get one. As one journalist told me, 'If I wanted to start a TV station, it could never happen. But Kopelipa got the licence for *TV Zimbo* in one month... Kopelipa is one of the princes of Angola.'[21]

Of the three newspapers taken over in 2010, *Seminario Angolense* in particular had launched several high-profile investigations of corruption in Angola and regularly published articles by the anti-corruption crusader Rafael Marques (see Chapter 4). After the takeover, Marques was told he will not be allowed to write again for *Seminario*; then the founding editor of the newspaper, Graça Campos, was forced to resign and was told he will not be allowed to open a new newspaper.[22] In an interview shortly after the takeover, Campos explained that his newspaper had been struggling financially due to a campaign of intimidation. He explained, 'As you may know, *Seminario Angolense* was deprived of publicity and information.' The result, he said, was that several Angolan companies, including state companies and large, recently privatized banks and telecommunications companies owned by people close to the president, withdrew advertising support. Campos contended that the withdrawal was political and that 'What is happening in our country is that the new stakeholders in media emerge from all of the same political family, and sometimes even the same actual family. Moreover, there is the suspicion that they are all supported with public money.'[23]

The Angolan state media (*Angola Press*, *Jornal de Angola* and *Rádio Nacional de Angola*, etc.) are notorious for refusing to criticize the government. Although some, like the activist interviewed above, believe that a small space is opening up, others do not. An Angolan staff member at a large NGO in Angola commented to me that the problem with the media is that they are all based in Luanda. 'You have to belong to the government to speak on *Rádio Nacional*, which is the only radio that broadcasts nationwide.' Therefore, he says, options to disseminate information and empower locals through the media are limited. As an example, he pointed to a recent project in which his NGO had recently attempted to use community radio as a means of dialogue between the government and its citizens, but it had met with only very limited success.[24] Another civil society representative confirmed that the state media are simply not a source of pressure on the government: 'everything is good, everything is progress.'[25]

An Angolan journalist and journalism professor admitted to me in July 2010 that in terms of media freedom, 'There have been some quite big set-backs.' He argues that there may actually have been more media freedom during the war because now dominant groups are using their resources to gain control of the independent private media. While noting that there are more private newspapers and a new private TV station (*TV Zimbo*), the professor recognized that 'they all belong to the same people... they control the media'. However, he remained optimistic for the future: 'I have been a journalism professor for many years. One thing I have learned is that, number one, you will never have all the media singing the same tune. Never. That is what history says. You will never be able to block information in this global village.'[26]

As an example, the professor used the case of forced evictions in Benguela and elsewhere in Angola in early 2010; despite the government imposing a blackout of the story on two radio stations (*Rádio Dois Mille* and *Rádio Provinciale da Huila*) and the TV stations, people still got the information anyway on the internet.[27] 'Everyone found out and there were cries of protest.' This has led the professor to argue that the situation will balance itself: 'In the end, I don't think they will succeed in denying the people their right to be informed or at least to have access to different angles on the same information. Of course they will try, especially because they still use Marxist methods, but they are no longer effective for the actual context.'[28]

Many journalists in Angola continue to press on. Another journalist I interviewed admitted that the government can come down hard on journalists who write negative stories, and that this phenomenon in Angola is aided by the strength of the ruling party and its access to oil wealth. However, he told me that he felt change was inevitable and that he would know Angola had changed when freedom of speech and freedom of the press were achieved:

> When the media change for good, that will be the sign that things are better in our country, things have really changed. Maybe 2010 is not the year for that... I think things will change when the state media change. When *Jornal de Angola* starts to be an interesting newspaper, it will be a new Angola. On that day, things will have changed, a new Angola will be born![29]

* * *

Finally, in addition to the tight controls on the media, the lack of transparency (both government transparency and oil sector transparency) prevents citizens and civil society actors from getting the information they need to hold the state and international oil companies accountable. According to one of Angola's most prominent civil society leaders, the 'culture of the state is still very closed'. The closed nature of the state, he argues, is the result of a lack of capacity and training in the institutions of the state which he attributes to a culture of 'secretism', a mentality of segregation and an anti-democratic sentiment that has origins in Portuguese fascism and a Leninist belief in the need for secrets. However, he argues, the West is also arrogant about the question of transparency.[30]

While transparency is not a well-established norm in Angola, the head of a domestic NGO argues that lack of transparency is an international problem for the oil sector. For this reason, he describes the transparency debate as 'Eurocentric' and argues that to publish information about Angola on a website does not mean transparency for the Angolan people. Transparency must be transparency to the citizens of Angola by the government and by corporations operating in Angola. This, he argues, is 'substantive transparency'.[31] By most measures of transparency, Angola falls short, but by this measure of transparency in particular, there is a long way to go before achieving a form of transparency that helps civil society keep state power in check.

A staff member at a different NGO laid out for me clear ideas of the mechanisms that would be needed to achieve substantive transparency, including clear laws and regulations on how the government manages oil and diamond revenues, institutions to apply the laws and combat corruption, sharing information openly at various levels and through various mediums and developing mechanisms of local participation through decentralized government. Without these mechanisms, he argues, the publication of audits and statistics online cannot allow citizens to follow up on this information even if they do have access to it. 'For me,' he says, 'website publications are just something for Englishmen to see.'[32] A member of the BD made similar comments when he argued that Sonangol should instead publish its disclosures in the *Jornal de Angola* and in the *Diário da República*, and 'not online where no one sees them'.[33]

Interestingly, when I interviewed two Angolan public relations officers at Esso Angola, my questions about transparency angered one of my interview subjects, who told me that he does not think that the US financial sector is very transparent. He told me, 'I don't know what transparency means. I can talk about cultural differences. For us Angolans, the Swiss are very corrupt. If there is one country in the world that accepts dirty money, it is them. Also, the US system of lobbies would not be acceptable in Angola.' Given this ambiguity in what transparency is and the concern of who defines what it is, he argued, all his company can do is follow existing laws. His counterpart quickly intervened after his statement to let me know that all of what he had just said was his 'personal opinion'.[34] Although he is clearly making a false comparison between Angola and Switzerland and even Angola and the US, the views expressed demonstrate the complexity of the issue of transparency in Angola.

The lack of transparency is central to the reproduction of accumulation strategies that allow the MPLA to maintain and deepen its dominant political and economic position. Therefore, it is unsurprising that the leader of the BD, Justino Pinto de Andrade, told me: 'no, we don't have transparency. In reality, corruption continues and a lack of transparency continues... People who say there is more transparency are lying. Things are very corrupt.'[35] Growing outrage over corruption prompted the President to announce the 'Zero Tolerance' programme and the MPLA to pass a new law on public probity. Questions remain, however, about what effect the new law will have. A senior member of the BD who has studied the new law in detail questioned whether the President is subject to it: 'In practice, the President is excluded. It is his decision that he should be excluded.' Therefore, he argues, 'The new Law of Public Probity doesn't do anything. It's just a piece of paper. Nothing is transparent. In fact, it's just the opposite. It is very opaque.'[36]

Given the realities of the MPLA's intrusion into and power over civil society in Angola, there are only very limited ways in which Angolans can participate in decisions and even discussions about the use of their petroleum resources and the way in which petroleum resources impact on Angolan politics, the Angolan economy and Angolan society. The situation is severe enough to remove the possibility of any bottom-up transformation under the current regime. There is only very limited space in which to challenge the regime's control over the state. The system offers only a few avenues for challenging top-down decision-making related to petro-policy, which is among the most sensitive topics for the Angolan government.

Non-Governmental Organizations and Civil Society in Nigeria

NGOs in Nigeria are more numerous and, since 1999, have generally been freer to advance their objectives—whether they are about poverty alleviation, citizen empowerment, human rights, or government or corporate oversight. When it comes to lobbying government, especially on oil and gas issues, one of the most established NGOs in Nigeria is the Civil Society Legislative

Advocacy Centre (CISLAC), based in Abuja.[37] According to its executive director, CISLAC was created to bridge the gap between CSOs and the work of the legislature and allow for an exchange of ideas. However, he acknowledges that legislators often do not have much experience with civil society and think of CSOs as groups there to attack them. In a context where 'many legislators are only interested in what profit they will make' out of a particular issue, it can be a real challenge in Nigeria to promote citizen input in decision-making.[38] This could lead in turn to a more substantial challenge to power relations in Nigeria.

The majority of the most interesting civil society work in Nigeria as it pertains to oil extraction is done by those organizations that actually work in the Niger Delta. Of these organizations, perhaps the most well-known is Environmental Rights Action/Friends of the Earth Nigeria (ERA), which focuses on defence of people's 'environmental human rights'.[39] ERA has field offices throughout the Niger Delta and has compiled hundreds of field reports documenting oil spills, the health effects of gas flaring and water pollution in various communities and other ill-effects of oil and gas pollution, such as extinction of crops (like the cocoyam) and aquatic life. While the IOCs continue to deny the link between oil pollution and negative effects on human health or plant and animal life, one ERA field officer in the Niger Delta told me that it was clear to him that 'locals attribute the extinction to gas flares and oil spills and I tend to agree with them'.[40] In compiling volumes of empirical evidence of such negative effects, ERA has been highly successful in countering the propaganda of the IOCs and advancing their message that oil should be left in the ground.

Working more to empower communities and groups affected by oil extraction in the Niger Delta, Stakeholder Democracy Network (SDN)[41] and Social Action[42] are two local NGOs fighting for social change in Nigeria.[43] SDN works on a series of issues such as transparency and governance, peace building, human rights, forced evictions and environmental degradation. Social Action works on similar issues of democracy, corruption and poverty alleviation. It also works on broader political economy issues, promoting knowledge of the global system of trade and debt and other forms of political education.

Both organizations monitor the oil and gas industry in Nigeria and have played an active role in lobbying for the perspectives of host communities in petroleum industry restructuring, though neither has specifically focused on the issue of local content. With reference to the current restructuring taking place with the proposed PIB, which aims at a complete overhaul of the industry in Nigeria, a staff member at Social Action commented that 'this is the moment the oil-bearing communities have been waiting for'. By this, he meant that Social Action would push for the PIB to represent a better deal for people living in the Niger Delta. At the same time, both organizations advocate that IOCs leave Nigeria and leave the oil in the ground.

Social Action has also been leading the way in monitoring the implementation of state and local governments' budgets through the Niger Delta Citizens and Budget Platform.[44] According to a Social Action staff member associated with the project, a key finding is that because the states and local governments are not dependent on collecting revenues from their citizens and instead rely on oil revenues, they do not feel accountable to their citizens.[45] This work is crucial to promoting better governance and better use of oil revenues.

Numerous organizations do important work in the Niger Delta and many of these organizations work very closely with each other. It is beyond the scope of this project to list them all and do justice to the work they do.[46] However, to compare the situation of women's empowerment in Nigeria to the situation in Angola described above, I think it is important to mention the work of Gender and Development Action Nigeria (GADA), which focuses on women's social, economic, cultural and political rights.[47] In the Niger Delta, GADA works closely with SDN with a focus on women's livelihoods and security. As a staff member of the organization told me: 'It's very ironic that the Niger Delta produces the nation's wealth and yet it is one of the poorest areas. It produces the nation's wealth, yet the nation's wealth does not translate to development. It does not translate to improvements in the situations of the people and the realities of the people's lives.'[48]

From its Abuja office, GADA also monitors the federal budget and works on gender budgeting. Like PMA in Angola, GADA seems not to have a great deal of capacity regarding gender budgeting, as evidenced by the lack of publications offering critical gender analysis of Nigerian budgets. However, its staff are knowledgeable on the budget in general. One of the organization's Abuja-based staff complained that at every phase, especially in the beginning with the estimates produced by the ministries, departments and agencies of the government (MDAs), 'budgets are overburdened with selfish interests'. According to her, the 'only consultation the government does [regarding the budget] is with the MDAs—there is no public consultation.'[49]

Unfortunately, while civil society organizations in Nigeria in general enjoy much more freedom than in Angola, they do not always have more ability to influence the state to promote positive social change and better use of state resources. Nigerian non-governmental development organizations do organize marches, press conferences, public consultations and many other activities that reach legislators. While some are mistrustful or do not understand what these organizations are attempting to accomplish and the role they wish to play, others are more responsive.

While the Nigerian press does face repression, the independent press in Nigeria is thriving. A thriving newspaper industry is not the same as a free one. Some of the most critical voices reporting on corruption and bringing to light information the government must publish information on the internet anonymously, or, as in the case of Sahara Reporters, be based overseas. Nevertheless, while there is political violence in Nigeria, Nigerian opposition parties and the media have much more freedom to discuss issues related to petroleum resources and contribute to the national debate. With the passage of the Freedom of Information Act in 2011, a long-standing demand of Nigerian CSOs and media institutions, access to information seems set to become even more open.

* * *

Transparency in Nigeria is important because the opaqueness of the oil sector allows the elite to maintain their privileged positions. Specifically, the enormous amount of stolen oil rents is the single biggest factor in Nigerian electoral politics and creates a direct link between the political elite and the 'godfathers' of Nigerian politics (massively wealthy rentiers and local elites) who appoint them and keep them in office. A discussion of transparency in the Nigerian oil and gas industry must begin with the Nigerian Extractive Industries Transparency Initiative (NEITI),[50] part of the global EITI movement launched in 2003. That year, President Obasanjo committed Nigeria to making public its revenues and requiring companies operating in Nigeria to do the same. In 2004, Obasanjo formally established NEITI under the presidency and set up the National Stakeholders Working Group (NSWG), a committee made up of stakeholders representing government, extractive companies and civil society to oversee the activities of NEITI. A bill giving legal backing to NEITI was first put to the National Assembly that same year. Its signing into law was one of the final acts of Obasanjo's presidency in May 2007.

By passing the NEITI Act in 2007, Nigeria became the first EITI-implementing country with a statutory backing for its operations and a model for other countries. NEITI produced its first audit of the oil and gas industry in April 2006 for the period of 1999–2004. It identified an initial US$232 million in revenue/receipt discrepancies and followed that up with an audit of 2005. The scope of the reports that NEITI and NSWG produced goes beyond the minimum requirements laid down by EITI principles and criteria by requiring the audits it conducts to go beyond looking just at financial flows. As the Chairman of NEITI in 2010, Professor Assisi Asobie, told me: 'The NEITI reports [for 1999–2004 and 2005] are unique among EITI-implementing countries because they cover financial flows and physical performance and processes.'

According to Asobie, who is also a member of the EITI global board, Nigeria is also the only EITI country that went back to look at previous years. NEITI is also unique in that it has a mandate to follow up on discrepancies and remedy them by working with other agencies to recover the money owed to the state from underpayment of royalties. Finally, the NEITI Act also requires NEITI to eliminate corruption and corrupt practices. 'Unlike other EITIs, we have the unique task of also being an anti-corruption agency, so we work with the other anti-corruption agencies in Nigeria.'[51]

Nigeria gained EITI complaint status in March 2011. Asobie notes that to date NEITI's work has been on historical data, which is less controversial. He feels that as NEITI begins to look at current data, it may generate more controversy. 'The biggest achievement of NEITI will be to put the current figures in the public domain. Then the controversy will increase. Also, when we begin to monitor expenditure, especially at the state and local government levels.' However, by Asobie's own admission, NEITI has not done much expenditure monitoring yet and it is unclear according to Nigerian law whether it has the power to look at state and local government budgets.[52] According to a Nigeria-based expatriate who has worked on NEITI issues and consulted for the organization, NEITI is mostly about revenues at the federal government level. So far, it has not been able to look at expenditure, even from the Excess Crude account, which has been identified as a fund used by successive presidents for political patronage with little oversight or accountability.[53]

It is also unclear how NEITI is going to monitor the physical loss of oil between the wellhead and flow terminal. One of the main reasons for this loss is the practice of illegal oil theft (or 'oil bunkering'). Oil bunkering remains a key aspect of elite accumulation in Nigeria and, as one source told me, is 'better understood as highly organized by the highest levels of the state'.[54] Unfortunately, as Zalik (2011) contends, campaigns against oil bunkering (such as Legaloil.com) risk changing the way in which abusive relations of extraction are understood—associating them with criminal activity rather than the state-sanctioned violence of the IOCs. This confusion prevents an understanding of oil bunkering 'not as the cause of socio-economic break-down but as its consequence' (Zalik, 2011: 188). There seem to be few scenarios for envisioning an end to bunkering. Even a shift towards more capitalist social relations in Nigeria seems unlikely to make an impact, given how high the corruption reaches (see Chapter 2).

NEITI is a commendable programme and an example that Angola could emulate if it wanted to promote greater transparency in its petroleum sector. The programme is an important step towards substantive transparency, because it sets up an independent agency with the power to audit both the government and the IOCs and distribute their findings widely. However, as made clear in a report by Nicholas Shaxson (2009), it is still unclear how NEITI's work can be used to promote social change. While some of Shaxson's criticisms have been dealt with, now that Nigeria has achieved EITI-compliant status and released two more audit reports, one of his main findings is still true, that: 'Measured against EITI's and NEITI's broader goals of fostering better governance and accountability, the initiative has not shown impressive results' (2009: viii).

According to Professor Asobie, NEITI would like to empower civil society to hold both the government and the IOCs accountable, based on their data. In fact, that is the point of the NSWG. However, while he maintains a vision of NGOs and trade unions working in coalitions to use the data provided by NEITI, he admits that 'The groups are reluctant to work with each other.'[55] This highlights another of Shaxson's findings, that 'Civil society is supposed to be a key end-user of EITI reports, but NEITI has performed poorly in this respect.' It may be that the reluctance of CSOs, the media and other actors to work with NEITI is founded on some of the same reasons and logics that drive the lack of interest in Nigerian content. While extensive research was not done into the full extent of this reluctance, some explanations may be found in the mistrust of any initiative that comes from the government, and a general scepticism among both CSOs and the general public that the government and IOCs will take seriously any concerns they may have.

The Question of Corporate Social Responsibility: Evidence from Angola

This section briefly introduces multinational corporations, including international oil companies and oil service companies as actors that influence oil policy and development potential through their participation in the sphere of civil society. The engagement of multinationals may be in the form of lobbying government (as discussed in Chapter 3), sponsoring research, thwarting the efforts of state regulators to monitor the sector, or refusing to implement government priorities. In Nigeria, it also involves hiring and equipping private security forces and dealing with aggrieved host communities. In this section, I focus on engagement through Corporate Social Responsibility (CSR).

Much has been written about CSR in the oil and gas industry, especially with respect to Nigeria.[56] For this reason, this section will focus on Angola. Multinational corporations are important actors in the oil industries of Angola and Nigeria; however, as the above list of forms of engagement demonstrates, many of their interventions in civil society are negative. In both countries, the debate still rages as to what effect oil companies can have on economic and (especially) social development.

In Angola, many of the PSAs specify amounts of social investment that must be made (with Sonangol's approval). These costs are repaid by the state through oil production. However, each company also has its own programme of social spending, generally in the range of a few million dollars per year. The first thing to note is that this is a very small amount of money compared to the profits extracted from the country. An Angolan employee of one of the IOCs in Angola acknowledged to me: 'The money is not enough; [my company] could invest more.'[57] However, in my interviews with oil company representatives, I began to see another trend in oil company CSR that specifically relates to the question of local content (more properly, Angolanization).

For the most part, corporations give as little as possible to CSR. Most companies believe, as a senior manager at BP responsible for CSR told me, that the main contribution a company can make is through paying taxes. The same lower-level employee quoted in the paragraph above told me: 'Oil companies won't increase investment in development themselves. Government must force them to. If not, they won't. They are foreign. They are not Angolans. They won't spend money on Angolan development; only to get more revenue... [my company] is exploring oil and is getting rich. But the money they are spending is not enough.'[58] However, there is, in my experience, one exception to the 'spend as little as possible' rule.

Every IOC has several priority areas for their CSR programmes. Invariably, every IOC has education and training as one of their priorities. These programmes usually involve scholarships in the sciences and engineering, support to national universities and institution-building related to petroleum engineering. The money for these programmes generally comes from the company itself, not from its PSA obligation. The companies are often quite reluctant to discuss the details of these programmes in terms of how many Angolans are trained, how they are found and how much money they spend on this area of CSR. In fact, one interviewee from an IOC who spoke to me about this subject even offered to give me access to data in exchange for information on what the other companies were doing with regard to education and training initiatives as part of their CSR. As he told me, these programmes are highly proprietary and deal with how the company is going to identify and recruit high-quality Angolan labour to meet its own needs and the increasingly stringent demands of the Angolan government. The case of educating and training its potential labour would seem to be a rare case where corporations are prepared to spend more than the minimum possible on 'CSR' (although it is not clear that such spending should properly be considered CSR at all).

The case of education and training aside, CSR carries many dangers for the advancement of social change. A well-known Angolan NGO representative put it succinctly when he noted that while funding from oil companies for development is increasing, the practice of contracting out development projects to NGOs could lead to the 'domestication of civil society'. Such a scenario has negative consequences in terms of CSOs being able to act as advocates for monitoring and affecting change in the petroleum industry.[59] While it is more common for international NGOs to carry out development projects on behalf of the oil companies, domestic organizations work with IOCs as well.

As described by the Country Representative of a US-based NGO, ExxonMobil announces a call for proposals once a year and holds an open meeting in Luanda to explain what it is looking for. In the case of this NGO, the organization carries out a school rehabilitation project and a malaria eradication project funded by ExxonMobil. The effect, however, on the organization's attitude towards oil extraction is telling. Regarding CSR in the oil industry, the NGO's Country Representative, a US citizen, says: 'On the oil companies, they're already paying lots of taxes. Their signing bonus is going to the government. Obviously, they are still making lots of money and it's profitable to be here and I don't know how much of their money goes to CSR, but at least it's having some effect.' He went on to say:

> I believe, and I can't say for certain off the top of my head, but I do believe our oil donors, at least Exxon, are giving more money than is required by the Angolan government. I think they're doing more than they're required to do in Angola... I'm not in a position [to say if what they're doing is enough]. I think what they're doing

is great. I've had a very positive experience with Exxon and obviously I hope to continue working with them and doing good work on their behalf with the funds from them.[60]

Multinational corporations are engaged on issues of oil and development in many ways. While they contribute negatively to economic and social development, corporate social responsibility is one way in which they attempt to mitigate the negative consequences of their activities (even if only to salvage their reputations in Europe and North America and deflect criticism). Struggles for better outcomes from oil extraction, including struggles over local content, involve corporate actors. Movements from below as well as movements from above are likely to encounter corporate resistance in which CSR activities are often held up to show the positive results of their presence. While social transformation does not depend on corporate actors, neither should their influence over civil society and political processes be forgotten.

The Labour Movement in the Angolan and Nigerian Oil Industries

Labour unions are often powerful membership-driven participants in the oil industry and the economy more generally. Historically, as Mitchell (2009) has shown, while there is less space for workers to influence the oil industry than there may have been in coal and other forms of mineral extraction, labour plays a key role in affecting the distribution of surplus value. There are important differences between Angola and Nigeria in terms of the relation of forces and the power of labour to influence oil policy. In Angola, unions struggle to perform even their basic functions; while in Nigeria, they have claimed enormous space not only to affect the distribution of petroleum revenues, but actually to shape industry policy.

In Angola, trade unions were officially tied to the MPLA through the União Nacional dos Trabalhadores until 1991. Hodges writes that 'the development of independent trade unionism has been held back by repression and intimidation' (2004: 94). Turning specifically to the petroleum industry, labour unions operate without much power to promote better working conditions for Angolans or to fight for workers' issues. Labour unions have been fighting the casualization of labour and the increasing use of private labour brokers to contract out employees. However, they have had little success in influencing the IOCs. The union representing employees of Chevron in Angola is the Sindicato Autónomo dos Empregados da Cabinda Gulf Oil Company (SAECGOC). The union went so far as to write a letter to the government in June 2010 complaining about the use of private labour brokers, which it argued is a violation of Decree 8/96 of 5 April 1996. However, privately they complain that their employer simply ignores them, while the government often ignores them too.[61]

Specifically, SAECGOC contends that the agencies are in violation of Article 8 of the law governing private labour brokers by claiming that workers are contractors carrying out work for clients instead of regular employees. In this way they are able to avoid the heavy taxes prescribed in Article 8. Additionally, since 1994, Chevron (through the Cabinda Gulf Oil Company, or CABGOC) has used clauses designed for temporary workers to employ labour from labour brokers in service provision. Finally, labour brokers have been charging employees fees and costs for their job placements even though this practice is explicitly prohibited in Article 10. SAECGOC also complained that Chevron organized its Angolan subsidiary in the 'tax haven' of Bermuda to 'streamline certain business in a globalized world and hide certain information about the company and its shareholders'. They conclude that 'Chevron and other companies, to avoid claims and threats of strikes by workers, as already happened with the workers directly employed and managed by it, chose to exchange those workers for agencies that perform the role of employers... This whole exercise was aimed at Chevron getting away with numerous violations of Angolan legislation (labour and environmental).'[62]

According to a representative of SAECGOC, salaries and benefits for Angolan CABGOC workers and subcontractors are too low: 'The salaries are not fair. They are not sufficient for living in Cabinda.' As the representative explained, if the salary paid to a Chevron employee is US$2,500 per month, a subcontractor would get only US$1,200 for the same work. However, after the cut of the labour broker, he would see only US$700–$800. This leads the union to conclude, as this official told me, that 'Our employer is only interested in making money—the more the better.'[63]

SAECGOC also complains of more basic intimidation that is specific to the oil sector and no doubt tolerated by the government due to the revenues it receives from the industry. The union representative explains that although there are strong labour laws in Angola and union rights are part of the constitution, the union has a lot of difficulty in practice. Strikes in the oil sector are really not an option. It is simply understood by the union that they would not be tolerated. Furthermore, Chevron does not even let union representatives on their base to talk to employees who have problems and prevents the union from doing its job. While Chevron claims they cannot do anything about the salaries or conditions of subcontractors, the union believes that Chevron actually sets the salaries for these agencies. With regard to local content, the union would like to play a role in implementing local content and informing MINPET of problems. However, it cannot play such a role at this time because, in the union's words, MINPET 'lacks capacity' to control the IOCs, while the union lacks regular access to CABGOC facilities.[64]

* * *

The labour movement in Nigeria is fighting very similar battles to labour in Angola around contracting and casualization of labour. However, unlike in Angola, Nigerian labour is highly organized and actively engaged on all of the important issues facing the oil and gas industry. Therefore, it exercises a great deal of power vis-à-vis the state and the IOCs. The two main trade unions in the oil and gas industry are the Nigeria Union of Petroleum and Natural Gas Workers (NUPENG) and the Petroleum and Natural Gas Senior Staff Association of Nigeria (PENGASSAN). Although there is not a clear division, NUPENG tends to represent lower-level blue-collar workers, while PENGASSAN represents white-collar or skilled labour. Both unions have a long history of pushing for better working conditions for their employees. They have also taken positions on issues of importance for the industry and the country as a whole, such as local content, the PIB and downstream privatization. Both unions strike frequently to exert pressure on the government for better working conditions and to advance their political agendas.

During PENGASSAN's national executive council meeting in December 2009, the union identified several issues of national importance that they needed to address. These included the PIB, anti-labour practices of certain oil and oil service companies, increasing casualization and contract staffing in the sector, the denial of labour rights in the new free trade zones, deregulation of the downstream sector and support for the national housing fund.[65]

When Goodluck Jonathan became Acting President in April 2010, the president and general secretary of PENGASSAN issued an open letter to him reminding him of several issues that mattered to the labour movement, including insecurity in the Niger Delta, the PIB, Nigerian content, the lack of a stable power supply, deterioration of the country's oil refineries, corruption and transparency, job insecurity, electoral reform and healthcare. The letter shows PENGASSAN's interest in a wide range of issues facing the nation. For example, on the power supply, the union wrote: 'We however urge the Acting President to go beyond the rhetoric of politics that have characterized the realization of constant power supply to the country in the past and confront headlong the hydra-headed monster of inadequate power supply that had crippled the nation's industrial, social and economic growth.' Additionally, on corruption, they wrote:

> Corruption is another major problem hindering the development of the country which this government must develop the required political will to stamp out. To this end, Government must strengthen the anti-corruption agencies (EFCC and ICPC), strive to conduct her businesses in more open and transparent manner; expose and prosecute all corrupt officials irrespective of their status in the society.[66]

In 2010, PENGASSAN went after service companies still refusing to enter into collective bargaining agreements (CBAs) to protect workers. PENGASSAN's national president, Babatunde Ogun, has spoken often about this issue:

> PENGASSAN and NUPENG will no longer tolerate a situation whereby companies in the oil and gas industry will be disobeying the laws of the land and turn Nigerians to slaves in their own country. CBA is part of the law and it is also recognised by the international conventions of the ILO and the Nigeria Constitution. If any company is not ready to put CBA in place, it means such company is disobeying the law and not worthy to operate in the country. We will go all out to disrupt operations of any company that refuse to put in place CBA, as this is an attempt to deprive their workers the rights to the freedom of association and lawful assembly and right to belong and participate in trade union activities.[67]

NUPENG and PENGASSAN have devoted the most effort to the issue of casualization and contract staffing. A report on casualization of labour in the oil industry in the Niger Delta underscores the significance of the fight:

> In the 1980s, union leaders were imprisoned and oil unions placed under military government control. Today, union organizers must contend with both legal obstacles and anti-worker violence... Nigerian oil workers are vulnerable to a new kind of attack—quiet but more potent—through an industry-wide shift away from regular, full-time work toward forms of cheaper temporary labour and short-term contracting. This process, called 'casualization' in Nigeria, attempts to lower corporate costs while breaking workers' strength... (Solidarity Center, 2010)[68]

Together, the unions launched several small strikes in 2010 to force the IOCs to provide lists of all senior management positions with the names and nationalities of the people filling the position so that it could monitor implementation of the Nigerianization policies included in the NCA. After threatening several strike actions, NUPENG and PENGASSAN pushed the Minister of Labour to set up a Technical Working Group to examine the issues in August 2010. This is a sixteen-person group made up of all the major stakeholders in the industry with a mandate to review existing MOUs on Casualization and Contract Staffing in the light of current socio-economic realities, review the outcome of the Stakeholders Forum held in March 2010, come up with guidelines that will ensure unionization and collective bargaining for the affected workers and proffer solutions to all identified unfair labour practices in the oil and gas sector.[69] The unions' ability to push for this arrangement demonstrates their influence and ability to participate in industry reform in a way that ensures representation of workers' interests.[70]

Labour unions are powerful actors on the terrain of civil society with unique leverage to influence not only the distribution of petroleum revenues but also wider economic and social policy issues. While Angolan labour struggles with many of the same forms of oppression faced by other civil society groups, Nigerian labour has asserted its right to weigh in on a diverse set of issues related to the industry. As in Angola, Nigerian labour is primarily concerned with the casualization of labour. However, Nigerian trade unions also make demands related to Nigerian content, deregulation of the downstream oil industry and reform initiatives such as the PIB.

Mitchell's comparison to coal mining notwithstanding, labour-power is crucial to oil extraction. This fact gives labour unions an ability to influence top-down implementation of new strategies for managing petroleum resources and for economic and social development. Additionally, as we shall see in the section below on new social movements, trade union support is crucial to movements for social change from below. Oil sector unions are uniquely positioned given the centrality of oil to the economies of Angola and Nigeria. For this reason, the actions of the labour movement bear directly upon the potential of the petro-developmental state.

Host Communities to Oil Extraction in Cabinda and the Niger Delta

The communities that host oil extraction and the infrastructure that transports oil across the land play a special role in Angolan and Nigerian civil society. Struggles that take place on the terrain of civil society around oil and politics often take place on the physical terrain of oil-affected communities. The following sections seek to explore the struggles and agency of individuals and groups living in Cabinda and the Niger Delta.

Host communities contain multiple and overlapping constituencies with various interests. The actors mentioned below include local business owners, artisanal fishermen, farmers, groups of disaffected youths with various degrees of organization, private militias, local governments, residents' associations and traditional authorities. Together, these groups seek to ensure that they have a voice in decision-making and a fair share of their resource wealth. Often the struggle for access to petroleum rents foments conflict among these groups and between communities on the one side, and the government, state oil company and IOCs on the other. While these individuals and groups reside in the locality that provides the justification for local content policy, they are often not the target beneficiaries of these policies. Addressing the development concerns of these locals must be at the heart of successful implementation of the petro-developmental state through local content.

Oil, Development and the Question of Cabinda

The impact of oil and the extent to which it 'curses' developing countries can only be understood by examining questions of development in the areas that host oil extraction. In Angola, much of the extraction is onshore and offshore from the Province of Cabinda, a small enclave separated from the rest of Angola by the Democratic Republic of Congo. The most extensive field research on the effects of oil extraction in Cabinda has been done by Kristen Reed, whose book *Crude Existence* (2009) is based on her doctoral fieldwork there and in nearby Zaire province.

Reed's work has shown the very real impact of oil extraction on people's livelihoods in Cabinda. Reed notes that there are nearly 35,000 artisanal fishermen in Angola and another 50,000 people who participate in the sector from over 100 fishing communities in the north (Reed, 2009: 10; citing FAO, 2004). Reed profiles the small fishing community of Fútila, just outside Chevron's large Malongo base. She describes the 'conflicting sentiments due to the wealth visible inside the base and the poverty outside'. As I mentioned in Chapter 1, there is a stark contrast between the water, electricity, air conditioning, etc. inside the enclave of the base and lack of these in the community:

> The contrast between Fútila's deprivation and Malongo's excess sparks resentment among Cabindans: if this truly were their country, it would be their oil. Many Cabindans feel that the Angolan government has colluded with the American government and Chevron to exclude them from their own resource wealth. Malongo's concentric barbed-wire fences enclosing a corridor laden with land mines reinforce this aspect of exclusion (Reed, 2009: 106).

Reed's findings correspond to my own interviews with Cabindans. When I interviewed an oil worker from Cabinda, he told me: 'I am from Cabinda, but you can't see the benefit of petroleum. The roads are still very bad in Cabinda and Zaire and people are not benefitting from the oil.' In recent years, the provincial capital has undergone something of a transformation. However, the unimpressed worker reminded me that if you go 20 km north of the city, 'there is nothing.'[71] The oil worker I spoke to is one of the privileged few. According to Reed, only 12 per cent of Cabindans between age 16 and 55 are formally employed (2009: 108; citing Government of Angola, 2003).

The approach of the Angolan government to the question of Cabinda has had the effect of denying Cabindans any role, not only in their political future but also in their own economic and social development. Nothing demonstrates this more than the situation of the dedicated individuals I met in Cabinda who have been trying to help their province's development by founding an NGO to work on basic education and literacy, information technology training and other poverty alleviation programmes. Founded by a Cabindan who worked previously for an international NGO, the organization has struggled for close to a decade to gain legal registration. Its founder notes: 'We are neutral as a civil society organization. We have our opinions. We are not a political organization. Civil society should be part of the dialogue. It has contributions to make... We will be training in computer skills—not giving political lessons!' Yet, the organization has been denied the permissions needed from the provincial government and operates without legal status. Unable to get backing from international donors, the organization plans to continue and raise funds for its computer training centre. According to the organization's founder, 'We're not waiting for provincial authorization.'[72]

One of the other members of the organization confirms that '[name of organization] is not a political organization'. Having lived in other parts of Angola, he told me that Cabinda faces a different and more serious problem because of the especially low levels of education, health, access to clear water and energy. His connection to the people of his community drives him to create an organization which he would ideally like to see working in partnership with the government on development and solidarity projects.[73] The third member of the organization I spoke with also told me, 'We want to help the government. We want to work in partnership with them.'[74] Far from being a threat to the government, its founder went to pains to assure me that '[name of organization] cannot support violence. That is why we advocate dialogue between all stakeholders. We cannot support violence.'[75]

With few options for employment, a reduced ability to lead a sustainable livelihood in farming or fishing and facing continued repression and collective punishment for an independence movement that can only grow stronger the longer poverty and state violence persist, Cabinda seems to be trapped. The situation breeds resentment. As the Cabindan oil worker I met said, 'The province is producing everything for the country. It needs to be helped in other ways.'[76] Yet, despite the promise of additional revenues for Cabinda, even a government official working in Cabinda told me what everyone in Angola already knows regarding the 10 per cent of oil revenue allocated to Cabinda: 'Right now, the reality is that the money doesn't arrive.'

For decades, the major development player in Cabinda has been Chevron (and its predecessor companies). Chevron indeed does run an impressive array of social programmes in Cabinda. Facing the most unrest of the oil companies, it is perhaps unsurprising that it is the most closed: Chevron was the only company to refuse even to grant me an interview with a public relations officer. When I finally did manage to meet someone at Chevron who worked on community development for an off the record chat, my interviewee told me that my contact had been passed onto him previously, but permission to speak to me had been denied by senior management. This fact shows Chevron operating with an unusually high level of secrecy—even for an oil company. The Chevron official I spoke to told me that 'Relations between Chevron and the local community and government have improved due to local investment and better communication with stakeholders.'[77] To an extent this is true. However, a former Chevron employee who is from Cabinda and still resides there told me: 'Considering that CABGOC is a subsidiary of Chevron and has been here for thirty years, I don't think they've done anything. They have small social programmes here and there, but to me Chevron is not doing what it should be doing. I don't think their projects have much of an impact...'[78]

While spending on social programmes is helpful, decisions that Chevron takes at an operational level are likely to have a larger and more lasting effect. The Cabindan oil worker cited earlier pointed to the decision by Chevron to relocate their Angolan headquarters to Luanda as a key decision that would negatively affect his home province:

> Life in Cabinda is conditioned by oil... Life in Cabinda is linked to the oil sector... When Chevron decided to bring its HQ to Luanda, why should it be in Luanda? Having the HQ of Chevron in Cabinda allows for Cabindans to benefit first, so those working in Cabinda can spend their money in Cabinda... our life here in Angola is totally linked to the oil sector.[79]

The comment points to a weakness in Angola's approach to local content: investment in the regions where the oil comes from has not been encouraged, and in fact has in many ways been discouraged. The 'locale' referred to in local content policies is the nation as a whole; and the benefits flow mainly to Luanda and the MPLA elite, as opposed to any subnational groups or jurisdictions.

Esso's public relations officers told me that the company considers the whole country to be its host community.[80] For those companies that operate entirely in the deep offshore, there is more justification for treating the nation as the primary stakeholder, although people living on the coast will continue to bear more of the burden in terms of health risks and loss of livelihood. However, while every IOC has social projects spread amongst multiple provinces, the economic benefit of Angolan participation in the oil sector flows to a few key locations—Luanda and a couple of major support bases along the coast. While the other IOCs have made little progress in switching to local content, Chevron has begun to lay the groundwork for a more serious effort. To that end, as one Chevron contractor told me, it is planning a new Malembo Support Base in Cabinda for all of its service providers. The project dovetails nicely with its goal of getting out of logistics, moving all non-Chevron employees off the Malongo Base and concentrating its own activities on exploration and production activities.[81]

In Angola, CABGOC was forced to take a more active role in logistics and services because it was operating in a context of civil war. Now that the war is over and oil facilities are no longer targets, Chevron is keen to push subcontractors off-base and into Cabinda, where they will have to rent office space, warehouses, houses for their staff, etc. A Chevron contractor I spoke to about this argued that it would have an impact on the community in terms of construction jobs, hiring of staff, etc. 'The benefit isn't huge,' he acknowledged, 'but you have to start somewhere.' Yet, even this company, exclusively a Chevron subcontractor, has its head office in Luanda because that is where Sonangol and the Ministry of Petroleum are located.[82] Furthermore, the company does not buy anything locally.

The main reason why this particular company does not engage in any local procurement is an unresolved issue over customs duties. Cabinda has its own customs regime, which is different from the rest of Angola (imports are taxed at a lower rate than they are for the rest of the country, but at a higher rate than for items brought in by the IOCs). On top of that, imports for the oil sector are governed by their own customs regime. The extra complications in figuring out the customs duties sometimes make it impossible for a local company to bring products into Cabinda and then sell them to an oil service company.

The subcontractor referred to above related a story in which he wanted to use products from a company based in mainland Angola and was willing to pay the difference between IOC customs rates and Cabindan customs rates, yet was told by customs officials that there was no way to do this. The result, he explained to me, is that 'it's not really feasible for us to buy local'. Instead, his company imports everything from the US or South Africa. In emergencies it buys office supplies and other routine items from neighbouring Congo or brings them to Cabinda from Luanda.[83]

Chevron's limited support for local content in Cabinda can be understood in a few different ways. In part, some of the steps they have taken are in line with their own strategy and plans. No doubt they are also influenced by what they view to be the prevailing mood in the Angolan government and in Sonangol. However, it is also true that the first steps the company has taken to implement local content are also cost-saving or potentially cost-saving (down the road). This is especially true of the switch, discussed in some of the case studies in Chapter 5 and above in the section on labour unions in Angola, from employing much of the labour in its own logistics operations to Chevron subcontracting this labour to private Angolan labour brokers. An Angolan former Chevron employee who worked in their human resources department explained to me that in recent years the number of subcontractors has surpassed the number of Chevron employees. In fact, Chevron has halted much of its hiring. He explains: 'Chevron does want to contain costs. There is little regulation on subcontractors. Also, the labour market is such that people need to work and have to accept whatever is offered.'[84]

An expatriate working for an Angolan service company in Cabinda confirms the assertions of the former Chevron employee: 'I think salaries are pretty low in general... There are a lot of unemployed, so the wages are correct for the market, but not for the cost of living.' He went on to say: 'When we hire the same labour companies that Chevron used to hire for the same services, the salaries will go down because we aren't going to pay what Chevron pays.'[85] For now, the situation remains unchallenged by the Angolan government. To begin with, local companies remain uncompetitive in terms of price due to the high cost of doing business in Angola. Additionally, as a former Chevron HR official acknowledges, 'the truth is that Angolan companies aren't at the standard Chevron needs right now... Angolans don't have what it takes right now.'[86]

That situation is likely to change as Angola recovers from decades of war and a new generation of Angolan entrepreneurs seek to provide services to the oil industry. However, the benefit is not likely to spread far beyond Luanda without the government encouraging it. On the contrary, right now the ability of those who are most affected by oil extraction to realize some of the economic benefit of local content initiatives is impeded by state policy towards Cabinda. A Cabindan businessman attempting to provide services to the oil industry told me: 'There are some political things going on between Cabinda and the rest of Angola. Sometimes this makes it difficult because they think if we make a lot of money, we will support the resistance.'[87] Ultimately, marginalizing Cabinda and estranging its people from the benefits of oil production will take the country down a path towards increased conflict and insecurity.

Insecurity and Underdevelopment in the Niger Delta[88]

The Niger Delta is a complex and chaotic part of the world. Underdeveloped by a history of foreign exploitation, slavery and, more recently, the negative effects of oil extraction, the region's inhabitants suffer greatly from poverty, conflict and the destruction of their environment. In 2010 at a consultative forum in Port Harcourt on the PIB, one audience member commented: 'We must in our poverty see if we can shout loud enough that they will hear us!'[89] The statement reflects a predominant feeling among residents that both the federal government and the IOCs, which make enormous profit by extracting the region's oil wealth, refuse to listen to the Niger Delta or to deliver a fair share of their profits to inhabitants, and ignore the damage that oil extraction does to their natural environment. The desire to claim rights of self-determination over natural resources and a fair share of the revenues from their extraction fuels conflicts over 'community content' that divide Delta communities.

Acts of sabotage and violence against the IOCs are well covered by the media, while the question of violence in the Niger Delta has been discussed in depth by many scholars.[90] However, there are many other ways in which host communities seek to assert themselves. Ukiwo (2008) lists five strategies for indigenes of oil-producing communities to access the 'rentier space': 1) Approaching IOCs for provision of social amenities (classrooms, health centres, electricity, etc.); 2) Stopping oil production until demands are met; 3) Demanding positions be reserved for their elites (Petroleum Minister, General Managing Director of NNPC, etc.); 4) Demanding a percentage of revenue to be allocated on the basis of derivation; and 5) Exclusion of non-indigenes from the rentier space through discourse of indigeneity. However, any discussion of struggles in the Niger Delta must begin by attempting to understand the situation of the host communities.

In the host communities where oil production takes place and through which crude oil is piped, the land and people have been adversely affected in a myriad of ways that are by now well-known and universally acknowledged. When a Nigerian general manager of the French oil company Total was asked if the benefits provided by his company outweighed the negative aspects of oil production, he forcefully responded:

> No! I will tell you no! Completely not. First of all, Total is a business organization. We have integrated sustainable development, but if you go today, I am from this area, many people have lost their land... Some people have lost completely their farmlands. They were farmers before. So how can a company fully compensate for this? The problem is it is really the responsibility of government. Most of the revenue is going to them, so Total is doing its best. If you're asking whether this best is enough, I will tell you absolutely not![91]

I was surprised by his comments, but after speaking to other Nigerians at senior levels in IOCs, I realized that these comments are typical of what many Nigerian employees, especially those from the Niger Delta, think about oil extraction. In another example, a manager working in the Nigerian Content Division of a major American IOC said: 'Oil has not been well managed. It has destroyed other sectors of the economy that were our mainstay before now—farming, solid minerals, etc. All those have died.'[92] Even the former Petroleum Minister Edmund Daukoru, now that he is out of government and holds a traditional position as ruler of the Nembe kingdom in Bayelsa state, acknowledges the damage that oil production has caused:

> The impact has been devastating—not just the temporary disruption of community activities, livelihood activities, but even the thoroughness of the clean-up is suspect... There is a layer of pollution that has caked up over decades over a vast area. To clean that up is going to take quite a lot of money! One day we will have to deal with this—the pollution and exposure to the negative aspects of the industry. There are quite a lot of negatives to go with the positives we are enjoying![93]

Oil pollution and environmental degradation from extractive industry must be understood as a key cause of discontent. Gas flaring and oil spills are two of the most serious forms of pollution affecting people's everyday lives. The frequency and cause of oil spills is greatly disputed. Until recently, the lack of hard data allowed Shell and other IOCs to claim that oil spills were not causing large-scale harm to human inhabitants of the Niger Delta or plant and animal life. However, in 2011, the United Nations Environment Programme

(UNEP) finally released a comprehensive environmental assessment of Ogoniland which indicates that pollution is far more pervasive than has previously been acknowledged. In one village surveyed, water contamination was 900 times the WHO standards, while altogether 28 surveyed communities were found to be using water from community wells far in excess of safe limits (UNEP, 2011).

In recent years Shell and other IOCs have also taken a new approach to the question of oil pollution—denying responsibility. This denial has mainly involved blaming sabotage by Niger Delta residents, specifically militants, for oil spills. When I asked a remediation specialist who works with SPDC what causes most spills, he immediately answered that 'corroded pipes cause most of the spills', explaining that after the spill has occurred it may attract 'local boys' hoping to profit.[94] Field office representatives of ERA agree that despite claims from the IOCs to the contrary, equipment failure is a much more common explanation for spillage than sabotage.[95] However, the sabotage excuse does not absolve the IOCs of responsibility. As a participant in the PIB consultative forum noted, it is unfair to make the community pay:

> Even when it's sabotage, oil companies are still responsible—if you bring something that is bad to my land, under law, you should be responsible. That is natural law, but the government and the courts have spoiled this... If it is sabotage, you look for the man that caused it to pay you, but if you are the company, you pay me first for the damage you are responsible for and then you look for that man.[96]

The attempt to blame oil pollution on militants is ironic given the practice all of the IOCs have of hiring local youths as private security militias to guard their facilities. This practice exacerbates conflict.[97] Over time, the security situation in the Delta has deteriorated into a crisis from which there seem to be few ways out. In community conflicts the single biggest catalyst is petroleum resources. As a staff member of an NGO that works in several communities in the Niger Delta told me, in terms of conflict, 'it's all for resources. That much is clear... it's also about employment contracts with [the IOCs].'[98]

The reason these contracts cause conflict is that contracts awarded by IOCs to local companies for the provision of goods and services are one of the main benefits to host communities from oil extraction. Such contracts may be for goods and services directly related to oil production (provision of fencing, oil spill clean-up, provision of labour, etc.), or they may be for activities carried out under the terms of the MOUs that the IOCs sign with host communities (road-building, construction of schools and clinics, electrification, etc.). A final category of contracts are awarded to private companies in the host communities for security and surveillance. Such contracts remain outside the normal processes for tendering contracts for operations or for community development.

* * *

In most villages in the Niger Delta, there are a few wealthy individuals and families who have benefited from oil extraction in their communities by providing services to the IOCs and collecting oil rents. An employee of a company that does surveillance and security contracting for SPDC in Bayelsa state noted that the owner of the company he works for is a wealthy man and part of the village elite because he benefits from oil production and can maintain a house in both his village and the state capital of Yenagoa. For those who are not part of the elite, this employee explained, there is no benefit. 'Apart from surveillance, there is no money. The land doesn't produce anything. The majority of the family used to be farmers and now they can't do anything due to the spills. It was a virgin area and now you can't farm on it.'[99]

On the one hand, using companies and employing labour from the host communities is an important mechanism for ensuring a return to the communities most directly affected by oil extraction. In discussing Dorman Long's work on the 'Sea Eagle' project (described in Chapter 5), Henry Okolo noted that success was ensured by the active involvement of the community: 'We even constituted the chiefs of the community into a labour supply company so that those boys we trained were hired by them and supplied to us.' Okolo went on to say that: 'The problem of the Niger Delta is more like the IOCs were not quick enough in coming to terms with the idea that they owe some obligation to the communities where they operate. They thought they could get away with anything. That is what created the situation we have now.'[100]

On the other hand, the politics of local content in the Niger Delta reinforce the view that the elite in Nigeria are defined primarily by their access to the benefits of the nation's oil wealth. Whether that access comes as a business person, a government official, or a traditional authority, the Nigerian elite are those who can manipulate the system to direct the dividends of an industry that impoverishes the majority. Often these elite work very closely with the oil companies that operate in their communities and are rewarded with contracts to provide goods and services to the industry.

While in public they proclaim their desire to give back to the community, in reality IOCs desire not to promote economic development but to promote a more stable environment for oil extraction. While the two objectives may seem to dovetail together when it comes to local content, the answer to who benefits from the contracts would be very different if the principle objective was developmental. Since the IOCs generally view the contracts they provide to host communities as protection payments, they are made not to the most qualified or entrepreneurial, but rather to those in positions of authority. This difference is an important source of tension in Niger Delta host communities, where conflicts stem from the region's marginalization and exclusion from a fair share of their own wealth.

According to an employee in the Nigerian Content Department of SPDC, Shell takes the idea of community content, or participation by SPDC host communities, seriously: 'We deliberately as a matter of policy ensure that we stipulate that unskilled labour is sourced from the community and even skilled, when available, should be sources from the communities.' There is also an intermediate level of community content where some preference is given to source contracts from the Niger Delta region. He outlined the types of contracts that are generally reserved for communities, which usually involve cleaning, security, surveillance, grass cutting and catering. In some cases, there is more that can be sourced from the community, including construction, marine logistics and even dredging.[101] Another employee in the same department added that 'sensitivities' involved in awarding a contract require the company to 'evaluate the risk' before a contract is awarded. However, he went on to say that 'Sometimes it doesn't work and there are grievances in the community that we didn't know about. Therefore we try to be fair and follow due process and to work within our basic principles.'[102]

A big part of the contracting problem is when contracts are not fairly tendered—even if it is just to the community. This most often happens in the case of so-called 'surveillance contracts', but can happen with all sorts of community contracts in order to give preference to favoured elites. A Total general manager admitted to me that in the JOA between Total and NNPC, there is a provision that if communities nominate someone, you do not have to follow the tendering process. Therefore, he estimated, '30 per cent of the time, jobs are done on sole-source contracts'. This may be changing, as now Total is trying to adopt a system whereby the communities must nominate more than one contractor for each job.[103] It is not clear though, and seems unlikely, whether this would apply to surveillance contracts.

The process at NAOC is quite similar. An employee in the Nigerian Content Division explained to me that beginning in the early 2000s the company would only choose contractors recommended by its host communities as long as a contractor could pass the technical stage of the tender. However, the communities used to recommend only one contractor for a particular job and then the tendering department would fulfil due process by sending the tender out to others (even though their policy was to use the community contractor). In the commercial stage of the tendering process, NAOC would compare the community contractor's bid to the lowest bid received. If the community contractor is close to the management idea of what the contract should be, the community contractor was offered the contract at the rate of the lowest bidder. As he explained, 'It was as if the other bidders were only involved for the purposes of due process and competition… the community-recommended contractor almost always got the job.' In 2007, NAOC moved to a new system where the community had to recommend at least three and no more than seven contractors for each project so that the contract could be awarded to the contractor with the lowest bid.[104]

Asked about the challenges his company faces, the NAOC NCD employee told me that the biggest challenge was that while communities can participate in contracts to carry out projects done for the community under the terms of the MOUs that NAOC signs with its host communities, they don't have the capacity to participate much in work that has to do with the company's production activities. He says, 'This is the gap we are trying to bridge so that contractors can participate in production jobs.' Another large problem is that community contractors often abandon jobs without finishing them, or finish them with poor quality. According to him, NAOC has had 14 abandoned projects in swamp areas and 20 abandoned projects on land in the last five years. Nevertheless, the company's system is that the community, through three stakeholder groups—the Council of Chiefs, Community Development Committee (CDC) and Council of Youths—must nominate community contractors.[105]

NAOC is very upfront though about the fact that it prefers to work with the elite of its host communities. An employee told me: 'The people who are signatories to the MOU are supposed to be the ones recommending the contractors. We consider this to be due process, but we have some problems.' The challenges he mentioned in this respect include the fact that while MOUs are for four years, the CDC chairmen in communities are elected to two-year terms. When a new CDC comes to power, there is often conflict because the new body wants to recommend its own people. This leads to unfinished or abandoned projects. Some the CDCs also like to propose projects for the next two to three years, knowing they won't be in power. When asked if he thought these groups might award contracts to themselves or accept payments to recommend certain contractors, he told me: 'They may have taken money to make these recommendations. We are not supposed to know anything about this and don't want to, but unofficially we know it happens.'[106]

Oil and Conflict in Two Niger Delta Communities

In my research, I found that most prominent community leaders, be they traditional chiefs or authorities in local government, have contracting companies. As a SPDC contractor from Ogoni confirmed, paramount chiefs are the most likely to be awarded contracts: 'If Shell is coming here, the big chiefs are the first people Shell will see. People in government are also aware of their coming, so they have to give some contracts to them. Definitely they will have companies getting contracts from Shell.'[107] The contractor contended that the oil industry uses only a few contractors from host communities known to them because of their official positions of authority. A second contractor from Ogoni, upset that he has been unable to secure work from SPDC, complained: 'I am from a host community. So I can say that we are not benefitting, I am not benefitting, nobody is benefitting. If you go to our place, we don't have lights, we don't have water, we don't have roads, we don't have hospitals, we don't even have schools, so we are not benefitting.'[108]

The persistence of bad feeling and lack of returns is not unique to Ogoniland, which successfully chased SPDC from its territory in the 1990s, though pipelines continue to run through their land. Contractors from other host communities in the Niger Delta—not ordinary citizens, but entrepreneurs and businesspeople—generally complain bitterly about the IOCs and fight amongst themselves over contracts, regardless of which IOC is present in their community. In this way, the contracting process has become a source of tension and conflict, woven into local politics and chieftaincy disputes.

In September and October 2010, I profiled two communities in the Niger Delta where two different IOCs operate in order to get a small sense of what impact oil production has in the Niger Delta and how issues of local content are related to questions of conflict and development. In a Total host community in Rivers State, contractors remain unsatisfied with the benefit to the community and with the amount of work they are given. According to one, 'Though [Total] is trying, they need to do more. What they are giving us is not commensurate to what they take away.'[109] In a second interview, a different Total contractor acknowledges the benefit while continuing to articulate a feeling that his community is being exploited: 'It is the oil companies catering to our infrastructural development. They provide us roads and scholarships, but it's not enough for what they are taking from our community.'[110] These sentiments help explain the anger felt, not only by residents of the Niger Delta towards the IOCs, but by all Nigerians towards oil production in general and the way the distribution of benefits is managed. In effect, their complaints concern the amount of 'local content' in the distribution of surplus value from oil extraction.

Those who benefit from oil production risk little by admitting that there is little benefit to their communities overall. Perhaps more concerning than the lack of overall benefit is the conflict and underdevelopment associated with local content. In the Egi kingdom of Rivers State, a key onshore location for Total, conflict over benefits from oil activity in the form of contracts has become intertwined with local politics. Complaining that the paramount ruler of the kingdom, the Eze Egi, takes all the contracts for himself through companies owned by his wife, a middle-ranking chief said: '[Total] is not doing well. They are cheating us seriously... For all this God has given us here, we are not supposed to be a beggar!'[111] The Eze Egi, whom Total in one of its glossy corporate affairs publications calls 'a bridge between the company and community' (TEPNG, 2010: 64), says that his own personal company has been unsuccessful in petitioning Total for work. Angrily, he explained: 'I used to tender many years ago but now they do not like to give contracts to me. Maybe they don't want me to stand strong. They leave me weak, but I keep the peace in my area of jurisdiction. I do not let any boys cause trouble or kidnap because I don't like trouble.'[112]

The Eze Egi made it clear that he feels entitled to benefit from Total's activities in his kingdom: 'They are willing to give me small gifts, but not contracts. I am supposed to be one of the richest men in this country. This, my jurisdiction, is the highest oil and gas producing area in the country!' He warned: 'My chiefs are worried. They want me to permit them to show Total E&P that they are operating in somebody's land.' When asked if that meant there could be violence, he said: 'Yes, this will cause some violence. My boys will resist and maybe soldiers will fire and somebody may die.'[113] He blames Total for a great deal of conflict amongst competing contractors, arguing that '[Total] loves only politicians.'

Indeed, Total has developed a very close relationship with the Egi People's Forum (EPF) and Egi Youth Federation (EYF), groups that in turn organize on behalf of the ruling People's Democratic Party (PDP). The leaders of these bodies and those officials who hold elected positions in the local government find it much easier to get contracts and even employment from Total, while those outside the EPF and EYF find it impossible to do business with the company. For this reason, the leadership positions in the EPF and EYF are fiercely contested, sometimes with violence. Opposition to the EPF and EYF by rival politicians and community leaders is also sometimes met with violence. For example, a community elder and local activist claims that Total sponsored youths in the EYF to attack elders when they organized a sit-in at the Obite Gas Plant: 'Through the EPF youths are employed for violence.' Another protest against the influence of the EPF was broken up by youths armed with machetes. According to the same elder, 'It's not a secret at all [that Total is involved]. They use the local chiefs against us. They will come and say we are creating problems... The police won't arrest anyone from EPF. They arrest people from our side and torture them. Then their relations have to raise money to bail them out.' He complained as well that there are limited ways of resisting the EPF because they are armed. Even to contest their candidates in elections is difficult because to run candidates against EPF (and therefore the PDP) in elections, 'you need to be supported by the moneymen who are the chiefs'.[114]

In this community, Total has multiple ways of controlling key members of the elite. The first and most important is the MOU between the company and the community. Another is a separate MOU between the company and families that are recognized as owning land that is used by Total for its operations. Together, these documents (which will be discussed further below) reward Total's allies in the community. Finally, through an advisory body called the OML 58 Consultative Committee, Total keeps a close eye on new developments. One member of the committee, a well-off contractor for Total, described the body as the 'eyes of Total in the community'. According to this contractor, there are positives to the influence of the EPF and EYF. He noted that the EYF can pressure Total when the community is unhappy (for example when there are problems with light, water and roads) by shutting down Total operations. It is because this has happened before that Total knows it needs to keep EYF happy.[115]

According to one local-level chief, the effect of Total's divisive relationship with the community is disastrous: 'You have to let the world know that where [Total] is operating, they are doing nonsense altogether. Now they are doing nonsense and nothing good they are doing to the communities. At least if they had impacted our lives, that would be a way forward for us to achieve our aims!'[116] The tensions caused by the EPF and EYF have made it difficult for other NGOs to work in the community. A programme officer for one such organization complained that questions about the transition between elected officials and 'divided interests' make the community very difficult to work with.[117] The same elder quoted above on the EPF and EYF laments the effect these divisions are having on the youth: '[Total] is distracting our youth from going to school so they can catch cheap money... Our boys are not interested in reading. They are just riding big cars, carrying women and all that. This affects the morals of our young men. They just want to be car owners and all that.'[118] In the tensions the community faces, Total sits right in the middle. However, the example of this Total community is understood herein not as the exception for IOCs in the Niger Delta, but as the rule.

The evidence from the first community shows a pattern of conflict in host communities centred on questions of access to and benefit from local contracting in the oil services sector. The pattern is not specific to one particular IOC. In a community in Rivers State that hosts some of NAOC's production, similar conflicts have broken out amongst the elite over access to contracts. In particular in one community, an ongoing conflict pits the current CDC chairman against the former CDC chairman. Both men have contracting companies to carry out contracts for development projects guaranteed to the community under its MOU with NAOC. When the current CDC chairman took office, he expected to benefit from contracts, as the former CDC chairman had, but he had still not seen any benefit. Angrily, he commented:

> The people at AGIP are not helping people in the communities. They don't give the people jobs except what is under the MOU... We have tried our best to see that our people are employed. We have a lot of trained engineers—mechanical, electrical. Our people can work with AGIP but they are refused employment and they bring people from outside to come and work here.[119]

The NAOC community in question has suffered immensely from forty years of oil extraction. Massive gas flares have been shooting flames into the sky non-stop for four decades. Entire generations have never experienced the darkness of night. A community informant told me that the rainwater is sometimes acidic, which means that rooves rust and deteriorate easily and must be replaced every two to three years. He also told me that he has seen the emergence of diseases formerly unknown in the area, such as unique rashes, respiratory diseases, various cancers and eye problems. Additionally, there are effects on livestock and fisheries. Livestock now go out to feed at night due to the flares and do not sleep enough, which decreases reproduction. Farm yields have decreased significantly, and, he claims, over twenty species of fish known locally can no longer be found. The informant, a community elder, told me:

'Oil spills flow into rivers, creeks and ponds destroying aquatic life. My people who were farmers and fishermen, their lives are destroyed.'[120]

During my time in the community, I was introduced to a farmer who has a farm less than 30 metres from three gas flares. He took me to the farm, where I could feel the heat of the three nearby flames, whose stacks rise roughly ten storeys high. He told me that the land came from his mother's family and has been in the family as long as anyone can remember. He grows cassava on the farm, though the yield has diminished significantly. Telling me that the flares have been lit non-stop for nearly four decades, the farmer told me: 'There is no real night. People don't know the natural night any more.'[121]

The community elder I spoke to told me a very similar story to the elder in the Total community. According to him, NAOC 'infiltrates leaders of the community' and these people 'become their advocates'. 'The interests they protect are not the interests of the people', he told me. 'They are the interests of the oil companies.'[122]

Like Total, NAOC maintains control through the benefits distributed in the MOUs signed with the community. The same elder quoted above told me: 'AGIP has infiltrated the community and these are the people with whom AGIP is supposed to negotiate [the MOUs].' The MOUs between IOCs and host communities are supposed to be confidential. In my research, I was able to obtain copies of the MOUs signed with the two host communities I profiled as well as the MOU Total signed with a group of oil and gas affected families in its community. Interestingly, the terms of the three contracts differ significantly. All three contracts are for four years. The main terms are laid out in Figure 6.1. The comparison shows that Total is paying significantly more to its host community. However, under the much more comprehensive agreements it signs, the stakeholders must agree to keep the peace and ensure no shut-down of company facilities. In return, the agreement specifies that Total will use local labour 'where possible' and that for the MOU with oil and gas affected families, the families can nominate projects and/or programmes within the budget envelope.

Local content, as it has played out on the ground in practice in the host communities of the Niger Delta, contributes to the enrichment of some and underdevelopment of others. There is nothing inherent in the policy that makes it so. However, Nigerian content in practice tends to foment unrest and fuel the general resentment of many Nigerians regarding the wilful mismanagement of petroleum resources. This feeling is summed up by a community organizer in Port Harcourt. When asked about Nigerian content, he responded:

Figure 6.1: Summary of Total and NAOC MOUs with Host Communities

NAOC MOU with Host Community	Total MOU with Host Community	Total MOU with oil and gas affected families
Projects: – 2X six classroom block at primary school – 2X 2km internal road with side drains – Renovation of staff quarters at grammar school – Rehabilitation of community water scheme – Electrification extension – Build and equip a mini library – Building of shops and fencing for market – Renovation of laboratory at school Other clauses: – NAOC employment will guided by list of applicants from chief and youths – Provision of scholarships **Total Value: N300 million**	Terms: – 200 post primary scholarships worth N45,000 – 30 post secondary scholarships worth N150,000 – 3 post-grad local scholarships worth N200,000 – 2 post grad foreign scholarships worth US$28,000 – 5 scholarships to clan members gaining admission to Petroleum Training Institute worth N150,000 – Support for Adult Education Initiatives – Support through seminars, workshops and performance incentives for teachers – Training for at least 85 youths in skill training (managed by committee) – 5 industrial training placements with service companies working for Elf – Microcredit scheme for entrepreneurs – Company agrees to hire indigenes for 12 senior and 4 junior positions – Company will send at least 5 eng grads from clan for intensive training to make them suitable for IOC hire **Total budget: N1.095 billion**	MOU is for just over 100 families/communities (families/communities can mean an individual, group, community of individuals, a village, or a group of villages belonging to, residing in or originating from the Egi Clan whose land was acquired by Elf for an upgrade project in OML 58) Terms: – Families nominate projects and or programmes within the budget envelope limit **Total budget: N740 million**

Source: Total and NAOC MOUs [internal documents].

'You say "Nigerian content, Nigerian content", but the local people have not been given the same opportunity. They have been robbed over the years, so they cannot benefit equally from Nigerian content.'[123] In light of this view, every step away from more equal distribution of oil wealth has to be viewed as a step towards the growing animosity felt by many Nigerians towards the government and Nigerian elite.

New Social Movements in Angola and Nigeria

Recent uprisings in Angola and Nigeria reflect increasing anger at chronic mismanagement, corruption and failed policy implementation. As the Arab Spring spread, observers began to ask where in SSA the movement would spread first. Zimbabwe, where Robert Mugabe has resorted to increasingly violent repression to maintain his hold on power, seemed an obvious choice. However, no new or existing mass movements in that country gained any traction from the global uprisings of 2011. Finally in Angola, where José Eduardo dos Santos has been in power since 1979 without ever being elected to office, a protest inspired by the struggles in Egypt and Tunisia was called. The 7 March protest to be held at Independence Square in the capital, Luanda, and at locations throughout the country, was all anyone could talk about for weeks after the protest was announced on the internet and through social media.

The announcement, backed by a well-known Angolan hip-hop artist, Brigadeiro Mata Frakus, led to panic in the ruling MPLA. It began a two-week campaign of intimidation to ensure that the protest would be stifled. Human Rights Watch documented 'anonymous death threats against opposition politicians and human rights lawyers, arbitrary arrests of journalists and activists, and misuse of the state media for partisan political purposes' (HRW, 2011a). Although a collection of small opposition parties announced on 28 February that they would participate in the protest, on 4 March they announced that they were withdrawing their participation and complained of death threats they had received by phone and text message. Previously, the Governor of Luanda had unlawfully banned the protest; however, a rally in support of the government was quickly organized for 4 March, bringing tens of thousands of Angolans onto the streets.

Human Rights Watch reported that they 'received a number of credible reports that government officials forced teachers and public servants in Luanda and several provincial capitals to participate'. Teachers were threatened with job loss or salary cuts and obliged to press their students to participate by threatening them with 'problems' if they stayed home. For good measure, people throughout Angola began receiving anonymous text messages warning them not to join the protests. The Secretary General of the MPLA, Dino Matross, was quoted as warning Angolans that 'serious measures' would be taken against anyone participating and for good measure added 'Anyone who demonstrates... we're going to get you.' The state media reiterated warnings in the period leading up to the protests not to join them. On 6 March, the streets were filled—but they were filled with a massive showing of riot police and soldiers. Seventeen rap artists were arrested earlier in the day for encouraging people to come to the rally. In the end, only thirteen people turned up at the rally in Luanda and they were all promptly arrested.[124]

Since March 2011, numerous protests have followed. On 3 September another protest, this time involving hundreds of protesters, was violently suppressed and at least twenty-four people were arrested (HRW, 2011b). Even more arrests took place a week later outside the courthouse where a hearing for those arrested on 3 September was taking place. Small but determined groups continued to defy the government into 2012 and 2013.[125] However, the mass movement in Angola has been stymied by the power and brute force of the regime.

In Nigeria, meanwhile, mass protests in early 2012 demonstrated the power of the Nigerian people. On 1 January, a decision by President Goodluck Jonathan to end Nigeria's fuel 'subsidy'[126] provoked massive demonstrations throughout Nigeria. The decision, which more than doubled the price of fuel, spurred indigenous 'occupy movements' to spring up in Abuja, Lagos, Port Harcourt, Kano and elsewhere, while 'occupy Nigeria' demonstrations were held by expatriate Nigerians in major cities around the world, including London, New York and Toronto.

The biggest rallies in Lagos, organized by the Save Nigeria Group (SNG), were reported to have as many as 2 million attendees.[127] The scale of the response to the increase in fuel prices even forced the government to put troops on the streets of its biggest cities—a first for the country since the return to civilian rule in 1999. Although the movement lost momentum after the subsidy was partially restored and the country's largest labour unions suspended the week-long general strike, simmering tensions remain. The SNG continues to organize public meetings and events backed by prominent Nigerians such as Wole Soyinka, Femi Kuti and many others.

The outcry and mass mobilization sparked by the fuel subsidy's removal can be understood as a response to the removal of the only tangible benefit most

Nigerians see from their nation's oil wealth. Speaking about the mistrust felt by residents of the Niger Delta, a Nigerian director of a national gender advocacy organization explained: 'You feel cheated. There is a strong feeling of injustice that people of this region feel. You know, they contribute 90 per cent of the nation's wealth and yet there is rising unemployment. You can't put food on your table and there are health problems due to oil exploration and oil activities.'[128]

While the rents from petroleum have flowed to the Nigerian elite, poverty and underdevelopment are the norm for the vast majority and are often seen as the underlying cause of militancy—not only in the Niger Delta, but, more recently, in the north of the country where Boko Haram has developed strong roots. Nigerians have clearly tired of policies that direct oil revenues into the hands of the elite. Seen through this lens, not only Nigerian content, but a much broader set of policy-making and state responses to crises, from the PIB reforms to the fuel subsidy debacle to the rise of militancy in the south and north, can be understood in terms of growing anger and widespread dissatisfaction. Additionally, as the evidence from the Niger Delta makes clear, the IOCs have their own role—perhaps even a leading role—in the underdevelopment of Nigeria and in making the country's resources into a curse.

The events of the fuel subsidy crisis, the uprising in the country's north and the simmering anger in the Niger Delta (only barely contained by a costly and unsustainable amnesty programme) suggest that Nigeria may be on the verge of a new period of more overt struggle to gain better access to the resources of the state and the benefits of its wealth. In Angola and Nigeria, the outcome of these struggles cannot be predicted in advance. Unfortunately, a model of social change in the Gulf of Guinea that relies upon new protest movements, or even the various civil society actors described in the sections above, from CSOs to labour unions and from multinational corporations to host communities, is a model based on wishful thinking. There is undoubtedly a role and a space for Angolans and Nigerians to promote more positive developmental outcomes through civil society engagement. However, given the limitations of civil society and new social movements discussed above, what makes the current moment unique and worthy of further study is the possibility of state- and elite-led economic and social development predicated on structural and conjunctural changes that alter the limits of the possible and open new possibilities that did not previously exist.

7

CONCLUSION

WHAT FUTURE FOR PETRO-DEVELOPMENT?

I end where I began: what has previously been understood about oil and development and about sub-Saharan Africa's place in the global economic system is outmoded and in need of re-evaluation. A new moment of opportunity may be at hand for Angola, Nigeria and the Gulf of Guinea as a whole if good policy for managing petroleum wealth and ensuring its developmental benefit is implemented and capitalist development is nurtured sufficiently to take advantage of the possibility for transformation. The geopolitical and technological realignment described above has been accompanied by changing strategies and realities for Europe, the US and China, as well as European, American and Chinese finance and petro-capital. Angola and Nigeria will not replicate the experience of the East Asian developmental states, although they may indeed produce their own petro-developmental states. This new moment presents opportunities emerging not only from changed external dynamics, but also from changed domestic circumstances and from the agency of struggles for social change and a better future.

In its previous iterations, the developmental state has emerged not out of movements from below, but out of particular structural factors in a specific historical conjuncture. Predicated on capitalist economic growth, the developmental state can later allow for greater citizen participation, social development and even redistribution to bring about greater stability and legitimacy (since legitimacy gained from delivering economic growth can only be sustained for so long). The developmental state can create the institutional foundations of an advanced capitalist economy. However, in the case of Angola and Nigeria, it is far from clear that the elite will in fact lead their respective countries into a new age of prosperity or that any of the wealth they attain will reach the majority of people in any meaningful way.

It is clear from the preceding chapters that in this period of rapid growth and fundamental restructuring of the petroleum industries in Angola and Nigeria, a transformation is underway. Yet the outcome of this transformation is still being determined. Angola, Nigeria and the other countries of the Gulf of Guinea face a unique opportunity, because global capitalism requires the petroleum resources they hold. As a former Angolan Minister of Finance from the Marxist–Leninist period told me, today there is a need to 'maintain the market as a mechanism for growth and development'.[1] Bearing in mind the devastation that oil has caused to Angola and especially to Nigeria, to sit back and wait for an anti-capitalist solution to the problems of extractive industry and underdevelopment is not a viable option. However, a large-scale movement to encourage a successful, democratic petro-developmental state has not yet taken hold.

Mark Robinson and Gordon White argue that: 'If the developmental state is to be genuinely democratic, it *should* be representative of the views of a wide cross-section of its citizens and reflect their needs and aspirations... Democratic developmental states *should*, by definition, cater to their poor citizens and produce policies which address their needs, rather than merely the exigencies of economic growth' (1998: 6, emphasis added). To ensure such progress, it is not sufficient to sit back and hope that the structural conditions favour developmental outcomes. Nor is it sufficient to expect that civil society organizations and actors, even new social movements, all operating within very difficult constraints in terms of bringing about social change, will be able to bring about effective management and use of petroleum resources.

Regardless of what we believe *should be* done, the reality of the current moment and the balance of forces, particularly in Angola, constrain civil society in myriad ways described in Chapter 6 and work against the emergence of a successful, democratic petro-developmental state. The emergence of the petro-developmental state despite the weaknesses of civil society will require a fortunate combination of elite interests, state autonomy, international forces and agency. The process of economic development will be aided by good policy choices, effectively implemented. The process of social development that will sustain the petro-developmental state in the long term will benefit from meaningful struggle and confrontation in the sphere of civil society to make oil work.

CONCLUSION

Policy Implications for Development Through Local Content

Important similarities and differences in the two cases emerged over the course of my study that allow for the development of policy implications from Nigeria and Angola's approaches to managing (or not managing) their respective oil resources and promoting (or not promoting) economic and social development. Through the adoption of good policy, state bureaucracies with relative autonomy can help ensure positive developmental outcomes. The current historical moment of competition between the US and China, along with the opportunity created by shifting strategies of elite accumulation, open up several advantages which may or may not be taken up in the move towards petro-development in the Gulf of Guinea.

To begin, there are obvious advantages to looking at the Gulf of Guinea as a region and for the Gulf's states to act with greater coordination. International capital views the Gulf of Guinea as a region. This fact drives processes of enclosure as well as competition for access to scarce resources. The size of their petroleum resources is what gives the countries of the Gulf of Guinea power vis-à-vis international capital and allows for local content policy to be implemented in the face of a global neoliberal doctrine which not only promotes but forcefully compels exactly the opposite from developing countries. Given the similarities of the current moment for these countries, they would certainly benefit from cooperation and an exchange of knowledge and best practice on a wide range of fronts, from environmental policy and social programming to industrial policy and petroleum taxation. This would require a much stronger and better-supported Gulf of Guinea Commission.

Coordinating relationships with global capital and the IOCs across the Gulf of Guinea can only strengthen the power of states vis-à-vis international actors. At the same time, such coordination can promote the industrial development of the region as a whole, particularly the indigenous oil service sector, which would benefit immensely from economies of scale. Cooperation on foreign policy and security will strengthen further the hands of countries in the region. Unfortunately, the internal dynamics between countries and leaders in the Gulf of Guinea seem to foreclose this possibility in the short to medium turn. There is however the possibility of a highly valuable and rich exchange between activists and interest groups in the different countries of the region to foster exchange in terms of advocacy and accountability and to address issues of mutual interest like oil spills and boundary disputes that require a coordinated response.[2] Nevertheless, the Angolan and Nigerian cases do show multiple ways forward towards petro-development.

Although both Angola and Nigeria were ravaged by the Atlantic slave trade, their histories diverge due to the perniciousness of Portuguese settler colonialism. The result for both countries was underdevelopment, conflict and malgovernance in the post-independence era. In Angola, China has gained an impressive foothold and offers a far greater possibility of development than does the West, though both remain interested in the region to meet their raw material needs. Angola represents a model for how the relationship with an emergent China opens the possibility of using China's interest in the continent's resources to improve bargaining power and promote infrastructure development and poverty alleviation.

Both Angola and Nigeria have made local content policies more palatable for a variety of stakeholders than older and more traditional forms of resource nationalism. The differences in implementation of local content, however, are enlightening. In Angola, smaller pieces of legislation provide some legal backing for local content, but the key provisions are in the production-sharing agreements with the IOCs. Angola's strategy involves negotiating and renegotiating the terms of their highly successful PSAs, while attempting to manage and enforce local content provisions effectively through the relevant departments of Sonangol. Angola has had only limited success enforcing Angolanization through the Ministry of Petroleum, but it has managed to make sure that all the multinationals operating in-country are aware of the priority they put on local content. IOCs have played important roles resisting certain changes (like new banking regulations and the use of TradeJango), while taking a role in others (capacity-building of Angolan oil service companies through CAE). Meanwhile, as discussed below, Sonangol has taken the lead in the development, implementation and monitoring of local content.

In Nigeria, IOCs have cooperated with foreign embassies—particularly the US embassy—to lobby against both the NCA and PIB. However, in both countries, the most the IOCs can hope to do is slow down the pace of local content. In reality, local content is not their primary concern. In fact, the IOCs have generally come around to supporting these policies. In any case, IOCs do not actually have the power to stop the implementation of local content policies. In Nigeria, they have so complexified issues that it is difficult for change to occur. While the oil sectors of both countries are dominated by foreigners, Angola enjoys significantly more power vis-à-vis the IOCs due to the effectiveness of Sonangol. The country's relationships with international oil companies have also benefited from the stability afforded by the long reign of President dos Santos. Angola, through Sonangol, has pursued a very different policy of local content. Neither country was previously successful in encouraging the employment of nationals in positions of authority, but since 2000 both have renewed efforts to increase national participation in the sector in terms of labour and subcontracting goods and services to national companies through policies of local content.

Local content was pursued in Nigeria through one key piece of legislation that took eight years to pass. Nigeria was in a stronger position from the beginning due to much higher levels of Nigerianization of labour, higher levels of education and human capacity, the presence of well-established E&P companies and service providers and a larger pre-existing industrial base. Until the passage of the NCA, the Nigerian Content Division of NNPC encountered several difficulties in the enforcement of its directives. With limited powers to monitor and evaluate, the directives did not have their intended effect. Also until the passage of the NCA, the NCD had little input into the NNPC's approvals process for oil service contracts and enjoyed only limited cooperation from the DPR, NAPIMS and other relevant agencies. Therefore, what seems like one of Nigeria's biggest local content successes, the NipeX electronic marketplace, had little to do with the NCD. Today, the NCDMB is building its own joint qualification system from scratch. Although the creation of the NCDMB is an important development, the completely unattainable (in the short term) targets in the schedule of the NCA serve more to deter progress than to inspire it.

The Theoretical Implications of Development Though Local Content

What does the use of local content solutions to development add to the theoretical literature on oil and development? For states seeking to nurture capitalist development, local content and the domiciliation of economic activity by foreign and domestic companies in-country offer a model of state intervention that would allow states to take advantage of the unique opportunities of the current moment to capitalize on oil rent with support among a broad base of local stakeholders and in a way that can also be tolerated by international actors, including international capital. While promoting economic development, local content strengthens the national bourgeoisie by providing autonomy for indigenous capitalist accumulation within the external structural constraints imposed by the capitalist world system. In effect, it represents a potential working model for reversing decades of underdevelopment and expropriation of surplus under global neoliberalism and moving once again towards industrialization, job creation and the alleviation of poverty.

The discussion of the elite of Angola and Nigeria in Chapter 4 clearly shows the ways in which, particularly in the Nigerian case, they have moved to embrace local content. This does not necessarily represent a shift from Boone's study of Senegal in which she concluded that rentierism is likely to be persistent. However, it does represent a shift in modes of wealth accumulation and strategies of maintaining political control in which a more capitalist social stratum could emerge, due to the alignment of their interests with the political elite, and challenge persistent rentierism.

The pursuit of local content represents a break from the path taken by the rentier states of the Middle East and an attempt to create backward and forward linkages between oil exploration and production and the domestic economy. Local content does this by applying the logic of capitalist development to the extraction of mineral rents so that, through domiciliation, the surplus created by the application of capital can promote further capitalist accumulation. This approach to oil and development represents the best and possibly the only successfully executed approach to addressing the acknowledged economic symptoms associated with the otherwise problematic resource curse concept. Going beyond simply addressing a 'curse', the conditions that allow the possibility of local content promotion represent a unique opportunity for economic growth in a wide range of non-oil sectors. However, they by no means represent the certainty of meaningful social development or even long-term and sustainable economic growth unless they are accompanied by redistribution of the oil benefit and other forces that will check grossly unequal power relations.

The new imperialism provides the necessary framework to analyze both the shift in domestic accumulation through capture of economic surplus from oil-rent extraction and the shift in the international context that allows petro-states to pursue policies of state protectionism in coordination with the domestic elite and acquiescence of international petro- and finance capital. Accumulation by dispossession is an ongoing feature of capitalist production. However, a certain amount of primitive accumulation, or accumulation of original capital, is one of the preconditions for a capitalist transformation. At that point, a dynamic theory of social change is needed to understand the role of shifting strategies of accumulation and shifting class interests in remaking the state and social relations. While accumulation by dispossession does not disappear, it does become more sophisticated. This process does not lead in a crude modernizationist view along one path towards capitalist development. Rather, it leads to uneven development—development in some areas and underdevelopment in others. Specific outcomes depend on the interplay of a number of forces.

Not only are there numerous possible outcomes, there are also a variety of mixed systems of accumulation dependent on the economic structures and class relations of the area being examined. Therefore Angola and Nigeria can exhibit different levels or types of continued rentierism within varieties of petro-developmental states. However, the Angolan cases suggest several features to look for in identifying other petro-developmental states. In Chapter 5, I argued that such states would show an increased number of indigenous companies and increased indigenous economic activity in the oil and gas industry along with movement towards more capitalist behaviour by the domestic elite.

Additionally, the petro-developmental state would likely possess a bureaucracy staffed by better-educated technocrats capable of implementing policy more effectively than the typical bureaucracies that many African countries had after independence. It would have to develop sufficient human capacity not only to increase indigenous participation in oil and gas, but also to exert some measure of national control over the exploration and production of petroleum resources. Ultimately, though the confluence of specific external and internal features brings about the structural conditions that allow for petro-development, the actual outcome of petro-development may depend on the agency of key actors within the state and civil society and their struggles to implement effective change.

State Agency in the Implementation of Local Content

Many of the differences in local content implementation come down to differences in the state bureaucracies responsible for local content. In Angola, Sonangol has spearheaded efforts. While the Negotiations Directorate leads long-term strategic planning on local content, many other divisions of the company also work on local content. The departments that approve oil service contracts evaluate the local content in various proposals to boost the benefit to the Angolan economy, while Sonangol is also involved in several high-profile joint ventures to try and deliver services that are beyond the capacity of private Angolan firms. Finally, an investments division of Sonangol, SIIND, is coordinating the development of manufacturing capacity in special industrial zones. While there are drawbacks to the control that Sonangol exercises over the Angolan economy, Sonangol's efficiency is a sharp contrast with Nigeria.[3]

The newly formed NCDMB has the potential to succeed where the NNPC-NCD failed. One of the first guidelines issued by the NCDMB in November 2010 covered the logistics of the 1 percent remittance that IOCs are supposed to make to the NCDMB from all oil service contracts.[4] These funds will enable the NCDMB to establish effective monitoring and evaluation of its policies. What remains to be seen, however, is whether the NCDMB is enabled to conduct itself competently and professionally—particularly when it comes to picking which companies to support (a key aspect of the role for state bureaucrats implementing the developmental state).[5]

The effectiveness of the bureaucracies of the D.NEG/DFE and NCDMB will be major factors in determining the outcome of any developmentalist project. As Evans notes with reference to East Asia, 'To focus on the East Asian developmental states is to focus on the importance of the capacity of public bureaucracies. Nearly everyone agrees that when East Asian public bureaucracies are compared with those of developing countries in other regions they more closely approximate the ideal typical Weberian bureaucracy' (2008: 6). Those bodies will need high-level support to implement local content policies successfully; however, effective oversight can only be guaranteed if civil society is given a role in local content policy. Importantly, they will have to be given a role in ensuring that the benefits of local content specifically, and oil extraction more generally, reach the majority of people.

In a sense, Angola has, through Sonangol, come much closer to the vision of an effective and autonomous bureaucracy most commonly associated with the East Asian developmental state. However, an important difference is that in the Angolan case the state bureaucracy appears somewhat less autonomous from business interests. Nigeria, meanwhile, has relied more heavily on legislation. As seen in the experience of the NNPC-NCD, the bureaucracy was unable to implement, monitor and enforce policy effectively until it was given the proper tools and authority through the NCA. The difference between Angola and Nigeria comes down to the respective levels not of local content, but of local control. As Chapter 2 described, policies of national content and control have been pursued in both countries for decades. While Nigeria has greater numbers of nationals working at higher levels in multinational corporations, Angola has pursued national control through the effectiveness of Sonangol and its ability to exercise power over the oil industry. Simply put, the various legal regimes governing the Nigerian petroleum industry and organizational structures of the Nigerian state oil company have failed to give the state power vis-à-vis international petro-capital. While the lack of control makes restructuring of state apparatuses necessary, and the creation of the NCDMB may finally have been a step in the right direction, it now seems that with the Petroleum Industry Bill Nigeria is moving further away from national control.

Both Sonangol and the NCDMB will face challenges in asserting autonomy from the interests of the political and business elite—especially in Angola where they are one and the same. Yet, South Korea faced similar difficulties in both promoting the interests of and remaining autonomous from its *chaebols*. The concern raised in Chapter 2 about the dual nature of local content goes to the heart of the concern over autonomy. The dual nature is the key pitfall in terms of successful implementation of local content. While the two aspects of local content do not have to work against each other, the Nigerian case shows that they can do precisely that if they stress the failed policies of indigenization over the more beneficial policies of domiciliation. In Angola meanwhile, the enrichment of the elite and the growth of their power over Angolan society has proceeded at such a rapid pace that the distinction between the state and the interests of the dominant class has been largely erased, leading to comparisons with fascist Italy in the 1930s.

There have been countless examples of poor policy choices made because of an inability to pursue the national interest over the interest of national elites. Chapters 3 and 4 describe the lengths the Angolan elite have taken to keep hold of political power. The case of the US company Cobalt, where the CEO of Sonangol (and likely presidential successor) actually owned the local partner, underlines the lack of separation between the state and private business interests. In Nigeria, this history goes back past the 'local content vehicles' programme to the history of indigenization in the 1970s and earlier. More recently, the case of Heerema in Nigeria, described in Chapter 3, shows the potential loss that can result from pursuing the wrong side of local content's dual nature.

Citizen Agency and the Petro-Developmental State

Evans also writes that the knowledge and skills embodied in the capabilities of individuals will be even more important to the twenty-first-century developmental state. He therefore sees 'ramping up the effective delivery of capability-expanding services' as an 'obvious starting point for aggressive state action' (2008: 13). This analysis, along with the comments by Mkandawire and Chang on social policy, fits nicely with the consistent demands of civil society in both Angola and Nigeria to invest more in education, health and agriculture and to redistribute the benefits of petroleum. Nigeria enjoys significant advantages in terms of human resources and capacity. With a much better-educated populace, a more successful record of integrating Nigerians into the oil sector, a headstart at building an indigenous oil sector and a much larger manufacturing sector to support its development, Nigeria is clearly ahead in terms of local content and the consolidation of a developmental state through human capacity development.

As conversations with civil society and the business communities in both countries make clear though, social investment must also be accompanied by greater investment in transportation and energy infrastructure. Here, Angola seems to be moving significantly faster, though it began only a decade ago and was much farther behind. The conditions for investing in Angola, despite the high cost of doing business in the country, are on the whole more favourable. Though it lacks Nigeria's reserves of oil and natural gas, in the judgement of many experts Angola has more potential reserves to be discovered and has a better system for capturing revenues from the oil sector through its PSA agreements. The higher cost of exploration and production in Angola, where oil extraction is increasingly taking place in the deep offshore, puts national E&P companies at a disadvantage. These companies are also at a disadvantage because there are relatively few protections for E&P companies, despite the new incentives put in place by Decree 3/12.

Both Angola and Nigeria also face their fair share of challenges in moving from rentiers to states that successfully nurture capitalist development. To begin, both the Angolan and Nigerian states and their citizens lack capacity to implement a developmental state and ensure its success. The primary weakness of the Angolan state related to local content is the lack of capacity and authority in the Ministry of Petroleum. However, low capacity in the Ministry of Finance and the national legislature contribute to the weak over-seeing of petroleum revenues while a lack of capacity is also a significant challenge for decentralization. Nigerian government agencies may have more human capacity, but they lack the institutional framework and governance structures to work effectively, as in the case of Sonangol. Nigerian regulators lack the basic necessities for doing their jobs, while the development pro-grammes put in place to assist the Niger Delta suffer due to gross incompe-tence and mismanagement. While Nigeria is well ahead of Angola in terms of human capacity, a lack of citizens with the necessary background and training is cited by multinational corporations in both countries as a key human resources challenge.

There are further challenges in terms of the capacity of the national bourgeoisie. It is unclear whether the local elite of Angola and Nigeria will begin to see greater advantage in reinvesting their assets at home in capitalist production, though there is some preliminary evidence from Chapters 4 and 5 that they may be ready to make this shift. There is also evidence that the 'dual nature' of local content may be encouraging less productive accumulation. While both countries have experienced strong economic growth in the past decade, demonstrating that economic development is possible within the capitalist world system for these particular countries, the fact that this development is premised on a very orthodox variant of economic liberalism suggests a weakness of legitimacy and susceptibility to crisis, since by now it should be beyond debate that the accumulated wealth of the elite does not simply 'trickle down' on its own.

Though both Angola and Nigeria suffer very weak civil society institutions, Angola must be singled out for the high levels of repression and unfreedom. Where Nigerian civil society may be disorganized or lack capacity, Angolan civil society is engaged in a struggle to assert basic demands. Freedom of the press is virtually non-existent in Angola. Though the press may have its problems in Nigeria, the problems simply do not compare. Similarly, though Nigerian labour at times struggles to assert the rights of workers, it is a force to be reckoned with and an effective and engaged contributor to debates on oil policy. By contrast, Angolan labour has not yet gained full practical independence from the MPLA. At times, it struggles even to represent its members. Its power vis-à-vis the IOCs is very limited. For this reason, unlike in Nigeria, Angolan labour cannot participate in the implementation or monitoring of local content.

Finally, an unfortunate similarity between Angola and Nigeria is the power of their respective coercive apparatuses. Hardened by decades of civil war, the Angolan military is one of the strongest on the continent and has been used with brutal effectiveness against the people of Cabinda. It has also been used to quell recent protests and new social movements (see Chapter 6). The massive Nigerian military is the power of the region. The elite Joint Task Force (JTF), which has been primarily responsible for combating militants in the Niger Delta, is notorious for its human rights violations (see Amunwa, 2011) and has even been used against Nigerian labour (Solidarity Center, 2010).

It is the similarities in the situations faced by Cabindans and Niger Deltans that are perhaps most troubling. While the violence, chaos and disorder of the Niger Delta are entirely different in their magnitude to the situation in

Cabinda, the root causes of the conflicts are remarkably similar. So too is the conclusion reached that a fair share of the benefits of petroleum must be used for the development of those communities that host oil extraction. Despite some progress, the Angolan and Nigerian states have yet to see fair redistribution as a prophylaxis for violent conflict and competition for state resources, though Nigeria has moved in this direction in recent years with the Niger Delta amnesty programme and provisions in the Petroleum Industry Bill to return some portion of revenues to host communities.

Final Thoughts on Local Content and the Petro-Developmental State

What makes local content important in the current moment of global neoliberalism is that it is a development strategy premised upon protectionism, state-led development, import substitution and other strategies consistently dismissed by the Washington and Post-Washington Consensus. The unique features of oil and oil rent combined with a variety of domestic and geopolitical shifts from a more educated and professional bureaucracy to new international anti-money laundering laws and the new Chinese engagement in Africa have combined to produce a changed historical moment for policy around oil and development and for capitalist accumulation strategies amongst well-positioned members of the domestic elite. Local content has already contributed to oil sector transformation in both Angola and Nigeria. Given the billions of dollars invested every year on oil extraction in each of these countries, capturing more of this spend through productive economic activity could have a dramatic impact on the economy. I have shown that a new combination of internal and external factors opens up a new moment of possibility in the Gulf of Guinea. The sheer size of investment in the oil sector combined with the unique power of the state when it comes to petroleum resources and the global economy (especially in Angola due to the power and effectiveness of Sonangol) have altered possibilities for economic development and opened new avenues for social development.

Besides the state, the key agents in the top-down implementation of the petro-developmental state are the emerging local capitalists and local oil and oil service companies. The case studies in Chapter 5 describe several aspects of the transformation that are already underway. The case studies in both Angola and Nigeria show the dynamism and potential of local capitalists while at the same time highlighting the mixed potential of some companies and their continuation of patterns of rent-seeking—further examples of the dual nature of local content policies in practice. These latter cases show the challenges that exist in making a real change beyond the ownership of companies in the sector. Nevertheless, a shift is undoubtedly occurring in both Angola and Nigeria. Angolan and Nigerian companies are moving into new areas of services that were previously dominated by foreign companies and Angolan and Nigerian labour is being mobilized (in some cases by the IOCs themselves, but more often by government policy and labour action) to make larger contributions in terms of labour-power and to be involved at all levels of service from unskilled labour to senior management.

The shift theorized in my study is from rent-seeking to productive investment of rents in capitalist accumulation. As discussed, many of the cases are not companies that fit either the 'pure capitalist accumulation' or 'pure accumulation by dispossession' ideal types. There may in fact be different varieties and of indigenous accumulation—a possibility that warrants further study to attempt a considered typology. Following from this insight, the shift is more accurately described as an increase in the number of indigenous companies and the amount of indigenous economic activity, coinciding with increased capitalist accumulation and decision-making based on the logic of capitalist growth.

Although indigenization is sometimes justified by the elite who benefit from it in terms of 'trickle down' theory, the kind of local content that actually leads to development is not premised on wealth trickling down from the elite. Rather, it is based on increased productive investment and opportunities for employment. Ground-rent in the form of surplus can be captured by successful local content initiatives and used by the state in many ways that make oil work for economic development. The state can also take its share of royalties and taxes to invest in education, health, agriculture, industry or social services to make oil work for social development. However, the ground-rents that have previously been captured or are still being captured by the Angolan and Nigerian elites can, under the logic of the capitalist world system, only promote development if the elite invest that rent in capitalist production. If incentivized to do this by changed structural realities and/or state action, positive social change and transformation of the social relations of production can occur without agency from below.

Economic growth alone can, along with external geopolitical change, translate over time into social development through shifting power dynamics and class relations. We are witness to a historical moment in which the countries of the Gulf of Guinea have an opportunity that did not previously exist to become petro-developmental states. As this possibility did not previously exist, development theory must adapt to accommodate and explain new limits of the possible while development practice seeks policy interventions that maximize the new potential. The outcomes of this new moment are far from certain. Better policy will produce better results, and more robust struggles by the state and civil society actors can discipline market forces to counter the so-called 'resource curse'.

NOTES

PREFACE

1. See, for example, Gereffi and Korzeniewicz (1994); Morris, Kaplinsky and Kaplan (2012); Gereffi (2014).
2. This term is more often associated with Latin America. See for example the work of former Brazilian Finance Minister Luiz Carlos Brasser-Periera (2011).
3. For more on this term, see Gudynas (2010).
4. See Pogge (1998); Wenar (2011); Armstrong (2014).
5. African Union, 'Africa Mining Vision', http://pages.au.int/sites/default/files/Africa%20Mining%20Vision%20english_0.pdf

1. INTRODUCTION: THE EMERGENCE OF THE PETRO-DEVELOPMENTAL STATE

1. Since 2011, Ghana has joined the group of oil-exporting countries in SSA.
2. According to Gilbert Rist, 'development' has become a 'plastic word', meaning a word that has been so widely adopted that it no longer has meaning beyond whatever an individual speaker wishes it to mean (1997). Therefore, I am obliged to define the term more concretely for my own purposes. In the work that follows, 'economic development' refers to a particular form of economic growth and industrialization associated with capitalist transformation and the appropriation of economic surplus. Economic development may have negative features, such as growing inequality or ecological destruction. Additionally, economic development in one area may also result in underdevelopment elsewhere through the appropriation of economic surplus. By contrast, 'social development' refers more directly to an improved quality of life in terms of health, education, housing, clean water and other basic needs, as well as to freedom from all forms of oppression. I view both economic and social development as necessary and desirable. Inequality,

underdevelopment, dispossession, loss of culture, loss of diversity and environmental degradation must be addressed through public policy; however, struggles of various kinds carried out on the terrain of civil society will ultimately be required to achieve greater social justice.

3. The concept of 'underdevelopment' here denotes the non-linear nature of development and acknowledges the role of neo-colonialism and continued surplus appropriation in modern African history. The concept as I use it is not a reference to a systematic or inevitable outcome of a metropolis–satellite relationship.

4. Chad's connection consists of a massive 1,070 km pipeline that bisects Cameroon and brings Chad's crude oil to the coast.

5. Although there are many examples to choose from, *The Economist*'s 'Africa Rising' typifies the enthusiasm that international finance now has, which has helped Africa transition from the 'lost continent' to the 'hopeful continent' in the eyes of Western investors. See 'Africa Rising', *The Economist*, 3 December 2011, http://www.economist.com/node/21541015

6. Calculations from this source are my own, based on the IMF World Economic Outlook Database, April 2013.

7. See 'Africa's impressive growth', *Economist Online*, Daily Chart, 6 January 2011, http://www.economist.com/blogs/dailychart/2011/01/daily_chart

8. Rodney (1974) is a classic text. See also Bond (2006); Saul and Leys (1999); and Amin (1977, 1974b).

9. African countries are not already capitalist simply because they trade and conduct commerce with the global economy. The presence of domestic and international markets, stock exchanges, or wealthy individuals with investments abroad also does not indicate that capitalism, defined by a particular mode of production, exists. Samir Amin (1976, 1974a) developed the term 'peripheral capitalism' to describe a situation where African countries participate in the capitalist world system in terms of the circulation of commodities but have predominantly non-capitalist social relations of production. In *Unequal Development*, Amin writes that: 'The pattern of transition to peripheral capitalism is fundamentally different from the transition to central capitalism' (1976: 200). The difference is that in peripheral capitalism, the social relations of production may remain primarily non-capitalist. The thesis of peripheral capitalism is still useful today to describe the countries of the Gulf of Guinea, and indeed much of SSA.

10. See Soares de Oliveira (2007b); El-Khawas and Ndumbe (2006); Klare and Volman (2006); Watts (2006); and Mohan and Zach-Williams (2005).

11. See Ayers (2013); Yates (2012); Southall and Melber (2009); Ampiah and Naidu (2008); Guerrero and Manji (2008); Ovadia (2008); Alden (2007); Manji and Marks (2007); Klare and Volman (2006); and Watts (2006).

12. Chinese loans to Angola since 2005 are conservatively estimated to be over US$14 billion by the international organization Global Witness. For more on Chinese

financing in Angola and elsewhere on the continent, see Ovadia (2013f); Corkin (2011); Alves (2010); Human Rights Watch (HRW 2010); Vines et al. (2009); Global Witness (2009); and Campos and Vines (2008).

13. More than US$20 billion in Chinese infrastructure projects in Nigeria have mostly stalled. However, China and Nigeria did agree to a US$1.1 billion low-interest loan in July 2013. See 'How the big projects fell short' and 'Diminishing returns in Beijing', *Africa–Asia Confidential*, 6(10), August 2013.

14. Similar arguments are made by Bunker and Ciccantell (2005).

15. J. Peter Pham, 'Securing the New Strategic Gulf', *World Defense Review*, 7 June 2007. http://worlddefensereview.com/pham060707.shtml [accessed 29 December 2007]

16. For more on the US Africa Command, see Ovadia (2008). On forced displacement, see Zalik (2009). The work of Stakeholder Democracy Network has been crucial to the fight against forced displacement in the Niger Delta; see http://www.stakeholderdemocracy.org/ending-forced-evictions.htm. Displacement has also occurred on a smaller scale in Angola. See, for example, Sylvia Croese, 'Angola: Rebuilding by Demolishing', *Pambazuka News*, Issue 475, 25 March 2010, http://pambazuka.org/en/category/features/63298

17. On petro-violence, see Peluso and Watts (2001).

18. For more information on such campaigns, visit http://www.sosyasuni.org/ (Ecuador) and http://www.eraction.org/ (Nigeria).

19. Even if one accepts the validity of discussing the Gulf of Guinea as a region, its boundaries are an open question. While Soares de Oliveira defines it as 'the coastal region that runs across Central Africa from Nigeria to southern Angola' (2007b: 5), I prefer to include the countries further west along the coast from Nigeria, which are also in the process of exploring and extracting petroleum resources.

20. Treaty establishing the Gulf of Guinea Commission [supplied by the Commission].

21. Interview, 5 August 2010.

22. Interview, 5 August 2010. It must be noted here that while Abeso's words are moving, there is little basis in fact for arguing that the Gulf of Guinea countries share the same ecosystem or environment, let alone that they are the same people and face common problems.

23. In Angola, research was conducted mainly in Luanda and Cabinda, although I also spent time in Huambo and Benguela. In Nigeria, my time was split between the Niger Delta, Abuja and Lagos. The time in the Delta was largely spent in Port Harcourt, with time spent in two oil-bearing communities in Rivers State and small trips made to Bori and Yenagoa. I conducted a total of 119 separate open-ended interviews with 129 interview subjects, split evenly between Angola and Nigeria.

24. In the context of the oil and gas industry, the 'upstream' sector refers to exploration and production activities, as opposed to the 'downstream', which refers to the

refining and distribution of products derived from petroleum as well as the distribution of natural gas.

2. WHAT IS LOCAL CONTENT, WHERE DID IT COME FROM AND HOW CAN IT SUCCEED?

1. The fact that the country-specific terms 'Angolanization' or 'Nigerian content' are now used more frequently reflects conscious efforts by those states to define the nation as the primary stakeholder in the oil and gas industry. At the same time, this minimizes the particular local claims of various subnational groups on petroleum resources—for example, in the Niger Delta of Nigeria and the Province of Cabinda in Angola. Both of these areas have seen widespread conflict and unrest due to such claims and both have also experienced significant environmental degradation and loss of livelihoods for local inhabitants.

2. This chapter draws upon material I first published in Ovadia (2012) and Ovadia (2013b).

3. O. Austin Avuru, 'Local Content Law: pitfalls in application'. Paper presented to the Nigerian Association of Petroleum Explorationists. Lagos, 25 August 2010. http://www.nape.org.ng/ [accessed 4 October 2010]

4. Several US diplomatic cables from Nigeria released by Wikileaks in 2010 and 2011 confirm what is already common knowledge amongst many in the petroleum sector—that members at the highest level of the executive, NNPC and the military are involved in bunkering. For example, one cable from 2009 marked 'SECRET NOFORN' (meaning that it was never meant to be shown to non-US citizens) names the Group Managing Director of NNPC, the First Lady of Nigeria and members of the President's cabinet and staff as figures, involved in bunkering, citing Shell's Regional Vice President for Africa. Another, from 2007, cites Chevron's Chief Nigeria Security Manager as a source for information that Nigeria's Joint Task Force (JTF) and Naval High Command aid and abet bunkering.

5. 2013 estimates from the US Energy Information Administration. However, it may be that Angola has greater potential for further exploration to lead to increased reserves—especially in the 'pre-salt layer' (2,000–5,000 metres below sea level), which is only now beginning to be examined.

6. For more on the 'success' of Sonangol, see Soares de Oliveira (2007a).

7. In fact, while the figure varies from year to year, actual annual investment is closer to US$12–15 billion.

8. Interview, July 2010.

9. In April 2014, Nigeria released more accurate GDP information after rebasing the measure to include industries like information technology, telecommunications, music, film and others that were not significant in the previous base year of 1990. The revised figures (see NBS, 2014), which also cover the informal sector better, provide an 89 per cent increase in Nigeria's 2013 nominal GDP. They also show

major growth in manufacturing and services. Previously thought to account for 1.9 per cent of GDP, the new figures put manufacturing at 9 percent. The biggest jump, however, is in services, which are now thought to account for half of Nigeria's GDP (previously they were thought to account for only a quarter). While these figures indicate that the importance of petroleum resources for Nigeria's economy is much less than previously thought (crude oil exports are now closer to 13 per cent of GDP), they also indicate the potential for local content policies to boost manufacturing and service provision and validate the thesis of a Nigerian economy in transition to capitalist social relations.

10. Barry Morgan, 'Local Content Regulations Come in Three Flavours', *Upstream*, 14 July 2006: 34–5.

11. Interview, August 2010.

12. According to MINPET (2010), investment in the oil industry was just under US$16.5 billion in 2009, up from US$13 billion in 2008. This investment came 74.2 per cent from IOCs, 24 per cent from the state (including Sonangol) and less than 2 per cent from national oil companies.

13. The Yar'Adua and Jonathan administrations have in recent years been trying to achieve a radical updating and consolidation of Nigeria's petroleum law, known as the Petroleum Industry Bill (PIB). To date, the legislation remains stalled in the Nigerian parliament. It has been rigorously opposed by the IOCs and foreign governments—especially the United States.

14. Meeting, November 2010.

15. The government has been trying to organize a new long-planned bid round for marginal fields since 2013. As of July 2014, IOCs and the Ministry of Petroleum Resources were still trading accusations over repeated delays.

16. Interview, December 2010.

17. Edmund Daukoru, 'The Nigeria 2005 Oil and Gas Exploration and Production Acreage Bid Round'. Port Harcourt: Keynote Address by the Presidential Advisor on Petroleum and Energy, 24 March 2005.

18. Interview, 26 November 2010.

19. Interview, 22 November 2010.

20. Interview, 19 October 2010.

21. Ibid.

22. The 'dual nature' refers to the notion that local content, while promoting economic growth and industrial development, has also become an important mechanism for unequal growth and elite accumulation in a changed geopolitical climate in which an emerging elite is seeking new and more legitimate methods of creating wealth. See Ovadia (2012).

23. Interview, August 2010.

24. Interview, August 2010.

25. Angolan Ministry of Petroleum and Norwegian Petroleum Directorate, Activity Plan 2010 [internal document].

26. Macaulay A. Ofurhie, 'The Role of a Regulatory Agency in Local Content Development'. Presentation to the National Association of Energy Correspondents. Lagos, 7 October 2004.
27. Interview, 26 October 2010.
28. Interview, 13 October 2010.
29. Interview, 30 November 2010.
30. Interview, 3 December 2010.
31. 'A Bill for an Act to make Provisions for Nigerian Content Development in the Upstream Sector of the Nigerian Petroleum Industry and for Matters Connected therewith' can be found in the *Official Gazette*, No. 72, 2 September 2003.
32. Interview, 26 November 2010.
33. Results of the gap analysis are reproduced in NNPC-NCD, 2008.
34. Interview, 26 November 2010.
35. Interview, December 2010. Building an online database has again become a priority of the new NCDMB. The latest version of the database they have built can be found at http://www.nogicjqs.com/
36. Interview, 26 November 2010.

3. THE PROMISE AND PITFALLS OF DEVELOPMENT THROUGH LOCAL CONTENT

1. This chapter draws upon material from Ovadia (2012); Ovadia (2013b); and Ovadia (2013e).
2. Interview, 18 November 2010.
3. Ibid.
4. Interview, May 2010.
5. Interview, August 2010 (author's emphasis).
6. Comment made at a social event in Abuja, October 2010.
7. Interview, August 2010.
8. Interview, July 2010.
9. Interview, August 2010.
10. BP Reputation Survey, May 2010 [internal document].
11. Interview, May 2010.
12. The three main liberation groups were divided largely along racial/ethnic identities, with the MPLA enjoying great support amongst *mestiços* (descendants of Portuguese settlers, mostly male, from the early twentieth century). In a few short decades these *mestiços* displaced the 'Old Creole' elite in the colonial bureaucracy. The Portuguese, like the French, had a category of '*assimilados*' (Angolans granted what Kristen Reed calls 'honorary whiteness'). However, in Angola, while some *assimilados* were black, most were *mestiços* (Reed, 2009; citing Bender, 1980). In the liberation movements, many MPLA leaders had received education and training in Lisbon, while those in the FNLA, for example, were educated in Leopoldville

(Kinshasa) (Reed, 2009). This division echoes some of the racial and neo-colonial dynamics found in the Angolan oil sector today.

13. Interview, June 2010.
14. Interview, August 2010.
15. Interview, 12 August 2010.
16. I. Esau and E. Means, 'Sonangol gives Total snub as DSME gains Clov vote', *Upstream*, 30 April 2010: 2–3.
17. Interview, August 2010.
18. Interview, August 2010. To date, no details of such a plan have been made public.
19. 'Results-at-a-Glance', *Wa Mukula: CAE—Apoio Empresarial Newsletter*. March–April 2010.
20. Interview, August 2010.
21. Interview, August 2010.
22. Interview, August 2010.
23. Interview, August 2010.
24. Interview, August 2010.
25. TradeJango, 'The Most Transacted Products in 2008', *TradeJango Newsletter*, 20 March 2009.
26. Interview, August 2010.
27. Interview, August 2010.
28. Interview, August 2010.
29. Interview, August 2010.
30. Interview, August 2010.
31. Interview, August 2010.
32. Interview, August 2010.
33. Interview, August 2010.
34. Interview, August 2010.
35. Sonangol's unparalleled influence in Angola was again seen in 2010 as the powerful Gabinete de Reconstrução Nacional (*GRN*), an agency created by the President to oversee projects financed by large Chinese oil-backed loans, was scrapped and its projects (largely in the areas of housing and construction) transferred to a new Sonangol subsidiary, Sonangol Imobiliária. GRN industrial development projects, such as the new Viana Special Economic Zone, were turned over to yet another new Sonangol subsidiary, Sonangol Industrial Investments (SIIND).
36. Interview, August 2010.
37. Interview, August 2010.
38. Interview, August 2010.
39. Interview, August 2010.
40. Interview, August 2010.
41. Interview, July 2010.

42. Interview, July 2010.
43. Interview, November 2010.
44. Interview, November 2010; December 2012.
45. Interview, November 2010.
46. Kunle Akogun, 'Nigerian Firms Now to Get Priority in Oil Sector', *This Day* [Lagos], 23 April 2010, http://allafrica.com/stories/201004230676.html [accessed 25 April 2010]
47. Oscarline Onwuemenyi, 'Nigerian Content: Measuring the Gains', *The Vanguard* [Lagos], Sweet Crude Supplement, May 2010, p. 6, http://www.vanguardngr. com/sweetcrude/2012/may/index.html [accessed 4 May 2012].
48. Interview, 13 October 2010.
49. Interview, 12 November 2010.
50. Meeting, November 2010.
51. Interview, 3 December 2010.
52. Interview, October 2010.
53. Interview, 13 October 2010.
54. Interview, 3 November 2010.
55. Interview, 7 December 2010.
56. As an example, Ben Amunwa of Platform London authored a report detailing eight case studies, all from after the return to civilian rule, in which Shell was directly involved in funding and supporting human rights abuses in the Niger Delta (Amunwa, 2011).
57. Interview, 3 December 2010.
58. Interview, November 2010.
59. Interview, December 2010.
60. Interview, 3 November 2010.
61. Interview, October 2010.
62. Interview, 3 November 2010.
63. Interview, 13 October 2010.
64. Interview, 7 December 2010.
65. Ibid.
66. Interview, 26 November 2010.
67. Interview, 3 December 2010.
68. Interview, 3 December 2010.
69. Interview, 18 November 2010.
70. Interview, 26 November 2010.
71. Interview, 26 November 2010.
72. Shawley Coker, 'Local Capacity Building in an Enhanced Enabling Environment'. Paper presented to the Nigerian Association of Petroleum Explorationists. Lagos, 25 August 2010, http://www.nape.org.ng/ [accessed 4 October 2010]
73. Interestingly, Beblawi (1987) also speaks about local fronts in Arab states. As he

describes, in Arab states a sponsor needed for foreigners to conduct business is called *al-kafil*. Beblawi writes that this leads to a '*kafil* mentality', part of the rentier mentality which Beblawi associates with the incentive to engage in unproductive work and make unearned income.

74. Ofurhie, 'The Role of a Regulatory Agency in Local Content Development'.

75. Interview, November 2010.

76. Ibid.

77. Interview, October 2010.

78. Coker, 'Local Capacity Building in an Enhanced Enabling Environment'.

79. Interview, 3 December 2010.

80. Interview, November 2010.

81. Interview, 26 November 2010.

82. For more on the measurement of local content in Nigeria, see Ovadia (2013c; 2014).

83. The lack of empirical data on local content in oil and gas has been remarked upon by several international organizations as they begin to pay closer attention to the question of local content. State protectionism not only has a long record of success in promoting development, as I argued in Chapter 1; it is really the only successful example of how capitalist development has occurred. The poor quality of quantitative data on the benefits of local content was a key factor in my decision to produce a qualitative study of local content through the case studies described in Chapter 5.

84. Internal documents and presentations of Heerema Nigeria.

85. Interview, December 2010.

86. 'Nigeria: While Heerema Quits' (Editorial), *ThisDay* [Lagos], 22 March 2010, http://www.thisdayonline.com [accessed 4 January 2011].

87. Interview, December 2010. Due to lack of corroborating evidence, I have decided to withhold specific allegations against individual officials.

88. Ibid.

89. Heerema seems to have found the investment environment in Angola more favourable. In 2009, working with a local construction contractor, it began setting up a US$160 million yard to support its contracts in Angola. See 'Heerema to Build Angola Yard', *Upstream Online*, 22 June 2009, http://www.upstreamonline.com/live/article181494.ece? [accessed 4 December 2010]

90. Simbi Wabote, 'Maintaining a Healthy Balance Between Local and Foreign Involvement in Oil and Gas Service Delivery'. Paper presented to the Nigerian Association of Petroleum Explorationists. Lagos, 25 August 2010, http://www.nape.org.ng/ [accessed 4 October 2010]

91. Interview, 26 November 2010.

92. The request for an audience was delivered to the Minister of Labour and Productivity, dated 3 August 2010.

93. Babatunde Ogun, 'Address by the President, PENGASSAN, to the National Executive Council'. Sasun Hotel, Port Harcourt, 7 October 2010.
94. Meeting, 17 November 2010.
95. Interview, December 2012.
96. Interview, 13 December 2010.
97. Interview, October 2010.
98. Interview, November 2010.
99. Interview, November 2010.
100. Interview, 7 December 2010.
101. Interview, 22 November 2010.
102. Interview, 3 December 2010.
103. Interview, 3 December 2010.
104. Interview, 7 December 2010.
105. Ibid.
106. Interview, 26 November 2010.
107. Interview, November 2010.
108. Ibid.
109. Meeting, November 2010.
110. Ibid.
111. Interview, 3 December 2010.
112. For a detailed study of Nigeria's power woes, see Olukoju (2004), who concludes that many small and medium-sized enterprises in Nigeria have collapsed due to the cost of using stand-by generators. As Okoigun's comment shows, many others have simply declined to enter production.
113. Meeting, November 2010.

4. ELITE ACCUMULATION AND POTENTIAL CLASS TRANSFORMATION IN ANGOLA AND NIGERIA

1. The discussion of the Angolan elites in this chapter draws upon material from Ovadia (2013f).
2. Interview, May 2010.
3. Interview, May 2010.
4. Defining exactly who make up the Angolan elite is not an easy task. Soares de Oliveira refers to the Angolan elite as the *Futango de Belas*, describing it as 'presidential clique' of 'unelected officials and businessmen' that surround the president (2007a: 606). In an interview, an Angolan informant of mine similarly described the elite as a collection of government figures, but also opposition politicians, the military and, importantly, the bureaucrats (known in Angola as '*funcionarios publicos*'). In Metz (2011), the author further distinguishes between two groups of Angolan business elites: the well-established *empresarios de confiança* (individuals from old families of *mestiço* Portuguese descent dating back to the colonial period)

and 'crony capitalists' (individuals with political connections to the current regime and ties to the president).

5. Privatization during the 1991–2 period of transition is discussed in greater detail by Ferreira (1995).

6. Some recent developments in the Angolan drive to gain international legitimacy include the country obtaining an average B+ sovereign rating, with positive outlook from three rating classification agencies in May 2010 (which removes the need to seek oil-backed loans); the negotiation of a stand-by arrangement with the IMF in November 2009, worth an estimated US$1.4 bn; moves to publish more data related to the economy and the oil sector (despite the many limitations described by Global Witness 2011); and the passage of the Law on Public Probity in 2010 (despite its many flaws).

7. Quoted in Henrique Almeida, 'Oil Corruption Menaces Angola, Nigeria, Global Witness Says', *Bloomberg Businessweek*, 8 February 2012, http://www.businessweek.com/news/2012–02–09/oil-corruption-menaces-angola-nigeria-global-witness-says.html [accessed 8 February 2012]

8. The discussion of the Nigerian elites in this chapter draws upon material from Ovadia (2013d).

9. Interview, 13 October 2010.

10. Interview, 7 December 2010.

11. Interview, 3 December 2010.

12. Interview, 2 November 2010.

13. Interview, 13 October 2010.

14. Interview, 3 December 2010.

15. Ibid.

16. Interview, 19 October 2010

17. Informal meeting, November 2010.

18. Interview, 3 December 2010.

19. Interview, December 2010.

20. Interview, 18 November 2010.

21. Interview, 22 November 2010.

22. Interview, November 2010.

23. Interview, 13 December 2010.

24. Interview, 7 December 2010.

25. Interview, 13 October 2010.

26. Interview, 26 November 2010.

27. Interview, 26 November 2010.

28. Interview, October 2010.

29. Interview, 26 November 2010.

30. While most Nigerians would agree with Kupolokun that one is better than the other, most would also think that neither should really be the aim of government policy.

31. Interview, 26 November 2010.
32. Interview, 13 October 2010.
33. Ibid.
34. Interview, August 2010.
35. Interview, June 2010.
36. Interview, June 2010.
37. Interview, July 2010.
38. Interview, July 2010.
39. Interview, July 2010.
40. Interview, July 2010.
41. Ibid.
42. Interview, July 2010.
43. Interview, September 2010.
44. Interview, 16 August 2010.
45. Ibid.
46. http://makaangola.org/
47. Tom Burgis, 'US to probe Cobalt oil links in Angola', *Financial Times*, 21 February 2012, http://www.ft.com/intl/cms/s/0/284a1c78–5cb9–11e1-ac80–00144 feabdc0.html [accessed 25 February 2012]
48. In Angola, I observed that the report was widely discussed for weeks after its release. Eventually, even the MPLA was forced to announce an investigation of the claims made in Marques' report, though I am unaware if the investigation was ever conducted.
49. Burgis, 'US to probe Cobalt oil links in Angola'.
50. While my research indicated that government officials had controlling or otherwise significant stakes in a handful of local oil companies that are partners in Angolan oil blocks, I am unable independently to verify or prove ownership by government officials. Marques (2011) makes more accusations against the local companies Somoil, Poliedro and Kotoil, claiming that they are owned by various high-ranking government officials. If true, this may implicate Total (operator of Block 17/06, in which Somoil may at one point have been a partner). Chevron, ENI (AGIP), Total, Petrobras and Statoil may also be or have been investors in blocks with Somoil.
51. Interview, June 2010.
52. Indeed, Statoil was awarded operatorship of ultra-deep Blocks 38 and 39 in late 2011. Its partners are all other well-known IOCs, although a stake in Block 38 is owned by China Sonangol. For more on China Sonangol, see Ovadia (2013a).

5. HOW COMPANIES ARE IMPLEMENTING LOCAL CONTENT IN ANGOLA AND NIGERIA

1. The discussion of the Angolan case studies in this chapter draws upon material from Ovadia (2013f).

2. For the sake of readability, each legal entity described as a case study is referred to as a 'Company' even when it represents a variety of formal conglomerates, informal groups of companies and other legal arrangements.

3. Interview, August 2010.

4. Interview, July 2010.

5. Interview, August 2010.

6. Interview, July 2010.

7. Interview, July 2010.

8. Ibid.

9. Interview, August 2010.

10. Ibid.

11. Personal correspondence; various media reports.

12. Interview, August 2010.

13. Interview, August 2010.

14. Ibid.

15. Interview, August 2010. As will be discussed in Chapter 6, SAECGOC, the union representing Chevron employees and subcontractors, estimates that private Angolan companies may pay as little as one-third the wage paid by Chevron for the same work.

16. Interview, August 2010.

17. Ibid.

18. Interview, August 2010.

19. Ibid.

20. Interview, August 2010.

21. Interview, August 2010.

22. Ibid.

23. Ibid.

24. Interview, July 2010.

25. The discussion of the Nigerian cases in this chapter draws upon material from Ovadia (2013d).

26. http://www.sahara-group.com/

27. Interview, December 2010.

28. Interview, December 2010.

29. This table excludes four indigenous companies expecting either to resume production or to achieve first oil before the end of 2012. These are Frontier Oil, Sahara Energy Fields, Prime Energy and Sogenal.

30. http://www.fhnigeria.com/

31. http://www.afren.com/

32. Interview, 22 November 2010.

33. The deal, reached in October 2010, was completed in November 2011. As part of the agreement, NNPC transferred its stake in the block to its subsidiary, the Nigerian Petroleum Development Company (NPDC), which will jointly oper-

ate OML 26 with FHN. See 'Shell Completes Sale of Two Nigeria Oil Blocks', Reuters Africa, 15 November 2011, http://af.reuters.com/article/investingNews/idAFJOE7AD00520111114 [accessed 25 November 2011]

34. Interview, 22 November 2010.
35. Ibid.
36. For more on the Ogoni struggle and the historical context in which it emerged, see Okonta (2008).
37. http://www.seplatpetroleum.com/
38. From a conference presentation that I wish to keep anonymous.
39. Interview, 26 November 2010.
40. Ibid.
41. http://www.aosltd.com/
42. Interview, October 2010.
43. AOS Nigerian Content Policy [internal document].
44. The drill bit project was described to me in an interview and an AOS presentation to NAPIMS on the project [internal document].
45. Interview, October 2010.
46. Interviews, October 2010.
47. http://www.intelservices.com/
48. Idris Akinbajo and Elor Nkereuwem, 'Atiku deals with the Mafia', Next. Lagos, 7 October 2010, http://234next.com/csp/cms/sites/Next/Home/5523881-146/story.csp [accessed 7 October 2010]
49. Interviews, October 2010.
50. Interview, October 2010.
51. http://www.dormanlongeng.com/
52. Interview, 7 December 2010.
53. Ibid.
54. Ibid.
55. http://www.nigerdock.com/main.htm
56. Interview, 26 November 2010.
57. http://arco-nigeria.com/
58. Interview, 3 December 2010.
59. http://www.cisconservices.com/
60. For more on the Nigerian Content Development Fund, see Ovadia (2013c).
61. Interview, 3 December 2010.
62. Interview, October 2010.
63. Ibid.

6. CIVIL SOCIETY, SOCIAL MOVEMENTS AND LOCAL CONTENT IN HOST COMMUNITIES

1. As I have noted elsewhere, I worked in partnership with ADRA during my

fieldwork in Angola and am deeply indebted to the organization and its staff for their support and for helping me find my bearings in Luanda.

2. Interview, 26 May 2010.
3. Some of these issues boiled to the surface in June 2010 when Luiz Araújo, coordinator of SOS Habitat, was forced to leave Angola in fear of his life. The incident garnered significant international attention. See Pambazuka News, 'Action Alerts: Calls for protection of Luiz Araújo in Angola', *Pambazuka News, 485, 9 June 2010, http://pambazuka.org/en/category/action/65072 [accessed 12 June 2010]*
4. Interview, August 2010.
5. ADRA, 'Proposta: Projecto Petróleo para Bem Comum' [internal document, author's translation].
6. Interview, June 2010.
7. Interview, 23 August 2010.
8. Interview, June 2010.
9. Like the Oil for Development project, PMA's activities are heavily supported by Norwegian People's Aid.
10. Interview, August 2010.
11. Interview, 23 August 2010.
12. Meeting, August 2010.
13. I attended two such NGO coordinating meetings on decentralization in June and July 2010.
14. Interview, June 2010.
15. Interview, May 2010.
16. Interview, August 2010.
17. Interview, June 2010. This activist is a very prominent Angolan with a large network of supporters inside and outside Angola.
18. Interview, June 2010.
19. Interview, June 2010.
20. Interviews, June and July 2010.
21. Interview, July 2010.
22. Interview, June 2010.
23. 'Não Danço a Música de Outro Patrão', *O Pais* [Luanda], 10 July 2010, http://www.angonoticias.com/Artigos/item/26628 [accessed 12 July 2010]
24. Interview, June 2010.
25. Interview, June 2010.
26. Interview, July 2010.
27. The banning of certain news stories and even censorship of newspapers is not uncommon in Angola. When I went to interview one official in the BD in August 2010, he mentioned to me that all the copies of the current week's *A Capital* had been seized and it was not allowed to sell the current edition on the street because there was an article about rising prices of gas that the government did not like.

28. Interview, July 2010.
29. Interview, July 2010.
30. Interview, June 2010.
31. Interview, May 2010.
32. Interview, June 2010.
33. Interview, August 2010. While basic information that is easily repeated verbally, such as information about housing demolitions, can get out with the help of the internet and other new technologies, the internet is not an effective medium in Angola for distributing an actual document or report.
34. Interview, 12 August 2010.
35. Interview, 22 July 2010.
36. Interview, August 2010.
37. http://cislacnigeria.org/
38. Interview, 26 October 2010.
39. http://www.eraction.org/
40. Meeting, October 2010.
41. http://www.stakeholderdemocracy.org/
42. http://saction.org/home/
43. I worked very closely with both SDN and Social Action in the Niger Delta and, as I note elsewhere, I am indebted to them for their support and assistance in helping to understand how oil extraction affects people and communities in their everyday lives.
44. http://citizensbudget.org/
45. Interview, October 2010.
46. I do however want to mention two other important CSOs in the Niger Delta because of the substantial contributions they have made. Firstly, the Movement for the Survival of the Ogoni People (MOSOP) has been fighting for the right of the Ogoni people to self-determination and control over their natural resources. Secondly, the Centre for Environment, Human Rights and Development (CEHRD) is an NGO that has been particularly effective in monitoring and mediating conflict in the Niger Delta.
47. http://www.gadanigeria.org/
48. Interview, September 2010.
49. Interview, November 2010.
50. http://www.neiti.org.ng/
51. Interview, 8 November 2010.
52. Ibid.
53. Meeting, November 2010.
54. Meeting, November 2010.
55. Interview, 8 November 2010.
56. See Zalik (2004); Watts (2005); Idemudia and Ite (2006); Akpan (2009); Idemudia (2010).

57. Interview, June 2010.
58. Interview, July 2010.
59. Interview, June 2010.
60. Interview, June 2010.
61. Interview, August 2010.
62. Letter from the Deputy General Secretary and Regional Coordinator of SAECGOC to the Minister of Petroleum, 28 June 2010.
63. Interview, August 2010.
64. Ibid. From my own visits to the HR department of MINPET, I would have to agree with the union's assessment.
65. PENGASSAN National Executive Council communiqué. De Nevilla Hotel, Kaduna, 18 December 2009.
66. Babatunde Ogun and Bayo Olowoshile, 'An Open Letter to the Acting President', 23 April 2010.
67. Undated PENGASSAN press release, November 2010.
68. The report was written by the US-based Solidarity Center, an organization funded by the American labour movement.
69. Technical Working Group Status Update [PENGASSAN internal document], 2010.
70. Of course, as I will describe with reference to the mass movements that emerged after the government's fuel price hike in January 2012, where workers' interests diverge from those of the general populace, the public may in fact lose out.
71. Interview, August 2010.
72. Interview, August 2010.
73. Interview, August 2010.
74. Interview, August 2010.
75. Interview, August 2010.
76. Interview, August 2010.
77. Interview, August 2010.
78. Interview, August 2010.
79. Interview, August 2010.
80. Interview, 12 August 2010.
81. Interview, August 2010.
82. Ibid.
83. Ibid.
84. Interview, August 2010.
85. Interview, August 2010.
86. Interview, August 2010.
87. Interview, August 2010.
88. Parts of the following two sections draw upon Ovadia (2013e).
89. Held on 15 September 2010, the 2nd Multistakeholder Consultative Forum on the Petroleum Industry Bill was organized by SDN and Social Action.

90. See Obi and Rustad (2011); Ikelegbe (2011); Allen (2010); Joab-Peterside and Zalik (2009); Omeje (2006); Zalik (2004); Peluso and Watts (2001).

91. Interview, October 2010.

92. Interview, October 2010.

93. Interview, 19 October 2010.

94. Interview, October 2010.

95. Meeting, October 2010.

96. 2nd Multistakeholder Consultative Forum on the Petroleum Industry Bill, 15 September 2010.

97. I came face to face with such a paramilitary group, who briefly 'arrested' me and assaulted my two Nigerian companions when I allegedly took photos of a gas flare at night outside Total's Obagi Flow Station in Rivers State. Such groups are convenient for the IOCs because they have plausible deniability for their actions. After a short time, the group decided it was better to let me go than cause further problems by bringing me to a Total facility.

98. Interview, September 2010.

99. Interview, October 2010.

100. Interview, 7 December 2010.

101. Interview, 8 October 2010.

102. Interview, 8 October 2010.

103. Interview, October 2010.

104. Interview, November 2010.

105. Ibid.

106. Ibid.

107. Interview, October 2010.

108. Interview, October 2010.

109. Interview, October 2010.

110. Interview, October 2010.

111. Interview, September 2010.

112. Interview, 29 September 2010.

113. Ibid.

114. Interview, September 2010.

115. Interview, September 2010.

116. Interview, September 2010.

117. Interview, September 2010.

118. Interview, September 2010.

119. Interview, September 2010.

120. Interview, September 2010.

121. Field visit, September 2010.

122. Interview, September 2010.

123. Interview, September 2010.

124. The account of the protest offered here is based on media sources accessed at the time and in the weeks that followed.

125. Ten protesters and two journalists were arrested at an anti-government rally in Luanda in early July 2012. More recently, three demonstrators were arrested at a protest in September 2013.

126. Many Nigerian commentators, including former Minister of Petroleum Resources Tam David-West and the Save Nigeria Group, have refuted the idea that the government subsidizes the cost of fuel, instead suggesting that corruption by middlemen involved in the process of refining and transporting fuel causes the federal government to incur large costs. See 'Why FG refused to build new refineries—David-West', *The Vanguard*, 25 January 2012.

127. 'PHOTONEWS: #Occupy Nigeria-Lagos 2 Million-Man Rally', SaharaReporters, 13 January 2012.

128. Interview, September 2010.

7. CONCLUSION: WHAT FUTURE FOR PETRO-DEVELOPMENT?

1. Interview, August 2010.

2. An example of such coordination is the Gulf of Guinea Citizen's Network (http://www.ggcn-rcgg.org/), a coordinating body for NGOs in the region co-founded by organizations in Nigeria and Cameroon, which has nevertheless encountered some difficulty working across regional boundaries.

3. For profiles and comparisons of the two national oil companies, see Victor, Hults and Thurber (2012).

4. See http://www.ncdmb.gov.ng/images/downloads/guidelines/one-percent.pdf

5. Under Section 48, the NCA gives the Minister of Petroleum the right to provide tax incentives to foreign and indigenous companies to promote local content. Angola has also awarded incentives to all Angolan E&P companies through Decree 3/12. While picking winners and losers is necessarily a part of state-led economic development and a key aspect of the East Asian experience, it also represents an opening for corruption and patronage.

REFERENCES

Abdel-Fadil, M. (1987) 'The macro-behavior of the oil-rentier states in the Arab region', in Hazem Beblawi and Giacomo Luciani, eds. *The Rentier State*. New York: Croom Helm, 83–107.

Adesina, Jimi O. (2007) 'Introduction', in Jimi O. Adesina, ed. *Social Policy in Sub-Saharan African Context: In Search of Inclusive Development*. Basingstoke: Palgrave.

ADRA and OPSA (2010) Orçamento Geral do Estado 2011: Elementos Para o Debate. Luanda: Acção para o Desenvolvimento Rural e Ambiente and Observatório Político e Social de Angola.

Africa Progress Panel (2013) 'Equity in extractives: stewarding Africa's natural resources for all'. Africa Progress Report 2013 (Geneva).

Ake, Claude (1982) *Social Science as Imperialism: The Theory of Political Development*, 2nd edn. Ibadan: Ibadan University Press.

Akpan, Wilson (2009) 'When Corporate Citizens are 'Second-class' National Citizens: The Antimonies of Corporate Mediated Social Provisioning in Nigeria's Oil Province', *Journal of Contemporary African Studies*, 27(1): 105–18.

Alden, Chris (2007) *China in Africa*. London: Zed Books.

Allen, Fidelis (2010) *Implementation of Oil-Related Environmental Policy in Nigeria: Government Inertia and Conflict in the Niger Delta*. University of Kwazulu-Natal, unpublished PhD dissertation.

Alves, Anna C. (2010) 'The Oil Factor in Sino–Angolan Relations at the Start of the 21st Century', *South African Institute of International Affairs*, Occasional Paper No. 55, February. http://www.saiia.org.za/occasional-papers/the-oil-factor-in-sino-angolan-relations-at-the-start-of-the-21st-century.html [accessed 7 July 2010]

Amaduobogha, Simon W. (2010) 'Communities and the Petroleum Industry Bill: The Endless Search for Social, Environmental, and Economic Survival'. Paper Presented to the Second Multistakeholder Consultative Forum on the Petroleum Industry Bill. Port Harcourt: 14 September.

227

Amao, Ibilola (2010) 'Human Capital Development for Economic Growth and Poverty Alleviation in the Niger Delta: Creating a New Generation of Nigerians and Niger Delta Youth'. http://www.lonadek.com/ [accessed 4 December 2010]

Amin, Samir (1974a) *Accumulation on a World Scale: A Critique of the Theory of Underdevelopment, Volume 1*. New York: Monthly Review Press.

—— (1974b) *Neo-Colonialism in West Africa*. New York: Monthly Review Press.

—— (1976) *Unequal Development: An Essay on the Social Formations of Peripheral Capitalism*. New York: Monthly Review Press.

—— (1977) *Imperialism and Unequal Development*. New York: Monthly Review Press.

Ampiah, Kweku and Naidu, Sanusha, eds. (2008) *Crouching Tiger, Hidden Dragon?* Cape Town: University of KwaZulu-Natal Press.

Amsden, Alice H. (1989) *Asia's Next Giant: South Korea and Late Industrialization*. Oxford: Oxford University Press.

—— (1992) 'A Theory of Government Intervention in Late Industrialization', in Louis Putterman and Dietrich Rueschemeyer, eds. *State and Market in Development: Synergy or Rivalry*. Boulder: Lynne Rienner Publishers.

Amundsen, Inge and Abreu, Cesaltina (2006) 'Civil Society in Angola: Inroads, Space and Accountability'. Bergen: Chr. Michelsen Institute, CMI Report #14.

Amunwa, Ben (2011) 'Counting the Cost: Corporations and Human Rights Abuses in the Niger Delta'. London: Platform. http://platformlondon.org/nigeria/Counting_the_Cost.pdf [accessed 10 October 2011]

AOGR (2010) 'Marginal Fields: Status update', *Africa Oil & Gas Report*, 11(6): 4.

—— (2012) 'Nigeria's Top Twenty Indigenous Crude Oil Producing Companies', *Africa Oil & Gas Report*, 13(6): 15.

Apter, Andrew (2005) *The Pan-African Nation: Oil and the Spectacle of Culture in Nigeria*. Chicago: University of Chicago Press.

Ariweriokuma, Soala (2009) *The Political Economy of Oil and Gas in Africa: The Case of Nigeria*. London: Routledge.

Armstrong, Chris (2014) 'Justice and Attachment to Natural Resources', *Journal of Political Philosophy*, 22(1): 48–65.

Atsegbua, Lawrence (2004) *Oil and Gas Law in Nigeria: Theory and Practice*. Lagos: New Era Publications.

Auty, Richard (1993) *Sustaining Development in Mineral Economies: The Resource Curse Thesis*. London: Routledge.

Ayers, Alison J. (2013) 'Beyond Myths, Lies and Stereotypes: The Political Economy of a "New Scramble for Africa"', *New Political Economy*, 18(2): 227–57.

Balabkins, Nicholas (1982) *Indigenization and Economic Development: The Nigerian Experience*. London: JAI Press.

Baran, P. A. (1957) *The Political Economy of Growth*. New York: Monthly Review Press.

REFERENCES

Beblawi, Hazem (1987) 'The Rentier State in the Arab World', in Hazem Beblawi and Giacomo Luciani, eds. *The Rentier State*. New York: Croom Helm.

Biel, Robert (2000) *The New Imperialism: Crisis and Contradictions in North–South Relations*. London: Zed Books.

Biersteker, Thomas (1987) 'Indigenization and the Nigerian Bourgeoisie: Dependent Development in an African Context', in Paul M. Lubeck, ed. *The African Bourgeoisie: Capitalist Development in Nigeria, Kenya, and the Ivory Coast*. Boulder: Lynne Rienner Publishers.

Bond, Patrick (2006) *Looting Africa: The Economics of Exploitation*. New York: Zed Books.

Boone, Catherine (1998) 'The Making of a Rentier Class: Wealth Accumulation and Political Control in Senegal', in Peter Lewis, ed. *Africa: Dilemmas of Development and Change*. Boulder: Westview Press.

Bresser-Periera, Luiz Carlos (2011) 'From Old to New Developmentalism in Latin America', in José Antonio Ocampo and Jamie Ros, eds. *The Oxford Handbook of Latin American Economies*. Oxford: Oxford University Press: 108–29.

Brown, Joseph Atibi (2010) 'Nigerian Content and Oil and Gas Exploration in Nigeria: An Individual Project Report'. Abuja: NNPC Chief Officers' Management Development Program.

Brunnschweiler, C. N. and Bulte, E. H. (2008) 'Linking Natural Resources to Slow Growth and More Conflict', *Science*, 320: 616–17.

Bunker, Stephen G. and Ciccantell, Paul S. (2005) *Globalization and the Race for Resources*. Baltimore: Johns Hopkins University Press.

Campos, Indira and Vines, Alex (2008) 'Angola and China: A Pragmatic Partnership, Prospects for Improving US–China–Africa Cooperation'. CSIS Conference Working Paper, 5 December. http://www.csis.org/component/option,com_csis_pubs/task,view/id,4510/ [accessed 29 January 2009]

CEIC (2010) *Relatório Económico Anual 2009*. Centro de Estudos e Investigação Científica. Luanda: Universidade Católica de Angola.

Chabal, Patrick (2008) '*E Pluribus Unum:* Transitions in Angola', in Patrick Chabal and Nuno Vidal, eds. *Angola: The Weight of History*. New York: Columbia University Press.

Chang, Ha-Joon (2002) *Kicking Away the Ladder: Development Strategy in Historical Perspective*. London: Anthem Press.

—— (2003) 'The East Asian Development Experience', in Ha-Joon Chang, ed. *Rethinking Development Economics*. London: Anthem Press

—— (2004) 'The Role of Social Policy in Economic Development: Some Theoretical Reflections and Lessons from East Asia', in Thandika Mkandawire, ed. *Social Policy in a Developmental Context*. Basingstoke: Palgrave Macmillan.

—— (2006) *The East Asian Development Experience: The Miracle, the Crisis and the Future*. London: Zed Books.

REFERENCES

——— (2010) 'How to "Do" a Developmental State: Political, Organizational, and Human Resource Requirements for the Developmental State', in Omano Edigheji, ed. *Constructing a Democratic Developmental State in South Africa: Potentials and Challenges*. Cape Town: Human Sciences Research Council.

Corkin, Lucy (2011) 'Uneasy Allies: China's Evolving Relations with Angola', *Journal of Contemporary African Studies*, 29(2): 169–80.

EIU (2010) *Angola Country Report*. London: Economist Intelligence Unit.

Ejituwu, Nkparom C. (2010) 'Atlantic Trade', in Ebiegberi Joe Alagoa and Abi A. Derefaka, eds. *The Land and People of Rivers State: Eastern Niger Delta*. Port Harcourt: Onyoma Research Publications.

El-Khawas, Mohammed A. and Ndumbe, J. Anyu (2006) *Democracy, Diamonds and Oil: Politics in Today's Africa*. New York: Nova Science Publishers.

Evans, Peter B. (1995) *Embedded Autonomy: States and Industrial Transformation*. Princeton, NJ: Princeton University Press.

——— (2008) 'In Search of the 21st Century Developmental State'. Centre for Global Political Economy, University of Sussex. Working Paper No. 4, December. http://www.sussex.ac.uk/cgpe/documents/cgpe_wp04_peter_evans.pdf [accessed 19 January 2012]

Fanon, Franz (1965) *The Wretched of the Earth*. New York: Grove Press.

Ferguson, James (2005) 'Seeing Like an Oil Company: Space, Security, and Global Capital in Neoliberal Africa', *American Anthropologist*, 107(3): 377–82.

Ferreira, Manuel Ennes (1995) 'La reconversion économique de "la *nomenklatura* pétrolière"', *Politique Africaine*, 57: 11–26.

Fine, Ben (2006) 'The Developmental State and the Political Economy of Development', in Jomo K. S. and Ben Fine, eds. *The New Development Economics: After the Washington Consensus*. London: Zed Books.

Frynas, Jedrzej George and Wood, Geoffrey (2001) 'Oil and War in Angola', *Review of African Political Economy*, 28(90): 587–606.

Gereffi, Gary (2014) '*Global Value Chains in a Post-Washington Consensus World*', *Review of International Political Economy*, 21(1): 9–37.

Gereffi, Gary and Korzeniewicz, Miguel, eds. (1994) *Commodity Chains and Global Capitalism*. Westport, CT: Greenwood Press.

Ghazvinian, John H. (2007) *Untapped: The Scramble for Africa's Oil*. New York: Harcourt Books.

Global Witness (2009) 'Undue Diligence: How Banks Do Business With Corrupt Regimes'. London: Global Witness. http://www.globalwitness.org/ [accessed 28 May 2010]

——— (2011) 'Oil Revenues in Angola: Much More Information but Not Enough Transparency'. London: Open Society Initiative for Southern Africa–Angola and Global Witness. http://www.globalwitness.org/ [accessed 18 April 2011]

Govender, Shun and Skagestad, Beatrice Mutale (2009) 'Civil Society and Oil for

Development in Angola: Ways to Enhance Strategic Cooperation Among Non-state Actors'. Johannesburg: IDASA.

Gudaynas, Eduardo (2010) 'The New Extractivism of the 21st Century: Ten Urgent Theses about Extractivism in Relation to Current South American Progressivism'. Americas Programme Report. Washington, DC: Americas Policy Programme.

Guerrero, Dorothy-Grace and Manji, Firoze, eds. (2008) *China's New Role in Africa and the South*. Oxford: Fahamu.

Haber, Stephen and Menaldo, Victor (2011) 'Do Natural Resources Fuel Authoritarianism? A Reappraisal of the Resource Curse', *American Political Science Review*, 105(1): 1–26.

Harvey, David (2003) *The New Imperialism*. New York: Oxford University Press.

Hearn, Julie (2001) 'The "Uses and Abuses" of Civil Society in Africa', *Review of African Political Economy*, 28(87): 43–53.

Heum, Per, Quale, Christian, Karlsen, Jan Erik, Kragha, Moses and Osahon, George (2003) 'Enhancement of Local Content in the Upstream Oil and Gas Industry in Nigeria: A Comprehensive and Viable Policy Approach'. Bergen: Institute for Research in Economics and Business Administration, Report No. 25/03.

Hilson, Gavin (2012) 'Corporate Social Responsibility in the extractive industries. Experiences from developing countries', *Resources Policy*, 37: 131–7.

Hodges, Tony (2004) *Angola: Anatomy of an Oil State*. Bloomington, IN: Indiana University Press.

——— (2008) 'The economic foundations of the patrimonial state', in Patrick Chabal and Nuno Vidal, eds. *Angola: The Weight of History*. New York: Columbia University Press.

Howell, Jude and Pearce, Jenny (2001) *Civil Society and Development: A Critical Exploration*. Boulder: Lynne Rienner Publishers.

HRW (2010) 'Transparency and Accountability in Angola: An Update'. New York: Human Rights Watch. http://www.hrw.org/ [accessed 13 April 2010]

——— (2011a) 'Angola: Intimidation Campaign to Stop Protest'. Human Rights Watch. 9 March. http://www.hrw.org/news/2011/03/09/angola-intimidation-campaign-stop-protest [accessed 1 March 2012]

——— (2011b) 'Angola: Stop Repression of Anti-Government Protests'. Human Rights Watch. 5 September. http://www.hrw.org/news/2011/03/09/angola-intimidation-campaign-stop-protest [accessed 1 March 2012]

Ibrahim, Ado Sule (2008) 'Nigerian Content Development and Capacity Building in NNPC'. Abuja: NNPC Chief Officers' Management Development Program.

Idemudia, Uwafiokun (2010) 'Corporate Social Responsibility and the Rentier Nigerian State: Rethinking the Role of Government and the Possibility of Corporate Social Development in the Niger Delta', *Canadian Journal of Development Studies*, 30(1–2): 131–53.

Idemudia, Uwafiokun and Ite, E. Uwem (2006) 'Corporate–Community Relations in Nigeria's Oil Industry: Challenges and Imperatives', *Corporate Social Responsibility and Environmental Management Journal*, 13: 194–206.

Ikelegbe, Augustine (2011) 'Popular and Criminal Violence as Instruments of Struggle in the Niger Delta Region', in Cyril I. Obi and Siri Aas Rustad, eds. *Oil and Insurgency in the Niger Delta: Managing the Complex Politics of Petro-Violence*. London: Zed Books.

Iliffe, John (1983) *The Emergence of African Capitalism*. Minneapolis: University of Minnesota Press.

IMF (2003) 'Sub-Saharan Africa Regional Outlook, June 2003'. Washington, DC: International Monetary Fund.

—— (2010) 'Angola: Second and Third Reviews Under the Stand-By Arrangement and Request for Waivers of Nonobservance of Two Performance Criteria'. Washington, DC: International Monetary Fund.

—— (2011) 'Nigeria: Staff Report for the 2010 Article IV Consultation'. Washington, DC: International Monetary Fund.

—— (2012a) 'Angola: 2012 Article IV Consultation and Post Program Monitoring'. IMF Country Report No. 12/215. Washington, DC: International Monetary Fund.

—— (2012b) 'Nigeria: 2012 Article IV Consultation'. IMF Country Report No. 13/116. Washington, DC: International Monetary Fund.

—— (2013) 'Regional Economic Outlook Sub-Saharan Africa: Building Momentum in a Multi-Speed World'. Washington, DC: International Monetary Fund.

Inikori, Joseph E. (2011) 'Transatlantic Slavery and Economic Development in the Atlantic World: West Africa, 1450–1950', in David Eltis and Stanley L. Engerman, eds. *The Cambridge World History of Slavery, Volume 3*. Cambridge: Cambridge University Press.

Joab-Peterside, Sofiri and Zalik, Anna (2009) 'The Commodification of Violence in the Niger Delta', in Leo Panitch and Colin Leys, eds. *Socialist Register 2009: Violence Today: Actually Existing Barbarism?* London: Merlin Press.

Johnson, Chalmers (1982) *MITI and the Japanese Miracle: The Growth of Industrial Policy, 1925–1975*. Stanford: Stanford University Press.

—— (1999) 'The Developmental State: Odyssey of a Concept', in Meredith Woo-Cummings, ed. *The Developmental State*. Ithaca, NY: Cornell University Press.

Karl, Terry Lynn (1997) *The Paradox of Plenty*. Berkeley: University of California Press.

Kennedy, Paul T. (1988) *African Capitalism: The Struggle for Ascendancy*. Cambridge: Cambridge University Press.

Kibble, Steve (2006) 'Can the politics of disorder become the politics of democratisation and development?' *Review of African Political Economy*, 33(109): 525–42.

Klare, Michael (2012) *The Race for What's Left: The Global Scramble for the World's Last Resources*. New York: Metropolitan Books.

Klare, Michael and Volman, Daniel (2006) 'The African "Oil Rush" and US National Security', *Third World Quarterly*, 27(4): 609–28.

Klein, Nir (2010) 'The Linkage Between the Oil and the Non-Oil Sectors—A Panel VAR Approach', IMF Working Paper. Washington, DC: International Monetary Fund.

Kolstad, Ivar and Wiig, Arne (2009) 'It's the Rents, Stupid! The Political Economy of the Resource Curse', *Energy Policy*, 37: 5317–25.

Le Billon, Philippe (2007) 'Geographies of war: perspectives on "resource wars"', *Geography Compass*, 2(1): 163–82.

Lewellen, Ted C. (1995) *Dependency and Development: An Introduction to the Third World*. London: Bergin & Garvey.

Lopes, Carlos (2006) 'Candongueiros, Kinguilas, Roboteiros e Zungueiros: uma Digressao pela Economia Informal de Luanda', *Lusotopie*, 13(1): 598–642.

Lubeck, Paul M. (1987) *The African Bourgeoisie: Capitalist Development in Nigeria, Kenya and the Ivory Coast*. Boulder: Lynne Rienner Publishers.

Luciani, Giacomo (1987) 'Allocation vs. production states: A theoretical framework', in Hazem Beblawi and Giacomo Luciani, eds. *The Rentier State*. New York: Croom Helm, 63–82.

MacLean, Sandra J. (1999) 'Peacebuilding and the New Regionalism in Southern Africa', *Third World Quarterly*, 20(5): 943–56.

Mahdavy, Hossein (1970) 'The Patterns and Problems of Economic Development in Rentier States: The Case of Iran', in M. A. Cook, ed. *Studies in Economic History of the Middle East*. London: Oxford University Press.

Maliki, Dauda Anako (2009) 'Nigerian Content Implementation and Policy Targets in Oil and Gas Industry'. Abuja: NNPC Chief Officers' Management Development Program.

Manji, Firoze and Marks, Stephen, eds. (2007) *African Perspectives on China in Africa*. Oxford: Fahamu.

Marques de Morais, Rafael (2010) 'The Angolan Presidency: The Epicentre of Corruption', *Maka Angola*. http://www.makaangola.com [accessed 7 August 2010]

—— (2011) 'Corruption in Angola: An Impediment to Democracy', *Maka Angola*. http://www.makaangola.com [accessed 14 October 2010]

—— (2012a) 'Kero Hypermarket: Manuel Vicente Goes Shopping with State Money', *Maka Angola*. http://www.makaangola.com [accessed 9 February 2012]

—— (2012b) 'Understanding President Dos Santos Rule and the Gaming of His Succession', *Maka Angola*. http://www.makaangola.com [accessed 9 February 2012].

Messiant, Christine (2008) 'The Mutation of Hegemonic Domination', in Patrick Chabal and Nuno Vidal, eds. *Angola: The Weight of History*. New York: Columbia University Press.

Metz, Forrest (2011) 'The Challenging Business Environment—Experiences of Angolan Small and Medium Sized Enterprises'. Unpublished working paper.

MINPET (2010) 'Relatório de Actividades do Sector Petrolífero, Referente ao Ano de 2009'. Luanda: Ministério dos Petróleos, Gabinete de Estudos, Planeamento e Estatística.

Mitchell, Timothy (2009) 'Carbon Democracy', *Economy and Society*, 38(3): 399–432.

Mkandawire, Thandika (2010) 'From Maladjusted States to Democratic Developmental States in Africa', in Omano Edigheji, ed. *Constructing a Democratic Developmental State in South Africa: Potentials and Challenges*. Cape Town: Human Sciences Research Council.

Mohan, Giles and Zack-Williams, Tunde (2005) 'Oiling the Wheels of Imperialism', *Review of African Political Economy*, 32(104): 213–14.

Morris, Mike, Kaplinsky, Raphael and Kaplan, David (2012) *One Thing Leads to Another: Promoting Industrialisation by Making the Most of the Commodities Boom in Sub-Saharan Africa*. http://www.prism.uct.ac.za/Downloads/MMCP%20Book.pdf [accessed 30 July 2014]

Moses, Jonathon W. (2010) 'Foiling the Resource Curse: Wealth, Equality, Oil and the Norwegian State', in Omano Edigheji, ed. *Constructing a Democratic Developmental State in South Africa: Potentials and Challenges*. Cape Town: Human Sciences Research Council.

NBS (2009) 'Nigeria Statistical Factsheets 2009'. National Bureau of Statistics.

────── (2014) 'Revised and Final GDP Rebasing Results by Output Approach'. http://nigerianstat.gov.ng/ [accessed 21 July 2014]

NCDMB (2010) 'Draft NCDMB Monitoring & Evaluation Directorate Procedure'. Nigerian Content Development and Monitoring Board [internal document].

NCLCD (2002) 'Report of the National Committee on Local Content Development in the Upstream Sector of the Nigerian Petroleum Industry', Volume 1. National Local Content Committee, April.

NNPC-NCD (2008) 'Nigerian Content Development in Oil & Gas Industry'. Abuja: Nigerian Content Division, Nigerian National Petroleum Corporation, July [Powerpoint presentation].

────── (2010) 'NCD–IOC Joint Fabrication Yards Audit and Final Report'. Abuja: Capacity Building Department, Nigerian Content Division, Nigerian National Petroleum Corporation.

Nwaokoro, J. Emeka (2011) 'Signed, Sealed but Will It Deliver? Nigeria's local content bill and cross-sectoral growth', *Journal of World Energy Law and Business*, 4(1): 40–67.

Obi, Cyril I. and Rustad, Siri Aas (2011) 'Introduction: Petro-Violence in the Niger Delta—the complex politics of an insurgency', in Cyril I. Obi and Siri Aas Rustad, eds. *Oil and Insurgency in the Niger Delta: Managing the Complex Politics of Petro-Violence*. London: Zed Books.

Ogbeifun, Louis Brown (2007) *The Role of Labour Unions in the Oil and Gas Industry in Nigeria: A Practitioner's Perspective*. Lagos: Concept Publications.

REFERENCES

Okonta, Ike (2008) *When Citizens Revolt: Nigerian Elites, Big Oil and the Ogoni Struggle for Self-Determination*. Trenton, NJ: Africa World Press.

Olukoju, Ayodeji (2004) '"Never Expect Power Always": Electricity Consumers' Response to Monopoly, Corruption and Inefficient Services in Nigeria', *African Affairs*, 103: 51–71.

Omeje, Kenneth C. (2006) *High Stakes and Stakeholders: Oil Conflict and Security in Nigeria*. Aldershot: Ashgate.

Orre, Aslak Jangård (2010) 'Entrenching the party-state in the multiparty era: opposition parties, traditional authorities and new councils of local representatives in Angola and Mozambique'. University of Bergen, unpublished PhD dissertation.

OSISA (2013) 'Angola's Oil Industry Operations'. Johannesburg: Open Society Initiative for Southern Africa.

Ovadia, Jesse Salah (2008) 'Development and Security in Africa's "American Lake": The Political Economy of Oil and Exploitation', in Mark Ayyash and Chris Hendershot, eds. *Violent Interventions*. Toronto: York Centre for International and Security Studies.

—— (2012) 'The Dual Nature of Local Content in Angola's Oil and Gas Industry: Development vs. Elite Accumulation', *Journal of Contemporary African Studies*, 30(3): 395–417.

—— (2013a) 'Accumulation With or Without Dispossession? A "Both/And" Approach to China in Africa with reference to Angola', *Review of African Political Economy*, 40(136): 233–50.

—— (2013b) 'Indigenization vs. Domiciliation: A Historical Approach to National Content in Nigeria's Oil and Gas Industry', in Toyin Falola and Jessica Achberger, eds. *The Political Economy of Development and Underdevelopment in Africa*. London: Routledge.

—— (2013c) 'Measurement and Implementation of Local Content in Nigeria'. Lagos: Centre for Public Policy Alternatives (CPPA). www.cpparesearch.org.

—— (2013d) 'The Making of Oil-backed Indigenous Capitalism in Nigeria', *New Political Economy*, 18(2): 258–83.

—— (2013e) 'The Nigerian "One Percent" and the Management of National Oil Wealth Through Nigerian Content', *Science & Society*, 77(3): 315–41.

—— (2013f). 'The reinvention of elite accumulation in Angola: Emergent capitalism in a rentier economy', *Cadernos de Estudos Africanos*, 25: 33–63.

—— (2014) 'Local Content and Natural Resource Governance: The Cases of Angola and Nigeria', *The Extractive Industries and Society*, 1(2): 137–46.

Peluso, Nancy and Watts, Michael (2001) *Violent Environments*. Ithaca, NY: Cornell University Press.

Petras, James F. and Veltmeyer, Henry (2001) *Globalization Unmasked: Imperialism in the 21ˢᵗ Century*. Halifax, NS: Fernwood Publishers.

PMA (2010) 'Relatorio Semestral', PMA 2010. Luanda: Plataforma Mulheres em Acção.

Pogge, Thomas W. (1998) 'A Global Resources Dividend', in David Crocker and Toby Linden, eds. *Ethics of Consumption. The Good Life, Justice, and Global Stewardship.* New York: Rowman and Littlefield.

Reed, Kristin (2009) *Crude Existence: Environment and the Politics of Oil in Northern Angola.* Berkeley: University of California Press.

Rist, Gilbert (1997) *The History of Development: From Western Origins to Global Faith.* London: Zed Books.

Robinson, Mark and White, Gordon (1998) 'Introduction', in Mark Robinson and Gordon White, eds. *The Democratic Developmental State: Politics and Institutional Design.* Oxford: Oxford University Press.

Rodney, Walter (1974) *How Europe Underdeveloped Africa.* Washington, DC: Howard University Press.

Ross, Michael L. (2001) 'Does Oil Hinder Democracy?' *World Politics*, 53: 325–61.

—— (2012) *The Oil Curse: How Petroleum Wealth Shapes the Development of Nations.* Princeton: Princeton University Press.

Rowell, Andy, Marriott, James and Stockman, Lorne (2005) *The Next Gulf: London, Washington and Oil Conflict in Nigeria.* London: Constable & Robinson Ltd.

Saad Filho, Alfredo (2007) 'Monetary and Financial Policy under Resource Booms: Toward a New Development Compact in the ESCWA region'. Background Paper for the Survey of Economic and Social Developments in the ESCWA Region.

Saad Filho, Alfredo and Weeks, John (2013) 'Curses, Diseases and Other Resource Confusions', *Third World Quarterly*, 34(1): 1–21.

Sachs, Jeffrey and Warner, Andrew M. (1995) 'Natural Resource Abundance and Economic Growth'. NBER Working Paper No. 5398. Cambridge, MA: National Bureau of Economic Research.

—— (2001) 'The curse of natural resources', *European Economic Review*, 45(4–6): 827–38.

Saul, John S. and Leys, Colin (1999) 'Sub-Saharan African in Global Capitalism', *Monthly Review*, 51(3).

Shaxson, Nicholas (2009) 'Nigeria's Extractive Industries Transparency Initiative: Just a Glorious Audit?' London: Royal Institute of International Affairs.

Silva, Ana (2012) 'Manuel Vicente: Transparently Corrupt', *Maka Angola*. http://www.makaangola.com [accessed 15 June 2012]

Smith, Adam (2007) [1776] *An Inquiry into the Nature and Causes of the Wealth of Nations.* Charleston: Forgotten Books.

Soares de Oliveira, Ricardo (2007a) 'Business success, Angola-style: postcolonial politics and the rise and rise of Sonangol', *Journal of Modern African Studies*, 45(4): 595–619.

—— (2007b) *Oil and Politics in the Gulf of Guinea.* London: Hurst & Co.

Sogge, David (2006) 'Angola: Global Good Governance Also Needed'. Working Paper No. 23. Madrid: FRIDE.

Solidarity Center (2010) 'The Degradation of Work: Oil and Casualization of Labour in the Niger Delta'. Washington, DC: Solidarity Center. http://www.solidaritycenter.org/files/pubs_nigeria_degradationofwork.pdf [accessed 5 July 2011]

Southall, Roger and Melber, Henning, eds. (2009) *A New Scramble for Africa? Imperialism, Investment and Development*. Scottsville, SA: University of KwaZulu-Natal Press.

Total E&P Nigeria Ltd—TEPNG (2010) *Total Upstream in Nigeria*. Abuja: Blake & Harper, Nigeria.

Turner, Terisa (1980) 'Nigeria: Imperialism, Oil Technology and the Comprador State', in Petter Nore and Terisa Turner, eds. *Oil and Class Struggle*. London: Zed Books.

Ukiwo, Ukoha (2008) 'Nationalization versus Indigenization of the Rentier Space: Oil and Conflicts in Nigeria', in Kenneth C. Omeje, ed. *Extractive Economies and Conflicts in the Global South: Multi-Regional Perspectives on Rentier Politics*. Burlington, VT: Ashgate.

UNCTAD (2011) 'Fostering Industrial Development in Africa in the New Global Environment'. New York: United Nations Industrial Development Organization and United Nations Conference on Trade and Development.

UNEP (2011) 'Environmental Assessment of Ogoniland'. Nairobi, Kenya: United Nations Environment Programme.

USS (2010) 'Keeping Foreign Corruption out of the United States: Four Case Histories'. Washington, DC: United States Senate Permanent Subcommittee on Investigations. 4 February.

Victor, David G., Hults, David R. and Thurber, Mark C. (2012) *Oil and Governance: State-owned Enterprises and the World Energy Supply*. Cambridge: Cambridge University Press.

Vines, Alex, Shaxson, Nicholas and Rimli, Lisa (2005) 'Angola: Drivers of Change: An Overview'. London: Royal Institute of International Affairs.

Vines, Alex, Wong, Lillian, Weimer, Markus and Campos, Indira (2010) 'Thirst for African Oil: Asian National Oil Companies in Nigeria and Angola'. London: Royal Institute of International Affairs.

Wade, Robert (1990) *Governing the Market: Economic Theory and the Role of Government in East Asian Industrialization*. Princeton: Princeton University Press.

Waterbury, John (1999) 'The Long Gestation and Brief Triumph of Import-Substituting Industrialization', *World Development*, 27(2): 323–41.

Watts, Michael (2005) 'Righteous Oil? Human Rights, the Oil Complex, and Corporate Social Responsibility', *Annual Review of Environmental Resources*, 30: 373–407.

——— (2006) 'Empire of Oil: Capitalist Dispossession and the Scramble for Africa', *Monthly Review*, 58(4): 1–17.

Wenar, Leif (2011) 'Clean Trade in Natural Resources', *Ethics & International Affairs*, 25(1): 27–39.

World Bank (2008) 'Doing Business in 2009: Country Profile for Angola'. Washington, DC: World Bank.

Yates, Douglas A. (2012) *The Scramble for African Oil: Oppression, Corruption and War for Control of Africa's Natural Resources*. London: Pluto Press.

Zalik, Anna (2004) 'The Niger Delta: "Petro Violence" and "Partnership Development"', *Review of African Political Economy*, 101: 401–24.

—— (2009) 'Zones of Exclusion: Offshore Extraction, the Contestation of Space and Physical Displacement in the Nigerian Delta and the Mexican Gulf', *Antipode*, 41(3): 557–82.

—— (2011) 'Labelling Oil, Contesting Governance: Legaloil.com, the GMoU and Profiteering in the Niger Delta', in Cyril I. Obi and Siri Aas Rustad, eds. *Oil and Insurgency in the Niger Delta: Managing the Complex Politics of Petro-Violence*. London: Zed Books.

INDEX